T0323386

Migration Matters

Migration Matters

Mobility in a Globalizing World

Gurucharan Gollerkeri

Natasha Chhabra

OXFORD

UNIVERSITY PRESS

OXFORD
UNIVERSITY PRESS

Oxford University Press is a department of the University of Oxford.
It furthers the University's objective of excellence in research, scholarship,
and education by publishing worldwide. Oxford is a registered trademark of
Oxford University Press in the UK and in certain other countries.

Published in India by
Oxford University Press
YMCA Library Building, 1 Jai Singh Road, New Delhi 110 001, India

© Oxford University Press 2016

The moral rights of the authors have been asserted.

First Edition published in 2016

ISBN-13: 978-0-19-946480-7
ISBN-10: 0-19-946480-4

Typeset in Adobe Garamond Pro 11/13
by Tranistics Data Technologies, Kolkata 700091
Printed in India by Replika Press Pvt. Ltd

For Sunshine, without whose light and warmth,
I wouldn't be.

Contents

Tables and Figures

Tables

Figures

Abbreviations

3D	dirty, dangerous, and demeaning
AAPI	American Association of Physicians of India
AED	United Arab Emirates Dirham
AP	Andhra Pradesh
BRICS	Brazil, Russia, India, China, South Africa
CAD	current account deficit
CARICOM	Caribbean Community
CBC	California Board Council
ECNR	Emigration Clearance Not Required
ECOSOC	Economic and Social Council
ECR	Emigration Clearance Required
ENT	Economic Needs Test
EU	European Union
FDI	foreign direct investment
FII	foreign institutional investor
FTA	free trade agreement
G-20	Group of Twenty
G-7	Group of Seven
GATS	General Agreement on Trade in Services
GATT	General Agreement on Tariffs and Trade
GCC	Gulf Cooperation Council
GCIM	Global Commission on International Migration
GDP	gross domestic product
GFMD	Global Forum on Migration and Development
GMG	Global Migration Group
GOPIO	Global Organization of People of Indian Origin
GSDP	gross state domestic product
HDR	Human Development Report
HLD	High Level Dialogue

ICCPR	International Covenant on Civil and Political Rights
ICHRP	International Council on Human Rights Policy
ICPD	International Conference for Population and Development
ILO	International Labour Organization
IMF	International Monetary Fund
INR	Indian Rupees
IOM	International Organization for Migration
IPR	Intellectual Property Rights
IRPA	Immigration and Refugee Protection Act
IT	information technology
LtG	Limits to Growth
MDGs	Millennium Development Goals
MERCOSUR	Southern Common Market
MGI	McKinsey Global Institute
MGNREGA	Mahatma Gandhi National Rural Employment Guarantee Act
NAFTA	North American Free Trade Agreement
NIROMP	New International Regime for Orderly Movement of People
NMS	new member states
NRI	non-resident Indian
NSSO	National Sample Survey Organisation
OCI	Overseas Citizen of India
ODA	Official Development Assistance
OECD	Organisation for Economic Co-operation and Development
PBD	Pravasi Bhartiya Divas
PGE	Protector General of Emigrants
PIO	person of Indian origin
POE	Protector of Emigrants
S&T	science and technology
SAARC	South Asian Association for Regional Cooperation
SSN	social security number
STEM	science, technology, engineering, and maths

TiE	The Indus Entrepreneurs
TN	Tamil Nadu
TRIPS	Trade-Related Aspects of Intellectual Property Rights
UAE	United Arab Emirates
UDHR	Universal Declaration of Human Rights
UID	Unique Identification Number
UN-DESA	United Nations Department of Economic and Social Affairs
UNDP	United Nations Development Programme
UNFPA	United Nations Population Fund
UNGA	United Nations General Assembly
UNHCR	United Nations High Commissioner for Refugees
UNODC	United Nations Office on Drug and Crime
UNSC	United Nations Security Council
UNSG	United Nations Secretary General
UP	Uttar Pradesh
USD	United States Dollar
WEF	World Economic Forum
WMO	World Migration Organization
WTO	World Trade Organization

Preface

After eight years of work in international migration I decided to take a sabbatical. My work had covered policy and practice as also bilateral and multilateral engagement at the higher echelons of migration governance. I wanted to reflect on the state of play in migration in the wider context of a globalizing world; understand the dynamics at the intersection of the transnational movement of goods, capital, and people; and ponder the future of migration in the post-2015 development context. A bright, young researcher joined this endeavour as my co-author. This book, *Migration Matters: Mobility in a Globalizing World*, is the result.

The book does not seek to provide a comprehensive survey of its overarching theme. It attempts to convey to interested general readers, students, academics, and policymakers some conception of the principles, the political economy of, and the dynamics that influence migration praxis at the global and the national levels. In this modest effort my co-author has carried the burden of researching the subject, mining the scarce data and bringing empiricism to bear on the analysis. My role has been to provide the real-world perspective.

We have tried to explore international migration as a broad process that can potentially democratize development, expand economic and social opportunities, and contribute in a small yet significant way towards a more equitable world. In developing the central arguments of the narrative, we have relied on this general approach extensively; drawn on empirical findings where necessary; analysed data that is relevant and used international comparisons to draw from the eclectic learning of different countries and people.

The object of this book is not to propagate a purely academic or a doctrinaire view of international migration. Academic research is often critiqued as narrow and detached from the real world. Policy and practice equally are criticized for not relying on empirical evidence and analysis. We have strived to strike a balance and provide in our treatment of the subject a bridge between research and the real world. It envisages a wider audience and aims to stimulate intelligent lay readers to depart from conventional theoretical frames and to think for themselves on the live and contentious issues that confront our collective future.

Several people have helped us in writing this book. We are grateful to Gaurav Gollerkeri and Gautam Gollerkeri for their perceptive insights and invaluable inputs on the central arguments and the analysis of the data. We wish to thank Rajiv Mehrishi for his unstinted support during the course of the writing of the book. Roulkhumlien Buhril and Shiv Ratan provided valuable help and we thank them. Philosopher–friend Parsa Venkateshwara Rao Jr prodded us on and we thank him for his encouragement. Our editor at the Oxford University Press was patient, indulgent, and helpful. We wish to place on record our deep appreciation for his support.

Renuka Raja Rao—my wife, companion, and better half in its truest sense—has been by my side on this journey, through thick and thin; thank you for your faith.

Gurucharan Gollerkeri

My mother, Shyamal, and father, Rajendra, have been a constant source of support and I am grateful to them.

Natasha Chhabra

Introduction

Migration is the oldest action against poverty. It selects those who most want help. It is good for the country to which they go; it helps to break the equilibrium of poverty in the country from which they come. What is the perversity in the human soul that causes people to resist so obvious a good?

—J.K. Galbraith

This book is about migration futures: the transnational movement of people and the portability of skills in a rapidly globalizing world. It seeks to explore why from the last quarter of the twentieth century, development has produced outcomes so different from what was proclaimed to be its goal and resulted in the 'Great Divergence'—a world as unequal as never before. The book is divided into two parts: Part I explores the migration future of the world while Part II deals with India's migration future.

In an irony peculiar to our times we live in a world in which the movement of goods and capital across borders is seen as a virtue but also one in which the movement of people has been rendered increasingly difficult. Moving forward, value addition in the global economy, our ability to sustain global economic growth rates and the prospects of expanding economic opportunity, democratizing human welfare, and progressing towards a more equitable and just global order will be predicated as much on the free movement of people as on the movement of capital and goods. International migration must be seen in the wider context of the political economy of development and as the natural corollary to international trade and capital.

While global governance for international trade and capital has received more than its share of attention, this has been at the cost of international migration—the orphan child of globalization. Never before as in the present day has there been a more urgent need for a global framework to govern transnational movement of people that is rule-based, non-discriminatory and democratic. Indeed, the defining feature of migration in this century will be the rapid pace at which socioeconomic forces will drive and be driven by migration, making it a phenomenon beyond the realm of national governments. A characteristic of this century is the rapid growth in knowledge-based and technology-driven sectors. Combined with the explosive growth of mobile devices and the virtual world, there is a remarkable de-territorialized skills market that transcends geographic and political boundaries. To foster competitive, efficient, and equitable economic migration, there is a need for a new innovative and forward-looking global governance compact.

Over time, both policy and practice on international migration of most countries have only become more restrictive. This 'tyranny of the global elite' hurts the poor and the weak the most while perpetuating the status quo. Even the sedate Global Commission on International Migration (GCIM) and its flamboyant child the Global Forum on Migration and Development (GFMD) have tread cautiously with the result that the United Nations General Assembly's (UNGA) initiative remains inadequate in its development impact. The consequence has been high costs—both fiscal and human—and less than optimal results. Worse still, the artificial barriers to freer economic migration, at the least, have distorted development outcomes globally.

In Chapter 1 we explore the asymmetric world we live in. Despite considerable economic progress the geographic and inter-generational equity deficit is a drag on future economic development. Should such a contradiction persist in the future, material progress and welfare could witness diminishing returns while raising human costs. International migration cannot be left to uninformed debate or populist rhetoric. It represents a facet of internationalism that has received little attention, more by design than default. There is an urgent need to move to a rule-based, binding set of broad principles that would require states to willingly cede to a multilateral process some degree of their sovereignty on matters related to economic migration. Evidence is growing that freer mobility of people across borders will be the next frontier of globalization.

Chapter 2 examines two interacting forces that influence all populations: the demographic and development transitions. The differences in the stages of development around the world have influenced the rate at which countries go through their demographic transitions resulting in youth bulges and surplus labour in developing countries and population ageing and labour shortages in the developed parts. The demographic transition in turn influences growth and development. Consequently, the rate of development affects emigration from and immigration into a country. This chapter discusses the effects of the demographic and migration transitions and suggests that mobility is a natural solution to the structural changes created by the demographic transition at a global level. We argue that migration is a positive-sum game, illustrating it through the case of Brazil.

Migration is one of the politically sensitive issues of the modern world. This notwithstanding, Chapter 3 argues that migration will likely be the dominant mode of globalization in the future. In fact, economic migration needs to be recognized as a global public good. The global imperatives for mobility of people cannot be brushed under the carpet for too long. Declining fertility and ageing societies have meant serious demographic deficits. The world will have to learn to cope with growing transnationalism and the rise of the global citizen with a global culture. The imperatives include significant economic gains resulting from the liberalization of international migration. There is no other more effective solution to combating poverty and reducing global inequality. Across major economies significant skills gaps are jeopardizing growth—there is evidence of mismatch between the supply of and demand for skills across a wide gamut of sectors. Excessive segmentation in labour mobility that resists and restricts the movement of low-skilled migrants is both short-sighted and counterproductive.

Chapter 4 attempts to deconstruct and separate rhetoric from reality and situate migration within the wider process of global transformation. The rhetoric of the 'right to emigrate' enshrined in the Universal Declaration of Human Rights is not an illogical or a clumsy attempt to foster mobility of people but in fact is a serious limitation by design. We also try to dispel the myth of the 'sense of crises' that countries in the Global North anticipate. Unlike the 'hordes, floods etc. of the poor' that they fear might arrive at their gates, statistics show that the existing migration reality across various corridors seriously challenges this rhetoric. The 'selection' of migrants and increasing securitization of borders have raised the tariff and non-tariff barriers against economic migration. Another reality is that there is a tacit approval of 'shadow economies' alongside the rhetoric of the 'battle against irregular migration'. Finally, we address the limitations of the existing multilateral agreements, especially General Agreement on Trade in Services (GATS) Mode 4.

There is an underlying conflict between the idea of the 'nation state' and the demands of globalization. The 'Bretton Woods' institutions sought to strengthen the states through a grand international system—John Maynard Keynes put it succinctly, "We have shown that a concourse of forty-four nations is actually able to work together at a constructive task in amity and unbroken concord" (Keynes, 1944: 101–2 in Moggeridge, 1983). Yet, by 1976, in less than three decades this effort had been all but abandoned with the world embracing the 'neo-liberal' doctrine of liberalization, privatization, and deregulation. The introduction highlights the conflicting interests of 'nation states' and the process of globalization and yet how these do not serve mutually exclusive interests. Chapter 5 examines whether 'global governance' is at all possible in a manner that can serve the interests of the 'globe' (and not just parts of it). It invokes Polanyi's theory of 'embeddedness' to argue that a 'self-regulating market' is a utopian endeavour. If we envisage that migration responds to the forces of the market (from regions of surplus labour to regions with labour shortages and skills gaps) then will we not need a body to govern this kind of transnational mobility to ensure that it is a positive sum game?

In Chapter 6 we examine the urgent need for global governance that is essential in the current neoliberal paradigm. This is especially true of migration. While economic migration ought to be determined by market forces it cannot be in a self-regulating market. There is a need for a global body to govern migration; currently, there is no global view on migration. The need for rules or a multilateral framework for migration has been expressed but has always been in the nature of 'voluntary, non-binding bodies for the management of migration'. It is time for a global compact on international mobility of skills eventually leading up to a multilateral framework for the governance of economic migrants.

The world of the twenty-first century should gear up to move to a global 'skills paradigm'. It is in the interests of all—including those in advanced stages of development—to recognize that liberalization of the mobility of skills is essential. Compelling forces of demographics, technological advancement, and rise in the number of in situ services—all require skills to be portable. By skills we mean not just high-skilled migrants, but also semi-skilled and low-skilled migrants. Chapter 7 also discusses the problems that the global economy faces and will continue to face in the 'de-territorialization of skills'. Through case studies, we attempt to establish the importance of the portability of different levels of skills. The world needs firm and unapologetic advocates for the democratization of development through a transformative shift to an international regime for skills.

Chapter 8 seeks to answer the question of who gets what and why from more liberalized transnational mobility or the lack of it, that is, the gains for an individual and the state in the presence or the absence of a Global Mobility Compact. A vast majority of migrants are denied access to social security, civic services, and economic opportunities based on their race, religion, and nationality because they are migrants. Access, especially for the mobile economic migrants, should be based on residence and not nationality or national identity. If obligations are on the basis of residence, rights should be too. This holds true at several levels: from the ethical perspective; from the perspective of the migrant; of the state and of the various regional groupings that have facilitated easier movement of people. Access for migrants also implies costs of migration. Who stands to gain and lose? Migration cannot be discussed without situating it within the wider context of the politics of belonging and the racial shadow on the movement of people.

We conclude Part I of the book with Chapter 9. The world is at the crossroads of an opportunity. But where do we stand vis-à-vis migration governance—as a global community and as nation states? The state of play on international migration governance at a global level from the International Conference for Population and Development (ICPD) held in 1994 to the High Level Dialogue (HLD) on international migration in 2013, has been characterized by some convergence and other areas of divergence. International migration needs leadership at the global level. There is a need to understand the fields of action—the policies of nation states—to assess whether such leadership might emerge, and from where. In doing so it is equally necessary to analyse the counterfactual to change—what would happen if we were to carry on business as usual?

Part II of the book dwells on India's experience as a major country of origin, transit, and destination in the Global South placing it in a unique position. The scale and spread of the Indian experience in migration as well as development and the intimate interplay of these two complex processes defy comparison. From a simple narrative shorn of doctrinaire theoretical interpretations the 'India migration' experience demonstrates in its size, spread, and depth, and across time and space that migration is integral to society. International migration is of more than strategic importance to India as well as to the world and cannot be left to uninformed debate or fragmented interventions. The challenge in the governance of migration that India faces is to articulate a coherent policy framework and undertake coordinated modes of engagement.

Chapter 10 argues that India is on the threshold of a great transformation through the unfolding in tandem of the processes of demographic and migration transitions that will occur over the next few decades. India has the opportunity that will soon come but once in its history, when its working-age population will be at its highest. It is a major country of origin, transit, and destination. Its migration transition is influenced by its history and experience that have also shaped its economic growth and transformation from a traditional to a modern society. India's migration future will likely see an increase in independent women economic migrants along with an increasing diversity in the states of origin. There are also challenges that India will face—the lack of a clearly articulated migration policy embedded in its development policy; loopholes in migration governance; and the challenge of temporariness of migration in the India–Gulf corridor which render migrants vulnerable.

India's migration story is inextricably intertwined with its colonial history. In Chapter 11, we take a bird's-eye view of Indian emigration and the nature of the flows and stocks as well as the pathways and destinations. From slave migration, convict migration, and the

indentured labour system to free migration; there is now a perceptible change in the attitudes towards migrants and migration. We
trace the successes and failures of Indian migration through the years.
Not all migration from India in the colonial period was coercive; it
provided avenues for poor people to start afresh and some of these
success stories are the stuff of legends. Indian-Americans are
amongst the most successful across the world and are a testimony to
the courage and enterprise of early Indian emigrants. Of late, India
has emerged as one of the leaders in its number of overseas students
as also its high-skilled professionals. Despite this, however, the most
active corridor in India is its migration to the Gulf where the majority of Indian emigrants are still of the unskilled/semi-skilled category.
Central to India's migration praxis in the future will be the imperative
to diversify the destination base and help move emigration up the
value chain. Indian emigration must grow out of its colonial shadow
and signal childhood's end.

There are fundamental challenges that Indian society faces and
will continue to face if appropriate policy and institutional interventions are not put in place. Chapter 12 acknowledges that the lack
of inclusive growth; inequitable development; an unconscionably
large number of absolute poor; pressures of population on land and
resources; and deprivation are all retarding human development.
India has missed the bus for the manufacturing stage in its economic
transition. The consequences of this on its economic growth and the
impact on employment opportunities for the youth of the country
are far-reaching. The stark divide between the urban and the rural
poses a challenge to India's development prospects. Demographic
transition is a one-way movement and follows the 'arrow of time'.
The youth bulge needs to be harnessed in the next two decades. If
skilled, the young workforce has the potential to move up the value
chain in different parts of the world. India also faces governance and
institutional deficits in intra-state as well as international migration.
How these are addressed will substantially shape its migration future.

Chapter 13 examines the lacunae in the Emigration Act of 1983
that constitutes the regulatory framework extant in India today. The
Act is dated and has not come out of the colonial shadow in the emigration process. We discuss the shortcomings of the Act—intrinsic
and instrumental. The intrinsic flaws stem from its emphasis on exit

control; the arcane institution of the Protector General of Emigrants (PGE); and the institutional constraint it faces. The instrumental flaws include the absence of policy coherence—horizontal and vertical; the top-heavy, excessively centralized regulatory framework that leaves little space for the governments at the subnational level to intervene; inadequate institutional apparatus to design and execute policy or make interventions on a real-time basis; and an inability to mobilize non-state actors who are important stakeholders in migration—civil society, migrant networks, and non-government organizations that are more proximate to the community. Through an illustration of well-intentioned but seriously flawed policy, we conclude that the scarcity in India's migration praxis is not of resources, nor even of virtue, but of understanding.

In Chapter 14 we look at India as an important country of origin. While the migration flows are small relative to its population, India's emigration represents features that characterize the complexity of migration in the twenty-first century—a composite mix of different skills levels, temporary and circular migration, significant student mobility, and the growing importance of the feminization of migration. While the bulk of the emigration is of low-skilled workers to the Gulf, the rise of the emigration of professionals of the knowledge economy from India outweighs the former. The size and spread of the overseas Indian community underlines the rise of trans-nationalism by which people straddle more than one country participating in full measure in the economy and society of both the country of origin as also that of destination. Overseas Indians have demonstrated how mobility and migrant networks spur creativity, innovation, and entrepreneurship. India is in small but significant ways also emerging as a country of destination, thus underlining the fact that no country can remain only a country of origin or destination.

Irregular migrants continue to be criminalized as irregular migration stirs up powerful emotions and attracts most policy attention and action. Chapter 15 explores why irregular migration continues to thrive, causing great harm to pathways for regular migration and undermining serious efforts towards migration governance. Dispelling myths and popularly held notions, it answers questions such as who is an irregular migrant, what her incentives are, and who helps her in the process. Some insights from a survey of irregular migrants from India in Abu Dhabi are presented. The findings are revealing and go against general perceptions and anecdotal evidence. The chapter also addresses the Kafala system that is at the root of the widespread exploitation and abuse of temporary contractual foreign workers in the Gulf countries. In doing so, it points to areas where migrant workers most need help.

In Chapter 16 we look at the importance and implications of the democratization of knowledge. We begin with a discussion of how high-skilled migration takes place in a policy vacuum, and considering the changing nature of Indian migration highlight the importance of student mobility. We also try to assess the nature and role of the overseas Indian community; and the need for a more nuanced and strategic tactical engagement for India with its diaspora. Following the gradual shift in recent times in perceptions of high-skilled migration from brain drain to brain gain and currently to the more virtuous circular migration, we explore the medium- to long-term dimensions to India's engagement as a knowledge economy, and its ability to influence the global discourse on migration.

Despite being a major country of origin, transit and destination, India's global engagement on migration is suboptimal. In Chapter 17 we argue that the primary reason for this, in our view, is the absence of a migration praxis framework that is coherent. Its institutional framework for migration governance is obsolete. Emigration from India is still exit-control based. We analyse the consequences that result—a one-dimensional view of migration, the paternalistic approaches to protection and welfare of workers as well as the inability to treat migration as a self-selecting process. Findings based on primary data of a pan-Indian survey of intending migrants point to gaps in policy and the felt needs of migrants. Not all is gloomy though. There are good practices that have worked. We conclude with some first principles for migration governance and the way forward.

The book concludes on an optimistic note with a postscript urging that the time is at hand for India to play a proactive role in shaping the international migration discourse, position itself as the preferred country of origin, and demonstrate the benefits of its demography. It also urges that it is time for the world to anticipate the future: to recognize that the mobility of the producers of goods and providers of services is as important, to work towards a robust global migration policy framework that provides for freer movement of people, and to move towards 'one world, one people'.

The grand dynamics of the historical patterns of the accumulation of capital have shaped the evolution of global inequality. To paraphrase Thomas Piketty: failure to address the primary driver of inequality—the tendency of returns on capital to exceed the rate of economic growth—today threatens to stir discontent and generate conflict of an order that will likely jeopardize the very basis of a modern, progressive, and democratic future for all (Piketty, 2014).

1

International Migration
The Next Frontier

> We are suffering just now from a bad attack of economic pessimism. It is common to hear people say that the epoch of enormous economic progress which characterised the nineteenth century is over; that the rapid improvement in the standard of life is now going to slow down … that a decline in prosperity is more likely than an improvement in the decade which lies ahead of us.
>
> —Keynes (1930: 358)

An Asymmetric World

The world has seen quite remarkable economic progress in the second half of the twentieth century. The golden age, as some describe the period from the end of the Second World War till the time of the oil crisis, also brought modest welfare gains to newer geographies and a larger population across the world. It did appear for a time that such rapid growth in prosperity might never end. "Just how and why capitalism after the Second World War found itself, to everyone's surprise including its own, surging forward into the unprecedented and possibly anomalous Golden Age of 1947–73, is perhaps the major question that faces historians of the twentieth century"

(Hobsbawm, 1994: 8–9). The first decade of the twenty-first century, though, has been a rude awakening to what is essentially an asymmetric world in which there is a semblance of political equality residing uneasily with widespread economic inequality (Desai, 2002). Between 1870 and 1990, the ratio in per capita incomes between the wealthiest and the poorest widened by a factor of five (Pritchett, 1997). As we turned towards the new millennium the income divide between the developed and the developing worlds deepened significantly and in 2000 the ratio was 81 to 19 per cent of the world income. During the same period, the world population share of the advanced world dropped from 20 per cent to 16 per cent (Castles and Wise, 2008). This great divide between the rich and poor countries, between those who control the transnational movement of goods and capital and those who do not, between countries that are growing old and those that are young has placed us on the path of an unsustainable development model of 'exclusion', seriously jeopardizing long-term prospects for the march of human progress. The geographic and inter-generational equity deficit is a drag on economic development. In the near term, market distortions are now beginning to impede future economic growth and welfare.

As we ponder the prospects for economic growth and the progress of the world we now live in, the reflections of Keynes at the time of the Great Depression come to mind with a compelling sense of foreboding. This could well have been written with some nuances in the present day. The developments in the global economy of the last few years—triggered by the financial crisis of 2007–8 resulting in a recession in some parts of the world and a grinding slowdown in others, thus subsuming all—has created remarkable enough stress to cause no small sense of trepidation. The first decade of the twenty-first century has been a wake-up call. The Great Recession—the unrelenting Eurozone crisis, the precipitous fiscal cliff that the United States faces, the slowing down of the Asian tigers—as some have chosen to describe it, raises several questions on the sustainability of the political economy model that has been pursued in the post-colonial world. The prolonged contagion of economic distress has only served as an urgent reminder of crises in which the fault lines run deeper and are systemic. Doubtless this was perhaps the biggest crisis that the world was facing after the Great Depression; a culmination of a series of intermittent financial crises that had become a regular feature since the 1970s (Harvey, 2011). The surge in state intervention in diverse countries across the world to bail out financial institutions as well as to kick-start the economy through measures such as quantitative easing and fiscal stimuli demonstrates the fragility of the neoliberal doctrine in furthering the interests of capital (Kotz, 2002).

The new world order and the 'Bretton Woods' institutions established following the Second World War, the oil crisis of 1973, the emergence of the neoliberal model in its aftermath and the dissolution of the Soviet Union in 1991 resulting in a unipolar world only served to reinforce the capital accumulation model of growth and exacerbated the historical and structural inequalities of wealth and power. Fukayama's the end of history was nigh. The class war had ended and capital had finally won. Or had it, when what stared us in the face at the end of the twentieth century was a world more unequal than ever before in history? Widespread poverty, hunger, and disease, and the unconscionable absence of human development or opportunity for close to a quarter of the world's population at the turn of the century compelled world leaders to recognize that "we have a collective responsibility to uphold the principles of human dignity, equality and equity at the global level .... We have a duty therefore to all the world's people, especially the most vulnerable and, in particular, the children of the world, to whom the world belongs" (UN Millennium Declaration, 2000: 55/2). The short twentieth century as Eric Hobsbawm describes the period from 1914 till 1989, witnessed much economic and social turbulence. All the events of this period—the two great wars, the intervening doom and gloom of the Great Depression, the cold war decades, the fall of the Berlin Wall and the collapse of the Soviet Union—were characterized by integration of economies across diverse geographies. The great powers of the time were those with high economic growth owing to the relentless accumulation of capital based on the rapid expansion of their markets for goods and capital, the remarkable technological developments and the emergence of multinational corporations. Equally, their growth was the result of the coercive mobilization of labour and the exploitation of human resources which also meant international migration of people of a great magnitude. At the turn of the century it was visible and widely recognized that growth in itself does not promote welfare nor do the narrow concerns of nation states. It was clear that in the new millennium, a global community faced global challenges that would require us to go beyond the limited vision of a nation state or that of an elite but small group of countries.

The Limits to Growth

A pioneering study, 'The Limits to Growth (LtG)' (Meadows et al., 1972), was the first to simulate projections for the future based on the past that cast a long shadow on the model of growth extant. The study forecast a rather bleak and somewhat frightening future that would result in the disruption of community, progress, and welfare as we know it. Forty years on, there is evidence to suggest, based on the data from 1970 to 2000, that the standard-run scenario projected by the LtG report has occurred for almost all outputs. Should we continue on the same trajectory, the possibility of the projected scenario of global collapse by the middle of this century that seemed a wild prediction at that time can well turn into a real nightmare (Turner, 2008). Clearly, there are intrinsic limits to future growth prospects. The limits to growth arising from increasing population and declining resources have been compounded by the political economy of globalization. The institutionalized approach that liberalizes international trade in goods and services and of the movement of capital but restricts international migration of the producers of these goods and the providers of these services has severely constrained the bases for growth. Should such inherent contradictions persist, moving forward, material progress and welfare will witness considerable diminishing returns while raising human costs significantly. Global economic development is at that stage where whatever can be leveraged, outsourced, pushed to its margins—free trade agreements, financial engineering and global supply chains—has been attempted. These innovations might help squeeze out some surplus yet. Further significant surplus generation, however, will potentially come from higher productivity catalysed by human endeavour, cross-fertilization of ideas and a multicultural milieu fostered by international migration—the orphaned child of globalization. The World Bank had estimated in 2006 that the global gains from a three per cent increase in the stock of migrant workers in high-income countries after adjusting for prices would be USD 356 billion in 2025 (World Bank, 2006).

In an irony peculiar to our times, we live in a world in which the movement of goods and capital across borders is seen as a virtue but also one in which the movement of people has been rendered increasingly difficult. It is peculiar to the current age because the movement of capital and labour cannot be separated as the history of the last two centuries has demonstrated. The enhanced movement of capital and increase in international trade has always been accompanied by enhanced mobility of labour. Recent history has also shown that in times of economic downturn, when the movement of capital and goods slows down, there is a corresponding deceleration in the transnational movement of people (Solimano and Watts, 2005). The asymmetry between the liberalized mobility of goods and capital and the restrictions on the movement of people is ahistorical. It is the direct result of the neoliberal doctrine pushing privatization, deregulation, and liberalization of the capital and goods markets globally but not liberalizing the movement of people. Borders are now mostly for people (Pecoud and de Guchteneire, 2007). In this century, value addition in the global economy and our ability to sustain global economic growth rates and, indeed, the prospects of expanding economic opportunity, democratizing human welfare and progressing towards a more equitable and just global order will be predicated as much on the free movement of people as on the movement of capital and goods.

Beyond Borders

From a political economy perspective, human history is the history of international migration. It is the history of explorers, soldiers, traders, priests, and slaves traversing great distances in search of new lands, resources and labour, dramatically altering existing mores and thus shaping social and economic transformation. It is at once the history of mass migrations—of vast masses of people moving across not just countries but continents and shaping the economic and political futures of a 'New World' as a corollary to "capitalist enterprise through the process of creative destruction of the old" (Schumpeter, 1975). In the present day, migration is characterized by growing complexity, significant stocks, consistently rising flows, new modes, multi-directional pathways, and global networks. The result is that there scarcely is any geography in the world untouched by the phenomenon of migration. The defining feature of migration is the rapid pace at which socio-economic forces drive and are driven by migration, making it a phenomenon well beyond the realms of national governments and placing responsibility squarely in the domain of global governance between countries and across regions. As we begin our journey into the third millennium, it is clear that neo-liberalism cannot address the problems that confront a globalizing world (Kotz, 2002). Globalization is changing the hitherto held notions of citizenship; it is challenging the concept of sovereignty and is eroding the territoriality principle and the idea of mono cultural societies (Castles and Davidson, 2000). Imagine a world without borders in which economic migration—the transnational movement of students, workers, professionals, entrepreneurs, scientists, technologists, business people, and independent service providers—is free across countries in the global market place and follows the flow of capital. Imagine too, in what will remain an imperfect global market, greater cooperation between countries to ensure that the mobility of people is driven by the needs of the world economy and calibrated by the demand for and the supply of skills and productive human resources and not by the sovereign compulsions of nation states. This is a future not too distant. Rapid progress in information and communication technologies, the unprecedented spread of interconnectivity in virtual space, and the growth of transnational networks of diasporas and migrants alike have resulted in the rise of a new class—the Global Citizen—unfettered by national boundaries. These social and economic relationships that transcend borders are rapidly changing the way in which economic, political, and social relations are conducted. While in the conventional lexicon, nationals might yet see migrants as 'the other' and thus differently entitled, there is an unstoppable process at work by which citizenship as the basis for access to economic, social, and welfare opportunities is increasingly under question.

International migration is of more than strategic importance to the world and cannot be left to uninformed debate or populist rhetoric. The public discourse on international migration has acquired a sense of urgency in recent years. There is growing recognition that migration is an inherently transnational issue requiring cooperation between states at the sub-regional, regional and global levels. International migration has gained policy attention simply because of the large populations and the number of the countries involved in the process. It also poses challenges and opportunities requiring focused policy attention (GCIM, 2005). The importance of liberalized movement of people arises from powerful forces—demography, democracy, and development—that the world cannot turn its face from. Liberalizing international economic migration—enabling market-driven mobility of people and skills across borders—as a natural corollary to international trade, finance, and global supply chains will substantially shape the pace and direction of future global economic growth. The opportunity before the comity of nations is to move to a rule-based, global migration regime and governance structure that is non-discriminatory, democratic, and can best serve the world over the medium- to long-term. For this to come about, the international community will have to resolve the contradictions between industry and government, and between global concerns and national priorities. The political economy of migration will be the crux of the discourse (GCIM, 2005). Liberalizing economic migration can catalyse technological innovation, entrepreneurial risk-taking, higher rates of savings and investment and drive humungous consumption. Both the supply and the demand sides of the market will be driven by the demographic dynamics of mobility besides meeting the global imperative of attracting the best and the brightest. Mobility of people will strengthen the global economic fabric. There are also issues of a growing shadow market of irregular workers and the emergence of international cartels of human smugglers and traffickers. In a notable disconnect visible on the ground—between policy intent and its effects—legal migration has been rendered so difficult that illegal migration circuits have a free run. There is a clear and widening gap between global economic needs and national political compulsions.

Global Governance

One of the imperatives of sustaining global economic growth is the global search for talent and the demand for and supply of skills across sectors and geographies. This will have to transcend the idea of a nation state and of national boundaries. "The employment opportunities of the lowest skilled will continue to decline, risking a lost generation, cut off permanently from labour market opportunity … where skills were once a key driver of prosperity and fairness, they are now the key driver. Achieving world class skills is the key to achieving economic success and social justice in the new global economy" (The Leitch Review of Skills, 2006: 3–9). It will also require countries to be prescient and its policymakers to see that good economics makes for good politics. Who will benefit and who will not, will be determined by the policies and the politics that national governments follow in the foreseeable future but evidence is mounting that bridges will yield more than barriers. The world order that emerged after the Second World War through the Bretton Woods institutions combined the idea of nominally equal sovereign states and a small elite group of superpowers. This is reflected in the United Nations General Assembly (UNGA) comprising all nations on the one hand and the Security Council with a handful of select countries on the other. This is also reflected in the voting and representation process at the International Monetary Fund (IMF) and the World Bank which is not based on the democratic principle of one country, one vote but on the basis of quotas where the G-7 dominate (Desai, 2002). The effect of this contradiction between economic inequality and political equality was to render these global institutions less than effective and decisively tilt the balance of power. There is a need for rebalancing power at the global level, not just in international trade and international capital but equally in international migration. To foster competitive, efficient, and equitable economic migration, there is need for a new, innovative, and forward-looking global governance structure for international migration based on a framework that will be rule-based, non-discriminatory, and democratic. This will have to be through national governments willingly ceding some sovereignty to a global organization on matters relating to economic migration. Global governance of migration should be circumscribed by establishing normative standards, international dialogue, multilateral cooperation, and building strong capacities for governance (Betts, 2011). This would be best met through a global migration compact. National governments can continue to deal with immigration of asylum seekers and refugees. A defining characteristic of this century is the rapid growth in knowledge-based and technology-driven sectors and the power of market research to devise innovative delivery models based on targeted market segmentation. Combined with the explosive growth of mobile devices and the virtual world, there is a remarkable de-territorialized skills market that transcends geographic and political boundaries. The growing demand for managers who are mobile and have the ability to work across a wide range of geographies and in diverse, multicultural environments has given rise to a global hunt for talent. Global corporations are fighting to attract the best talent from across the world, just as various countries are. One statistical measure of the beneficial impact of high-skilled immigrants is that in the United States, both international graduate students and skilled immigrants were found to be positively correlated with patent applications (Chellaraj et al., 2005).

Historically, international borders and travel restrictions are of fairly recent origin. Less than a hundred years ago there already was liberalized movement of goods and capital, as well as people, not just across countries but continents. Over time, though, both policy and practice on international migration of most countries have tended more towards preventing freer mobility even of economic migrants with the barriers being erected becoming higher and more difficult. The absence of a rule-based framework for and the opposition to establishing a global institution to enforce it across and between countries and regional formations has simply meant that a handful of the 'rich and the powerful' set the rules of the game. Indeed, even the frame within which the discourse is held and the terms of reference are determined by precisely those countries that see migration as a political problem rather than an economic opportunity. Ex ante, therefore, the bias is to prevent, rather than enable mobility. This excessive influence of the 'naysayers' is evident in both the grammar and the nature of forums in which migration is discussed. This 'tyranny of the global elite' hurts the poor and the weak the most while perpetuating the status quo. The international discourse, quite understandably, has followed this path of trepidation, ever so reluctant about free movement while stridently pushing for newer and more stringent policy instruments to make border control more rigid and at considerable cost. This has been true even of the dominant strains of the discourse in the multilateral forums as well. Even the sedate Global Commission on International Migration (GCIM) and its flamboyant child the Global Forum on Migration and Development (GFMD) have treaded cautiously with the result that the United Nations General Assembly (UNGA) initiative remains a high-profile talk shop. The consequences over the last few decades of such reluctance, which is far removed from the reality on ground as well as from the empirical evidence on the imperatives for freer mobility, have been high costs—both fiscal and human—and less than optimal results. Worse still, the artificial barriers to freer economic migration, at the least, have distorted development outcomes globally. These market distortions have taken different forms—adverse selection, low-level equilibrium traps, cost–benefit inefficiencies, adversarial engagement, and fragmentation—and have rendered the global economic process less efficient. The asymmetry on a global economy-wide basis is stark. If social and economic disparities cause migration, they also catalyse social and economic development. It is counterintuitive that migration should be restricted or opposed. It is also a specious division to look at countries as silos of 'origin' and of 'destination'. In the age of globalization most countries are a little of both.

Goods, Capital, and People

As we progress towards a more integrated economy globally the challenges are to find ways in which we can enable freer movement of people as the natural corollary to the movement of goods and capital. Currently, there is no global view on economic migration. How often does the G-7 or for that matter the G-20 discuss the international mobility of people and skills? They talk about markets, global financial cooperation, the changing global architecture and much else but seldom, if at all, about international economic migration. On occasion, when they do, it is mostly about remittances and their impact on development, often seeming to imply that remittances substitute for overseas development assistance (ODA). How do we ensure that the global economy's needs for labour, skills and services are substantially met? How do we ensure that the dichotomy between the global market's need for migrants and the barriers to their movement raised by nation states do not result in an adverse selection process—of irregular migration, grey labour markets—and the resultant low-level equilibrium trap? These are not questions just about growth rates or demographics—both, no doubt, of significance. These are questions about structural problems in the global labour market resulting in a serious skills crisis where demand will far outstrip supply. These are only exacerbated by the barriers to the free movement of economic migrants, ironically by the growing securitization of migration. Quite simply, across countries, the migration policy and practice has been a case of poor economics and poor politics too—raising barriers and preventing their legal entry while being unable to stop the cartels that push them in illegally. How do we balance the competing demands of sovereignty and internationalism? How do we construct a global governance structure that can best meet the economic, social, and human development goals for the future? These are important questions. The challenges of the new century centre on the ethical as well as economic imperative of bridging the growing divide—social, economic, digital—between and across countries and its peoples. Central to our success will be to ensure that economic progress—measured not merely in terms of the aggregate value of the goods and services produced—catalyses the expansion of economic opportunity and welfare making for a more equitable world in which prosperity is democratized. This will require transcending discriminatory boundaries—social, geographic, political—and policy-related barriers to move towards a global regime of freer economic migration.

International migration represents a facet of internationalism that has received little attention, more by design than default. The Bretton Woods institutions have for many decades now served the cause of governing global capital flows, albeit less than democratically and, arguably, in less than an even-handed manner. The protracted negotiations under the General Agreement on Tariffs and Trade (GATT) concluding in the Uruguay Round and the emergence of what perhaps has some likeness to a global governance institution, the World Trade Organization (WTO), is testimony to the willingness of countries to cede some part of their sovereignty to an international organization in the interests of implementing a rule-based regime for international trade. Though migration has been a significant international process increasingly impacting countries engaged in it, there has been little effort, if any, at establishing a similar rule-based framework and an organization to administer it. It is arguable whether the GATT–WTO framework has resulted in a fair and just international trading regime; perhaps not. The developed world still determines tariffs and access-related issues, though this is beginning to change. What is heartening is that movement of goods is being subjected to minimum standards and global trading rules, applicable equally across and between countries and should there be a dispute, there is a mechanism for its resolution. More important is the fact that an international rule-based framework subordinates national legislations to advance the cause of lowering of barriers and promoting opening of economies. Contrast this with the often unilateral national or regional bloc–policy responses imposing restrictions on mobility of people and skills.

Imagining the Future

We must dare to imagine the future, be progressive and anticipate what the future economic imperatives are. The march of capital can progress into the twenty-first century and democratize economic development and welfare only if capital accumulation and surplus generation can be sustained in the future. This will require us to address the asymmetry of an unequal world as well as the asymmetry between the free movement of goods and capital and the restrictions on the movement of people. It is less a matter of choice, except with perilous consequences, and more an economic imperative to advance the migration praxis for the liberalized transnational movement of economic migrants. This imperative would be best met by establishing a global migration governance framework that would administer an international economic migration regime efficiently. We need to move to a rule-based, binding set of broad principles that would be binding on states on matters related to economic migration, through a global process of which they would be part. There is also need to draw up the lowest common denominator—minimum policy harmonization, if you will—set of migration practices to deal with the transnational movement of economic migrants, to be enforced across all states. Such a multilateral regime must include a compensatory adjustment arrangement that will engender reciprocity and enable an appropriate cost–benefit sharing mechanism that is enforceable. This governance structure will not deal with asylum seekers and refugees, which will remain within the sovereign domain of national governments. The WTO framework rather than the institution itself can be a rudimentary starting point that can be mimicked with appropriate changes to deal with international economic migration. There is an urgent need for countries to sit together in the UNGA to engage and draw up an action plan to transit to the new regime in a time-bound manner. The idea of an open society, a liberal economy and a democratic polity has been the bedrock of human civilization and progress. The march of capitalist development has been in the vanguard of this remarkable journey. As humanity travels through a new century, human endeavour faces its biggest threats—both secular and non-secular. The pursuit of human happiness, the ideals of an equitable, just, free, and fair world, and an egalitarian society in the new millennium will require a fundamental shift in the development paradigm with 'one world and one people' as the guiding principle of our new world order. Ironic as it might seem, Marx was prescient and envisioned global capital thus:

> The need for a constantly expanding market for its products chases the bourgeoisie over the whole surface of the globe. It must nestle everywhere, settle everywhere, and establish connections everywhere.... In place of the old local and national seclusion and self-sufficiency, we have intercourse in every direction, universal interdependence of nations.... National one-sidedness and narrow-mindedness become more and more impossible.... It compels all nations, on point of extinction, to adopt the bourgeoisie mode of production; it compels them to introduce what it calls civilization into its midst.... In one word, it creates a world after its own image. (Marx quoted in Laski, 1948: 123–5)

The international community has pledged to place people at the centre of the post-2015 development agenda. There is no better expression of this commitment than recognizing the indispensable role that migrants play—and protecting their rights. To this end, the agenda must create the basis for sustained and meaningful global partnerships on migration and human mobility, similar to efforts under the Millennium Development Goals (MDGs), to make trade and technology-transfer work for development. But not everyone stands behind these goals. A handful of national leaders could veto the inclusion of migration, owing to misplaced fears of its domestic political consequences (Sutherland and Swing, 2014). Such an outcome must be averted.

In the material and intellectual march of this world, do we have the perspicacity and the sagaciousness to work together to break down barriers, build bridges, and make international economic migration globalization's next frontier for the greater good of greater numbers?

2

The Disequilibria of Transitions

Mankind has a disconcerting way of dealing with problems only when the clock has begun to strike twelve. It solves problems which are upon us, not those which experts anticipate for the future. Yet once some of the problems cited here are upon us, it will be too late ... Yet we do not want to allow anyone to tell the rest of us precisely what needs to be done ...

—Dahrendorf (2002: 342)

Demographic Dynamics

The much-spoken-of and oft-misunderstood process of demographic transition can be stated as a partial cause for the level of development in a country (Dyson, 2001). The demographic dynamic has also resulted in deficits in parts of the world and surpluses in others, adversely impacting growth and development. The spatial and temporal distribution of people across geographies and the division of resources between them are doubtless the consequences of a historical process. The past in the present, it would seem, but the challenges and concerns, in fact, are of the future. In the ageing world the difficulties are obvious—low labour market participation, critical skills gaps, low productivity, high health care costs, higher dependency ratios and serious intergenerational equity issues. On the contrary, in the young world, with high levels of population, there is tremendous pressure on land and resources. There is a downward pressure on wages and widespread poverty. Demography is a drag in both parts of the world. Given that the fertility rates are below replacement level in most of the developed world, where will economic growth come from? The rather optimistic demographic dividend of the early twenty-first century may well turn out to be a curse owing to woefully inadequate human development resources. This causes economic slowdown as well as social disruption of a high order. The youth bulge in Egypt played a major role in its political transition. There has been a demonstrated intersection between demography, security, and the Arab Spring (LaGraffe, 2012). A large number of unemployed youth presents a recipe for unrest and an extremely dissatisfied society looking for a sense of purpose. What is striking is that demographic transitions work across space and time and the problems that they bring in their wake are structural and not cyclical. They will not go away with time and in fact will only make worse the dependency ratio and hence the development dynamic. A spatial factor mobility programme to logically ensure the mobility of the surplus young population based on the demand for and the supply of labour and skills to meet the deficits in other parts will be necessary to address the problem. There needs to be a global view of demography rather than a national or even a regional view. The Malthusian–Darwinian dynamic will not work if we do not allow for mobility.

The loosening of the Malthusian knot to reach sustained economic growth and the related phenomenon of the 'Great Divergence' has shaped the modern world. The manifestation of the twin forces of the Malthusian and Darwinian dynamics provides an important context for determining the future trajectory of human development. Our ability to evade local resource shortages and population crashes through innovation and migration has allowed continual growth (Nekola et al., 2013).

We live in a divided world—of haves and have-nots. The roots of this disparity are abundant and embedded in the history of humankind. If anything, the process of globalization has worsened this inequity within countries and across regions. Globalization, while giving impetus to expansion of trade in goods and transnational capital investments with the emergence of large multinational corporations, has also reinforced structural asymmetries in the global economy and society. The facets of globalization that have advanced the most are international trade and transnational capital, but the corresponding mobility of people not as much. International trade and capital, it is argued, open immense opportunities, and hence lowering of tariff and non-tariff barriers to their mobility is sought even if their benefits are uneven. International migration, on the other hand, the dominant discourse would have you believe, is a problem that needs to be tackled. So raise barriers and strengthen border controls. This is not by default but by design. Advancing the frontiers of international trade and capital was not inevitable and was in fact hard fought. It needed leadership that was provided by the United States and an appropriate institutional architecture. Equally, the growing restrictions on mobility of people are also the result of policy bias led by the developed world's view. This asymmetry is now beginning to distort the development process across the world. Correcting this will require mutualizing the gains and losses that arise from the forces of demography. We must move beyond the international governance architecture extant simply because the governance needs of the global economy are changing rapidly and are considerably more than what it provides for. The subtle but sure changes in the spheres of influence and balance of economic power need to be recognized, even if with a touch of nostalgia.

The growth in human population has often been termed unprecedented. From a laboured increase in 1750 to 728 million people to the dramatic rise between 1950 and 1990, we entered the twenty-first century with more than 6 billion people (Todaro and Smith, 2011); the best of soothsayers of the eighteenth century may not have predicted this but the high growth rates that various parts of the world have experienced are not astonishing. The world's population is rather unevenly distributed by geographic region, by fertility and mortality levels, and by age structures (Todaro and Smith, 2011). A large part of the world's young population (more than three quarters) lives in what is now fashionably called the Global South whereas the populations of the North are decreasing. In the year 1950 the three continents of Latin America, Africa, and Asia held 70 per cent of the world's population. This is expected to rise to 88 per cent in the year 2050. Technically, there are two reasons for population increase—natural increase and net international migration. Natural increase is a result of the difference between fertility and mortality rates. This is expected to contribute to a major chunk of population growth because population growth due to international migration is minimal. This was not the case in the nineteenth and twentieth centuries when movement of people was an extremely important source of population growth in North America, New Zealand, and Australia and a corresponding decrease in Western Europe (Todaro and Smith, 2011).

Economic demography has offered us the theory of the demographic transition. Societies undergo a change in their population numbers and structure from high mortality, high fertility rates to high mortality, low fertility and, finally, low mortality and low fertility rates. The remote or underlying cause for the transition is a decline in mortality rates which then ultimately lead to a decline in fertility rates (Kirk, 1996: 379, cited in Dyson, 2011). The falling death rates are a function of the gradual progress in the control of morbidity and disease through innovations in medicine and public health technologies. Due to transfer of these technologies to countries in the South, their mortality rates fell rather rapidly while fertility rates were still high. Fertility rates cannot be reduced drastically as they are rooted more in social attitudes and cultures. The time lag between the reduction in mortality rates and fertility rates causes population growth and this can continue for many years even when fertility rates have declined. Most parts of the developing world are at a stage of the transition characterized by a high proportion of young people, low dependency ratios and the working-age population constituting the majority of the population. This demographic condition holds the potential for many of these countries to achieve rapid economic growth. The expectation is that the young population will contribute greater productivity to the economy—by working, saving, investing, and consuming. These countries are in possession of what has come to be described as a demographic dividend that can potentially catalyse both the supply side and the demand side of the economy. However, to reap the benefits of this dividend, these countries need adequate support—the ability to provide these teeming potential economic multipliers with the basics: education, health, and skills. The unfortunate fact, however, is that many of these countries are unable to do so. This, coupled with high rates of unemployment, make this demographic explosion a significant drag on the economy unless some of the pressure of the weight of numbers is relieved.

However, there are differences among countries in the South. The 'one-child policy' was not the sole or underlying cause of fertility reduction in China. The process of fertility reduction had already begun when the policy was implemented. The policy only served to speed up the process of fertility reduction. This has put China in a rather interesting position. It is still a developing country with a huge demand for young labour but it already has the 'ageing society' problem of developed countries. It is now a reluctant country of immigration as it faces labour shortages and skills gaps because of its dwindling work force. The neo-Malthusian anticipation for lowering birth rates (through preventive checks) has backfired for some countries which have reached an advanced stage of the demographic transition much before their economies can afford it. India on the other hand is set to emerge as the youngest country in the world in the next two decades. But it is an uncertain future that the young India and its teeming millions will face as things stand, notwithstanding the hype surrounding the rise of India's economy, led by the flamboyant information technology sector. India continues to have poor human development indices—in some parts nearly as bad as sub-Saharan Africa. It faces a skills deficit of a significant order, especially in the rural population, and crippling infrastructure bottlenecks. The absence of a strategic economic roadmap over the last decade has meant a period of lost opportunities. India may yet make the cut, but that will need economy-wide reforms and countrywide mobilization of its latent talent and dormant productivity. As we proceed in the journey of the twenty-first century, what is clear is that China and India will be significant growth drivers over the coming decades.

On the other hand, countries in the North have gone through the demographic transition at a very different pace. They are mostly in an advanced state of the transition where their fertility rates have dropped below replacement levels. This eventually leads to dwindling populations. The countries in an advanced stage of the transition face a demographic deficit. The policy measures to combat these problems include raising retirement ages, incentivizing participation of women in the workforce, and outsourcing of manufacture. However, these are not long-term solutions to the structural problems faced by these economies. The long-term solution that is envisaged is to reverse the low fertility rates but this seems rather unlikely, as populations in the North have demonstrated.

The demographic transition creates a classic surplus–deficit situation but a restriction on the movement of people has rendered the problem of unequal distribution of population a huge challenge of our time. Not all young people from poor or developing countries migrate. It is only a small proportion of the young population that has the ability, the aspiration, and the wherewithal to migrate, that actually does. The fear of millions of the poor from the South flooding the gates of the rich countries if the restrictions on transnational movement of people were to be liberalized is wholly unfounded. Global emigrant numbers have remained largely stable. Relative to the global population, the number of international migrants remains relatively small. In 2013, international migrants comprised about 3.2 per cent of the world population, compared to 2.9 per cent in 1990 (OECD, 2013). It is also worth noting that South–South migration slightly exceeds South–North migration. In 2013, some 82.3 million international migrants who were born in the Global South resided in the Global South, slightly exceeding the number of international migrants born in the Global South who were living in the Global North at 81.9 million (OECD, 2013).

Migration Matters

The problem of immigration, the dramatic consequences of which we are witnessing, can only be addressed effectively … through an ambitious and coordinated development (plan) to fight its root causes.

—Manuel Barroso, President of the European Commission, 2005
(quoted in de Haas, 2007)

We now turn to why migration actually occurs. We review some of the migration theories in the discourse on migration. Thorough reviews of these theories have already been attempted in the past—and rather well; the effort here is to relate them to the larger discourse on migration. Indeed, our interest is to understand how the migration dynamic actually manifests itself and why. The two seminal papers on migration theories, one by Massey et al. (1993) and the other by de Haas (2010a), are widely cited. In a recent blog post, an extremely relevant question was asked, "Why is migration a 'Cinderella' issue in development?" (Green, 2012). This was in response to a talk by Dr Michael Clemens, one of the few voices of reason on the issue of migration and development. Dr Green deserves praise for his use of terminology. Migration is indeed a 'Cinderella' issue in development and there is indeed a sedentary bias in development. It is widely believed that development in poor countries will be a disincentive for people to migrate. The rhetoric that follows is that development will lead to a decrease in mobility of people. It is based on the popular notion that the poorest, 'the hungry and the desperate' (King and Schneider, 1991: 62–3) have the greatest propensity to migrate (de Haas, 2007). In fact, the justification for sending aid (and gathering popular support for it) to developing countries is often that it will reduce the burden of people immigrating to the developed parts of the world. There is an assumption of an inversely proportional relationship between income and other opportunity differentials and migration rates. The fear that liberalizing migration would open the floodgates for the poor from the developing world is counterfactual. The truth is that migration is never from the poorest parts of the world. The supposed inverse relationship between development and migration is based on the assumption that the two are substitutes; that development would stop people from moving altogether. Theories attempting explanations of migration give us a peek into the thinking on migration over the years and the resultant conventional wisdom on migration that has come about.

The roots may be discovered in the late nineteenth century, when Ravenstein (1885, 1889) formulated the 'laws of migration', which are described as the "starting point for work in migration theory" (Lee, 1966: 47). Lee (1966) himself contributed to migration literature by formulating the 'plus' and 'minus' factors that cause people to move across geographies. This later came to be known as the 'push–pull framework' (de Haas, 2010a). The 'common sense' understanding of migration; the ubiquity of the push–pull framework in policy circles; and the rhetoric flowing from the framework is testament to its powerful message.

Push–pull frameworks were made more sophisticated by the neo-classicists. However, the equilibrium assumptions also underlie these theories. Todaro (1969) and Harris and Todaro (1970) are the pioneers of these theories. They attempted explanations for rural–urban movements and these were later adapted for international migration. Borjas (1989: 482) argued that the two underlying assumptions of the neoclassicists were that individuals seek to maximize their well-being and an exchange of commodities (labour and capital) leads to equilibrium in the market place.

These theories popularized the belief that no migration will take place under equilibrium conditions; that migration is a linear and inversely proportional function of wage differentials (de Haas, 2010a).

Stark (1991) challenged the equilibrium assumptions held hitherto by arguing that the flow of people does not imitate the flow of water. 'The New Economics of Labor Migration' (Stark and Bloom, 1985) stated that the migrant is not necessarily the only decision-making body. In fact, migration decisions are jointly made by the migrant and a group of non-migrants. Migrants enter into voluntary contractual arrangements with their families. It viewed migration as a 'calculated strategy' and not as an act of 'desperation or boundless optimism' (Stark and Bloom, 1985: 174–5). This theory has offered a new way of thinking about migration.

However, it is not wrong to suggest that one of the most celebrated theories of migration is the Mobility Transition theory by Zelinsky (1971). It integrates the demographic transition with modernization and economic growth (vital transition). Zelinsky's vital transitions had five phases starting from the pre-modern traditional society to the future 'super advanced' societies. Each phase of Zelinsky's vital transition was linked to a distinct form of mobility and this came to be known as the mobility transition. The theory was further enriched by the work of Skeldon (1990, 1997) who added the spatial dimension to it. He also introduced the vital role of state formation to migration theory that helps us understand the role of colonization and decolonization in influencing migration in various parts of the world (de Haas, 2010a).

Moving away from a direct attempt to explain migration is the World Systems theory which treats migration as a tool to further the cause of the core states; it suggests that market penetration into the periphery by capitalist economies has caused migration and that migration is a natural outgrowth of disruptions and dislocations that inevitably occur in the process of capitalist development. The growth of the core countries is therefore incumbent upon the impoverishment of the periphery. De Haas (2010a) points out that this diametrically opposed the fundamental assumption of functionalist theories such as the push–pull model or the neo-classicist theories that predict that there will be convergence through factor price equalization.

Other theories like the network theory and the theory of cumulative causation have been used to explain the burgeoning/unprecedented numbers of immigrants. The network theory states that the proliferation of migrant networks plays a role in reducing the costs of migration and therefore causes more migration. The theory of cumulative causation states that each act of migration alters the social context and the structural conditions within which subsequent migration decisions are made, typically in ways that make additional movements more likely. Therefore, flows of remittances and the like encourage migration flows (Massey et al., 1993; de Haas, 2010a).

Evidence suggests that emigration takes place even from the developed parts of the world and within the developed parts of the world. Along with several macroeconomic factors, whether a person migrates or not is a function of several meta and micro factors: the ability to migrate (which may include education, skills, resources, family support, networks, and so on) and the willingness to migrate (which may include aspirations, desires, family, peer pressure, etc.) This, in fact, results in a relatively smaller number of people who actually take the decision to migrate. This has been proven by de Haas (2010a) who included individual agency as an essential component to existing migration theories. Individuals, after all, are not passive recipients of developments at the macro level. Also, there cannot be uniformity in experiences of all individuals; they may or may not react in the same way to the same set of external stimuli (de Haas 2010a).

While several theories attempt to understand the causes of migration, it is necessary that migration is placed within the wider context of development and social change if we are to understand it better (de Haas, 2010b).

Temporary versus Permanent Migration

Recent discourse in international migration policy refers to different kinds of migration, as if to suggest that they are distinct conceptual categories. Temporary migration, permanent migration, circular migration, step migration, and so on, are in essence artificial constructs. They are neither mutually exclusive nor divorced from the market. They are different forms of labour mobility representing different structural characteristics of the labour market on the one hand and the needs driven by the political economy of migration. They are all in equal measure influenced by market conditions—the demand for and the supply of productive labour and necessary skills.

The easier battles in migration have been those that advocate 'temporary migration'; the ones that allay fears of permanent settlement of outsiders. Similarly, it is politically easier and perhaps expedient to tilt towards high-skilled immigration, often to the exclusion of lower-order skills. Fundamental to understanding the dynamics of the mobility of people and the portability of skills is for policymakers to recognize the essential difference between labour market flexibility based on economy-wide needs and the politics of restrictive labour market segmentation. Policy prescriptions that seek to promote temporary as opposed to permanent migration and high-skilled migration to the exclusion of low-skilled mobility fail to recognize that development is organic and that these categories are not just the underlying linkages that bind the development process but are necessary complementarities in the economy. Restrictive labour market segmentation policies based on artificial constructs are necessarily counterproductive since they constitute 'ex ante' conditionalities that seldom influence 'ex post' objectives. In fact, they only fragment the productive process.

Whenever gaps of labour supply and skills shortages arise, mobility is always posed as a 'temporary solution'. There always seems to be some reservation about the acceptance of mobility as something natural and obvious. In fact, there are studies to prove that immigrants are not a solution to the labour shortages and skills gaps problems as they assimilate and become like the host societies—that is, they will eventually have low fertility rates and hence immigration is not the 'answer'. Is temporary migration, then, the answer? It has been articulated that there is some benefit in the 'temporariness of migration'; temporariness is a good thing and will give a lot of people the opportunity to migrate and offer more employment opportunities for everyone. After all, these migrants will return home and share their skills. Also, temporary migration will resolve a lot of the social problems that arise due to absence of parents (Rodrik, 2007). It has been argued that temporariness restricts the scope for migrants to make their way up (*The New York Times*, 2007). Even beyond the formation of an 'exploited underclass', the problem that seems to be most pertinent in this case is the fact that there is conditionality. A conditionality that seems to go against a few basics is that markets should not have an ex ante conditionality. Temporary, semi-permanent, or permanent—the nature of the skill required and the market conditions including the nature of the demand should determine the stay of the immigrant. A well-developed temporary migration programme can lend flexibility to labour markets across the skills spectrum. However, to argue, that only 'temporariness' in migration is a good thing is a misconstrued argument. This is political rhetoric common in many countries of immigration today.

Guest-worker programmes were first initiated by Germany in Europe (Gastarbeiter). However, this led to the intended 'temporary migration' resulting in a large number of migrants staying on and becoming permanent residents and citizens. Why did this happen? Temporary worker programmes ignore three things: first, the propensity of a migrant to stay on and lead a better life in the host country than her own (especially if aspirations and individual agency are taken into account. Now contrast this with expectations of the country of destination). Second, that there is a dichotomy between the demands of the industry and the compulsions of political agenda and, third, that the dynamics of integration and the multiplicity of identity do not allow the immigrant to remain just a 'worker' in her new country. The debate on permanent versus temporary migration needs to recognize three important causes of shortages of labour: first, the demographic dynamic that creates structural shortages; second, the stage of development reflected in educational attainments and social aspirations resulting in mobility up the value chain—typically, people move away from what are seen as 'low-skilled' jobs; and third, technological change causing skills shortages. The structural gaps that demography creates are not temporal and hence can surely not be met by temporary migration. These are gaps that require more permanent solutions. Some countries of the developed world have acknowledged this. Their policies are progressive and long-term and hence encourage immigration. Others, however, fail to do so. It is important to keep in mind that certain in situ services like farming, mining, construction, hospitality, geriatric healthcare and so on require people and the demand will be compelling. These are not jobs that can be outsourced nor replaced by machines. Quite simply, these shortages have to be met through immigrant workers. Demography also causes macroeconomic imbalances and intergenerational inequities by slowly and steadily altering the dependency ratio. So, on an economywide basis, there will be need to infuse a young workforce that can drive up productivity as well as ensure high rates of savings and investment. This means that over the medium to long term ageing societies may have little option but to liberalize their immigration regimes. Technological changes while reducing the demand for lower-order skills do result in skills shortages at the upper end of the skills spectrum. Often, these skills require tertiary education. Evidence on the ground suggests that student mobility enabling foreign students to pursue higher degrees, for instance, in the United States has been the best pathway to attract the best and the brightest at the higher end of the skills ladder. Regimes that do not enable such students to live and work with the expectation of permanent residence if not citizenship have fallen well short of meeting the demands of industry and the knowledge economy for talent. In this case too, skills shortages are unlikely to be overcome merely through temporary migration.

The migration to the Middle East is worth keeping in mind with regard to the case against temporary migration. Labour migration to the Gulf countries remains temporary and contractual in nature. This gives rise to several ethical issues relating to human rights as well as concerns about exploitation of the employees. The recruitment processes are dubious, the living and working conditions poor, the terms of the work contract coercive and the visa status, sponsorship based. The 'Kafala' system requires that the temporary work visas are 'sponsored'. The moment the sponsorship is withdrawn, often at the whims of the employer, the emigrant worker becomes 'illegal'. This

makes a migrant vulnerable, and lends the bullies of the industry—
the ones who want to employ cheap labour and discard them at will,
legitimacy. It distorts the market forces of demand for and supply of
labour. Worse still, it removes incentives for better skills, for improving productivity or contributing to the host society. This represents
a suboptimal solution to endemic labour shortages. A major concern
of the world is irregular migration. It is generally agreed that irregular migration might be less prevalent and tackled more effectively
if there were more avenues for legal migration and the barriers to
regular mobility of labour and skills were progressively reduced. This
is especially true in the case of economic migrants looking for better
opportunities and feature in the low-skilled and semi-skilled categories. There exist grey markets for this labour in developed countries.
Policies raise barriers and place restrictions on the movement of
labour. As if this were not bad enough, there is a growing populist
rhetoric fuelling uninformed debates on migration and building
anti-immigration sentiments. This helps the grey market to grow
as there are always people willing to migrate and employers willing
to exploit. Clemens and Pritchett (2013) have offered a solution to
the problem by arguing for well-designed temporary migration programmes, especially for low-skill, non-substitutable jobs. They argue
through an illustration of the case of the United States that welcoming immigrants for low-skilled jobs such as healthcare aides, janitors,
childcare providers, etc., will not only benefit the migrant workers
but also create more jobs for the middle-classes, stimulate demand
in their country of destination and keep farms and industries alive.
Large-scale entry for workers also addresses the concerns of border
security and irregular migration.

The debate on the transnational movement of people needs to
recognize that migratory movements are influenced as much by the
development dynamic as the demographic imperatives. The demographic transition combines with the causes and the consequences
of development to catalyse mobility to and from a country. It is
therefore not unsurprising that several countries can be significant
countries of origin and destination at the same time. Brazil is a case
in point.

Brazil is at that crucial point in its history when its demographic
and migration transitions are occurring simultaneously. It is an

excellent study of how the processes of demography and migration transition have placed it in a unique position. This case also serves to illustrate that we are moving towards a new paradigm where the division between sending and receiving states is no more possible. Brazil is a high middle-income country but still has its can of worms with high rates of poverty in the northeastern part of the country and in-your-face kind of inequality. In fact, until South Africa stole the top spot recently, Brazil had the highest inequality rates in the world. However, it is also amongst the leaders of the Global South with a large demographic dividend waiting to be reaped. Recent research (Quieroz et al., 2006; Turra and Lanza, 2012) suggests that demographic changes (read an increase in the number of producers over consumers) might favour economic growth although this requires appropriate policies and institutions to be in place. However, evidence suggests that Brazil is failing to take advantage of the positive impacts of its short, 'demographic dividend'. Intuitively and only considering its demographic situation, it should be considered a country with high rates of emigration. It should only be exporting a great number of people. However, Brazil also increasingly gets immigration from countries both in the South and the North. Why is this so? This rather strange phenomenon has recently been explored by Adriana Marcolini in an article called 'Flying South', where she explores what it is about Brazil that attracts a large number of immigrants. Should not the high number of youth in the country be a deterrent for foreigners? The answer is no. Brazil is attractive for foreigners. In the year 2000, 56.3 per cent of Brazil's total foreign population came from Europe, 21 per cent from South and Central America, and 17.8 per cent from Asia (with major populations from Portugal, Japan and Italy) (Amaral and Fusco, 2005). The multi-ethnic milieu makes it easier for newcomers to assimilate despite Brazil being the only Lusophone country in the Americas. Also, a large number of migrants from Brazil are now returning home. In fact, according to the latest census data, returning Brazilians represented 65 per cent of the immigration flow to the country between 2000 and 2010 (Marcolini, 2013). The fact is that Brazil's situation would have been impossible to understand if we were to rely only on the study of 'push–pull' factors, only its demographic transition or without an understanding of its levels of development.

Brazil is infamous for its difficult and slow bureaucracy but it follows the principle of reciprocity in the functioning of its visa regime. Does this suggest that Brazil has recognized that mobility of people is essential and will take place with or without the monstrous visa regimes that unfortunately represent our times? The answer may not be a clear yes.

Brazil receives a considerably high number of illegal migrants from its neighbouring states of Bolivia and Peru. Some travel from as far as Bangladesh, Pakistan, and Senegal in search of job opportunities. In April 2013, the Brazilian state of Acre declared that it was in a state of emergency after it received an 'alarming' number of illegal migrants. Following this, the Brazilian government decided to issue work permits to more than 900 Haitian immigrants so that they could stay back and work in Brazil. There was much protest from immigrants of other countries. They were denied work permits because they were not Haitian. The State Governor believes a 'broader strategy' is needed and told BBC Mundo, 'We cannot imagine that Brazil is going to solve the problems of the world and Africa'. Brazil is no exception, however. Other countries in the South that receive a huge number of poorer immigrants from neighbouring countries have similar attitudes. It is the new 'countries of immigration' that get large numbers of irregular migrants. Countries like the Czech Republic, Poland, Republic of Korea, Turkey, Kazakhstan, Malaysia, Thailand, Costa Rica and Chile, Lebanon and Libya along with the Gulf countries, South Asia, China and the CIS countries. One common solution that is proposed is developing well-designed temporary migration programmes keeping in mind certain basic principles such as ensuring the rights of the migrants, recognition of migrants' skills and so on to address the demands for workers without pushing them into the grey market (Abella, 2006).

It remains to be seen whether countries with demands for immigrant labour will be able to build in this flexibility in their labour markets.

The Disequilibria of Transitions

Apart from lending human beings the agency to move and look for better opportunities, there are other compulsions that drive movement of people. In this chapter, we discussed the disequilibria caused by the demographic and migration transitions. These 'transitions' are dynamic processes that take place across time and space. They create conditions that make mobility of people inevitable—in some parts to keep up the economic growth and in others to ease pressures on already overstretched systems. The world of today will not necessarily be the world of tomorrow. Societies and economies change and necessarily go through processes of 'creative destruction'. Natural and inevitable processes of demographic and migration transitions are important drivers. These transitions are creating structural gaps in populations. However, because these processes occur differently and at different times over the world, there is a classic surplus–deficit situation. There are compulsions on both the surplus (supply side) and the deficit (demand side). Apart from these, technology and higher educational attainment is resulting in rapid social mobility resulting in skills gaps and labour shortages. Also, there is a limit to outsourcing that may soon be reached. The liberalized transnational mobility of goods was not easily and widely accepted. It took a combination of an opportune time and visionary leadership. In the global capitalist system, the mobility of people follows the movement of goods and services. Mobility addresses the problems faced by the world as a whole. Mobility of people—as we envisage it, the movement of economic migrants according to the demand for and supply of skills across countries and continents will relieve labour shortages and skills gaps in countries in the advanced stages of the transition and concomitantly relieve some of the pressures in the countries that have huge 'youth bulges' and do not have the capacity to absorb their huge workforce. Also, the benefits of mobility for development are well known and include but are not restricted to remittances, transfer of technology, skills, and so on. We highlight from the migration transition theories that the poorest of the poor neither have the ability nor the willingness to migrate and therefore the apprehensions of the developed world that liberalizing the mobility of people causing a flood of migration to the developed world are unfounded. De Haas has pointed out that a society may be a high population growth and high economic growth country such as most oil-rich Gulf States and have low emigration whereas some countries may be ageing, stagnant, and have declining populations and may still be high emigration societies (de Haas, 2010b). While demography and development are not the only processes affecting migration, they are certainly objective conditions that make a compelling case for greater liberalization of transnational mobility of economic migrants. If, despite this, international migration is an orphan of the global system it is more a matter of underlying attitudes.

> Certainly, a wave of relativism is sweeping the world, especially the old developed world. Anything goes, either because it serves the self-interest of those who do not want to be told by others what not to do, or because it seems the logical end of the road from liberal to libertine predilections. Such relativism, however, will not help us square the circle in an age of globalization. It will make things too easy for those who believe that two of three objectives are enough, wealth and cohesion without liberty; wealth and liberty without social cohesion; solidarity and liberty without prosperity. (Dahrendorf, 2002: 342)

The perverse truth is that we need astronauts to take pictures of the Earth from space to bring home to us that we are indeed 'one world'. Nothing seems more natural to us than boundaries and restrictions on movement of people that are fairly recent and artificial constructs. But our memory is short and we fail to acknowledge what has shaped our societies and made them what they are. The world needs to learn to cope with the disequilibria that a shift in the balance of power brings with it and prepare for a more equal world.

3

Global Migration Imperatives

For most of those who have attempted it, it has served well, for their children even better. It has only rarely required any active effort on the part of governments. Most often it has only needed their acquiescence and, more often, in recent times, only their non-vigilance.

—Galbraith (1979: 120)

The Inter-generational Challenge

The objective conditions of global development and the inter-generational challenges that several countries across the globe face raise many concerns about future global growth prospects. They also set to rest the debate on international migration. Notwithstanding the 'naysayers', migration matters and will be a dominant mode of globalization in the future. In turn, the globalization of migration will affect a much greater number of countries and will spur cross-border movement resulting in a significant rise in the volume as well as in the diversity of the pathways of economic migration. The countries comprising the Organisation for Economic Co-operation and Development (OECD), because of their high incomes and shrinking populations as a result of both decline in fertility and ageing, serve as strong pull factors for migrants from the developing countries. There is growing demand in the OECD area for young workers who can replace the ageing work force, raise productivity and bolster their social welfare support system. There is also increasing demand for caregivers to tend to the elderly. In the developing world a young population and economic development are together giving impetus to greater migratory movements. Migration from non-OECD countries will continue to accelerate as a consequence of these demographic, economic, and social factors at play (OECD, 2009). The question is no more whether the world needs migration because migration is the 'missing link' between globalization and development (Ricupero, 2001). Rather, the question is how the international community might put in place a more liberalized regime for international migration, how such a regime might work and how it will be governed. A good beginning is to recognize that the main beneficiaries of liberalized migration will be the migrants themselves, whose average incomes grow several-fold by working overseas. If countries of origin and destination alike are to reap the development dividends of migration—remittances, skill-enhancement, entrepreneurship, productivity gains, and technological innovation—economic migration must be seen as a global public good, the gains and losses from which will be unevenly distributed. Hence the need for international cooperation to govern the stocks and flows of people across borders. To connect the missing link there will have to be a multilateral migration regime that is rule-based, reciprocal, and binding.

Indeed, where the world is today is the result of migration driven by a myriad of causes. Human history is full of narratives and imagery on migration: Moses leading his people to the promised land; the Celts moving from Central Europe to settle in France; the Pilgrims setting sail for the New World; the Irish, Italian and Eastern Europeans migrating to North America; and the East Germans moving West after the fall of the Berlin Wall. Migration has shaped our world. History aside, the movement of capital, goods, and people, together constitutes an integral element of the process of globalization (LeBlang et al., 2007: 1–32). Yet, it is clear that the transnational movement of people is infinitely more complex and fraught with greater political economy-challenges than the movement of goods and services which is why the dominant modes of globalization have hitherto been international trade in goods and capital while international migration remains a minor facet. The movement of goods and capital is a simpler process;

it comprises one-dimensional transactions the relationships from which are not enduring. The movement of people across borders is more complex and multidimensional. People move with families, cultures, and dreams. They have myriad needs—education, health, and social security. Their movement results in longer-term relationships that impact a host of others—governments, employers, and local communities (Trachtman, 2009).

Ironically, even as the rapid advances in transport and communications technology have made mobility easier and cheaper, restrictions on the transnational movement of people and the barriers to immigration are growing. International trade liberalization has behind it decades-long, sustained and outcome-driven regional and multilateral negotiations. Despite the long and inconclusive Doha Round, the view from the North is to push for further liberalization of markets and reduction in tariffs. Similarly, after the breakdown of the Bretton Woods system in the 1970s the neoliberal doctrine of transnational capital has made significant advances notwithstanding the widespread concerns about speculative finance arising from the recent financial crisis. Thus the policy rhetoric is imbued with anticipation of the potential gains to the developed world from the transnational march of goods and capital. This is a good time to pause and reflect on the global development dynamics. Even a die-hard neoliberal would recognize how far-off the intended path the World Trade Organization (WTO) has moved. The WTO agreement sought laudable objectives of promoting prosperity for all—raising standards of living, improving incomes, full employment, expanding production and trade, and equitable and sustainable development (WTO, 1995). In practice, however, these two goals—promoting development and maximizing trade—have come to be increasingly viewed as synonymous by the WTO and multilateral lending agencies, to the point where the latter easily substitutes for the former. The net result is a confounding of ends and means. Trade has become the lens through which development is perceived, rather than the other way around.

The Sovereignty Barrier

Contrast this with international migration, which is seen as the sovereign right of the nation state to prevent. It is this asymmetry that sets apart globalization today from its forbears. It is axiomatic, however, that good economics makes for good politics, especially in times of crisis. Tragically for the world, the international migration discourse has been dominated more by power politics than the rationale of economics. In fact, right-wing politics has gained ground in many countries riding on the back of anti-immigration sentiments whipped up by populism. "If international policy makers were really interested in maximizing worldwide efficiency, they would spend little of their energies on a new trade round or on the international financial architecture. They would all be busy at work liberalizing immigration restrictions" (Rodrik, 2001: 214). The discourses and the conclusions from international or global conferences on migration and related matters, though, make for interesting reading. The thrust of the argument has always been on how to restrict migration than enable it. The recommendation of the expert group meetings of the International Conference on Population and Development held in Cairo in 1994 was reviewed at a special session of the United Nations General Assembly in September 2014 and a framework for action to 'deliver a world of equality of opportunity and freedom to all of the 7 billion people—and more—who share it', was adopted (ICPD, Cairo, 1994). Liberalizing transnational mobility of people did not find even a passing mention. In fact, the summary report at the end of the conference urged countries of origin to follow policies for development that would best ease migration pressures. Ten years after, the Global Commission on International Migration despite well-meaning platitudes did not go any farther along the path of freer mobility of people. After a grand title, 'A World of Work: Migrants in a Globalizing Labour Market', admittedly based on the principle 'Migrating Out of Choice: Migration and the Global Economy', the commission speaks with trepidation and makes the rather tame recommendation that states while formulating policies must take note of the trend of increased international migration as a result of the differences in demography, development, and governance between countries (GCIM, 2005). So, when it comes to goods and capital—all the world's a stage, and all the men and women merely players, they have their exits and their entrances; but when it comes to people, the globe shrinks to small, disparate states and their sovereign rights gain primacy. The view from the North flies in the face of historical facts. Sixty million Europeans are estimated to have migrated to North America in the nineteenth and the twentieth centuries. From an annual average of about 300,000 migrants till 1875, the numbers grew to over one million immigrants leaving Europe each year by 1900 (O'Rourke, 2004: 2). Clearly though, what is sauce for the goose is not sauce for the gander. The economic argument for migration is rather straightforward. The gains from the mobility of workers from a low marginal productivity economy to a high marginal productivity economy are significant and the empirical evidence overwhelming. Indeed, if anything, the ageing economies will benefit most from higher rates of saving, investment, and productivity gains than anybody else. Yet many countries follow policies aimed at restricting immigration imbued as they are with protectionism and racism. In 2013, a United Nations survey of developed-country policies showed nearly three-quarters (73 per cent) of all governments either had policies to maintain the level of immigration or there was intervention to change the existing policies; 15 per cent followed policies designed to reduce immigration while 11 per cent had policies to raise the level of immigration. This is ironic because there is no more effective solution to combating poverty and reducing global inequality. The great transatlantic migration is a case in point. The escape from poverty in Europe for the millions who went to America in search of a new future has an aura of pioneering heroism to it. But the current rhetoric on migration does not recognize that migration remains the most effective development strategy in which nobody loses. Ironically, the dominant migration policy regime in most of Europe today is to prevent migration by raising barriers of different kinds. In the two centuries prior, most of the European migrants were poor and sought to migrate for a better life. Several European countries and European families were able to use migration to achieve a degree of convergence, escape from poverty, and raise their standards of living. Most of these countries not only actively prevent migration but cause harm by actively pursuing discriminatory labour market segmentation policies to allow only select high-skilled workers (O'Rourke and Sinnot, 2003).

The Contradictions of Globalization

The contradiction between the idea of international migration as integral to globalization and the idea of the right of a sovereign nation state to exclude 'outsiders' and the manner in which this contradiction is resolved represents the central dynamic within global governance in the modern world. This resolution will also be central to global economic prospects. In the past, international migration has influenced countries and communities. What sets apart the process in recent years from its past is the fact that it is global in scope, impacts domestic as well international politics, and has a significant socio-economic impact (Castles and Miller, 2009). The economic imperatives of international migration are compelling states to rethink political economy around the world. The lines that separate countries of origin and destination are getting blurred as economic migrants move where opportunities emerge and employers search for talent from across the world. In the global search for workers, work, and skills, geography is history. "The twentieth century assumption that migration is strictly a national problem to be handled independently by nation states is no longer valid" (Goldin et al., 2011: 215). But there is another perspective—that migration does not matter. While the patterns of global demographics will perhaps result in significant labour market imbalances one must recognize that there are several other factors that influence labour market participation. Labour market conditions, employment and wages are determined more by macro-economic factors, stage of development, and technological progress, than by demography. Equally, most countries are globally integrated and do not anymore function as closed economies. Their ability to produce goods and services is not dependent on the domestic labour force alone. Global capitalism has ensured that the mode of production and the accumulation of capital do not recognize 'artificial' national boundaries. Firms can today take recourse to foreign direct investment, offshoring, outsourcing, and subcontracting. Simply put, putting capital to work where a reserve army of workers and low wages exist seems a neater solution than having to grapple with the complex problems that immigration brings with it. Table 3.1 presents a bird's eye-view of the working-age population in the major economies of the world.

It has been argued with dramatic effect that with the integration of China, India, and Russia into the global economy there has been 'the great doubling' of the global work force. This assertion is predicated on the assumption that these countries prior to the 1990s were isolated from the world market as a result of trade barriers. They

Table 3.1   Trends in the Working Population Aged 15–59 years

Country/Region	1975	2000	2025	2050
US	132	176	196	217
Western Europe	99	113	100	86
Japan	71	79	65	49
US Share of (%)	44	48	54	62
China	497	829	913	787
India	335	594	869	939
World	2223	3636	4818	54104

Source: UN Population Division, DESA, World Population Ageing 1950–2050, available at: http://www.un.org/esa/population/publications/worldageing 19502050/index.htm.

operated largely in a self-contained manner and after the breakdown of the Soviet Union, the marketization of China and the economic reforms in India, these countries are now part of the global market. The result, it is argued, is a greatly increased supply of labour to the global capitalist system. Indeed, there has been 'a great doubling' of labour supply from 1.46 billion workers that would have been in the global economy, had these countries remained outside, to 2.93 billion since they are now integrated (Freeman, 2005). It would be a classical error of economic forecasting to assume that the current employment level is a fixed quantity and that migrant workers simply replace the domestic workforce. It would seem facile to suggest that China, India, and Russia would remain small economies even after their integration into the global system or that they will not on the back of high growth have a humungous demand for workers. As it happens, since the great prediction of the great doubling, these three countries have been growing rapidly and their workforce has been substantively absorbed in their own countries to meet the needs of rapid growth. In the west, meanwhile, the Great Recession has once again exposed the inherent contradictions of capitalism.

The unravelling has manifested itself in high unemployment rates, high fiscal deficits, surplus capital and surplus labour residing together uneasily and with little to cheer about even five years after the financial crisis. If there is one aspect of the recession that stands out it is the need for higher productivity, savings, and investment.

In the foreseeable future the economy will of course grow and with increasing returns. Technological progress is revolutionizing the modes of the production of goods and the delivery of services. In the transnational chain of production the question is less about the supply side and more about the demand side of labour. The central question really is of the shortage of specific kinds of skills. It is less about how many workers enter the labour market and more about the quality of the skills sets they bring with them. While it is true that at a global level labour shortages are unlikely given the stock, the spatial distribution of this stock is highly skewed with India and China accounting for a large part of the workforce. Equally, one must also factor in the effects of growth in capital stock and the steady rise in educational standards and technological development in India and China which will likely raise production capacity and hence the demand for workers.

The view from Europe is less global and more local. It is also somewhat dim with a broad even if grudging acceptance of the fact that immigration from third countries in significant numbers will be inevitable in the foreseeable future. Demographics will force most of Europe to increasingly rely on immigration from third countries to help balance supply and demand in labour markets, in particular through addressing shortages of young workers and severe deficits in specific skills necessary to maintain standards of living and to drive economic growth (see Figure 3.1).

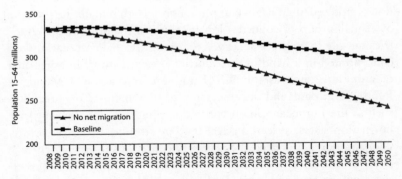

Figure 3.1 Projected Working-Age Population (Aged 15–64) in the EU-27, 2008 to 2050

Source: Eurosat, EUROPOP 2008 population projections.

The OECD in a recent long-term forecast of global growth prospects noted that sustained and substantial migration over time can help stabilize population growth and the working-age population. Even so, net migration rates projected till 2060 suggest they will not be able to offset the adverse impact of an ageing population on the labour force (OECD, 2012).

Skills in a Globalizing World

The global imperative for economic migration also arises from the mismatch between the supply of and the demand for skills across a wide gamut of sectors. A recent report of the McKinsey Global Institute noted that the global labour market is experiencing considerable strain owing to the mismatches between the skills workers can offer and those that employers need. In the absence of a global effort to enhance skills, the developing world just as much as the developed world might face serious skills shortages. This will also mean far too many workers with low or no skills (MGI, 2012). The idea of a global labour market in which labour as a factor of production moves freely across borders and skills are deterritorialized is an idea whose time has come. However, liberalized movement of economic migrants is still a bridge too far. International migration has a lot of catching up to do with international trade and capital. The evidence though is far from encouraging. Most accounts of globalization are exaggerated. By no measure is the growth of international trade or international capital flows unprecedented relative to production. Both remain the preserve of a small group of countries leaving the vast majority of the countries outside these processes. Even the multinational corporations are concentrated in a handful of countries. The growth of international organizations such as the WTO and the International Monetary Fund/World Bank and the emergence of supranational organizations such as the European Union create the mirage of global governance but nation states, at least a select few, are stronger than ever before. Globalization has created the necessary conditions for the emergence of an international labour market but labour mobility still faces excessive segmentation with a bias for highly skilled workers and restrictive policies that seek to keep out low-skilled workers. The UNDP notes that despite the fact that the larger share of international migration comprises unskilled workers; their entry is being restricted by national barriers. On the other hand, very early on—in fact, at the turn of the century—it was recognized that the market for high-skilled migrants is more integrated; they are more mobile and are paid standardized wages (UNDP, 1999). How important has migration been for globalization? As of the year 2005 it was estimated that about 200 million people or approximately 3 per cent of the world's population lived outside the countries of their birth. This would appear to pale in significance relative to the volumes of international trade and capital flows (see Figure 3.2). The average trade–GDP ratio at 45 per cent in 2005 and for the FDI–GDP ratio at 20 per cent far outstrip the migrant population to population ratio (Martin, 2008).

But the impact of migration must be judged more by the flows than by the stock. To better understand migration as one of the drivers of globalization, it is necessary to look at disaggregated migratory flows. Between 1990 and 2010, the number of international migrants grew from 155 million to 214 million and 56 per cent of this growth or 46 million migrated to the developed world. Almost 60 per cent of the world's migrants were living in the countries of the North. It is not the case, however, that people migrate only from the poor countries to the rich. Though a section of the western media and academia would have you believe that hordes of poor people will inundate their land, this is counterfactual besides being xenophobic. Similarly, many

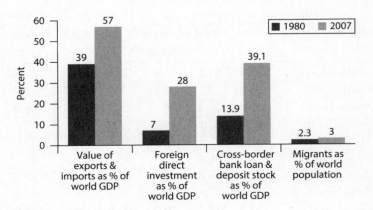

Figure 3.2 Indicators of Globalization
Source: Wickramsekara, 2011 (based on data by Guillén, 2010).

would have you believe that the bulk of the migration occurs from the poor to the rich countries. This is far from true since such movements comprised only one-third of the global total. In 2005, South–South movements accounted for 32 per cent and North–North movements made up 28 per cent of the total (Wickramasekara, 2011). As of 2010, the South–South corridor accounted for the same proportion of migratory flows as did the South–North corridor accounting for about 34 per cent each (see Table 3.2).

The number of international migrants in the world has been stable at about 3 per cent for the last 50 years. This is despite the remarkable pressures of ageing in some countries and young populations in others combined with cheaper transport and communications. Barriers to mobility raised by national governments are constraining migration despite demand for workers in the rich countries (UNDP, 2009). The approach of most countries in the developed world of 'cherry-picking': of unabashed preference for high-skilled migrants and the unreserved opposition to the migration of low-skilled workers is counterintuitive. It is also far removed from the ground reality in countries that face the double jeopardy of population decline and population ageing.

Besides driving up the dependency ratios sharply in most of the developed world, the economy-wide effects of a shrinking workforce,

Table 3.2 Number of International Migrants by Origin and Destination, 1990–2010

Origin/ Destination	Migrant Stock (millions)			Migrant Stock (percentage)		
	1990	2010	Absolute Change	1990	2010	Percentage Change
North–North	42.1	53.5	11.4	27.1	25.0	27.0
North–South	13.3	13.3	(0.1)	8.6	6.2	(0.4)
South–North	39.9	74.3	34.4	25.7	34.7	86.0
South–South	82.0	127.8	45.7	52.9	59.6	55.7
Total in North	82.0	127.8	45.7	52.9	59.6	55.7
Total in South	73.2	86.4	13.3	47.1	40.4	18.1
Total from North	55.4	66.8	11.3	35.7	31.2	20.4
Total from South	99.8	147.4	47.7	64.3	68.8	47.8
Grand Total	155.2	214.2	59.0	100.0	100.0	38.0

Source: Report of the Secretary General, UN, 2012.

rising costs of health care, and fiscal fragility are already beginning to impose unsustainable stress on governments across both the Eurozone and elsewhere in the OECD. That this constitutes the single-biggest threat to future economic growth of the developed world is beyond question. The size and scale of the problem was considered serious enough for the UN to debate as early as in the year 2000 the impractical and politically contentious idea of 'replacement migration'. Since then, however, governments in the ageing economies have been exploring non-migration-related solutions: increasing the retirement age, encouraging higher labour market participation by women, rolling back public services, and imposing austerity measures—the best 'band aid' no doubt but wholly inadequate. There is no doubt that the knowledge economy will see technology steadily reducing opportunities for low-skilled work. However, machines cannot replace humans in some of the basic but necessary functions such as in health care, geriatric care, and the care of children. The resistance to and the restrictions on low-skilled migrants is both short-sighted and counterproductive. There are a myriad sectors in which are jobs that cannot be done without young workers with appropriate skills: caregivers, nurses, housemaids, nannies, fruit pickers, cooks, chauffeurs, plumbers, carpenters—the list goes on. These jobs can neither be offshored nor can technology serve as a substitute. Several countries are already experiencing a perceptible contraction of the supply of workers to carry out these tasks and the situation will only get worse with the passage of time. The problem is not cyclical but structural and hence, annoying as it is, will not go away with time. Another dimension that exacerbates the labour and skills shortages is higher educational attainment. The rush for tertiary education has closed the door on vocational and skills education to an extent that there is a perceptible shortage of young school graduates with skills but a surfeit of people with higher degrees but poor employability in the developed world. Besides, the local workforce is averse to undertaking difficult, dirty, and dangerous jobs.

The Business Case for Migration

The most striking feature of the discourse on international migration at the global, regional, and national levels is the near-complete absence of the private sector. Critically, industry and business are mostly missing in the dialogue. This is an important gap because migration is directly related to competitiveness. Industry and business generate jobs and represent producers and service providers. Their importance also stems from the fact that migrants provide a huge new market for diverse businesses—financial services, consumer goods, hospitality services, logistics, money transfer, information and communication, health, and education, to name just a few—and are giving impetus to innovative business models. Much of the space in migration services currently occupied by the state is the functional area where the private sector can excel. There is often an undercurrent of antagonism between government and business and it is necessary that the voice of industry and business is heard in migration policy discourse, if only to lend balance to the debate and realism to the policy action that might follow. There have been some half-hearted attempts at bringing the private sector to sit at the migration high table—the Business Advisory Board established by the International Organisation for Migration in 2005; the round table organized in the lead-up to the GFMD at Athens in 2008; and the round table organized again in 2013 to consult with the private sector on future population dynamics. The private sector's engagement in the discourse has been a mix of circumspection and trepidation when in fact it ought to be taking the lead.

Following the global slowdown since 2008, high levels of unemployment have persisted in many countries especially in some of the member states of the European Union as also in the United States. Yet, organizations around the world report that they cannot find the talent they need and when they need it. Shortages exist at all skills levels, hindering the efficiency and competitiveness of industry. Business and industry are constrained by four key problems: widespread unemployability, skills gaps, information gaps, and private and public constraints on mobility (World Economic Forum, 2012). Ironically it is also the case that migrants are often employed in jobs not commensurate with their skills resulting in waste of trained, skilled talent. An efficient labour market is a prerequisite for competitiveness. Relatively liberal policies on migration provide the flexibility to business and industry to access and allocate skills across job needs efficiently thereby enhancing competitiveness. The mobility of talent can serve as an instrument to enhance competitiveness and profitability, and to create jobs. The intersection of ageing and migration has significance for business. Ageing creates job opportunities for migrants; it can also be a market opportunity in itself for competitive new businesses to provide geriatric care and home care by marshalling migrants' skills as an alternative to expensive healthcare currently in play. In fact, global sourcing opportunities are transforming the sector creating new business opportunities locally as also globally. Migrants are big business both as producers and consumers. Industry and business must be seen and heard in the migration discourse simply because the economic case for migration rests on the intersection of talent, innovation, entrepreneurship, and investment.

Between Economics and Politics

Thus while the political economy of migration remains a deeply dividing and complex challenge in global governance it is the dichotomy between economic imperatives and political compulsions; between the needs of employers and the policy regimes extant; and between industry and governments on how to meet the growing human capital deficits that poses the greatest threat to our global future over the medium- to long-term. The immediate downside of restrictions on low-skilled migration is that despite physical barriers in the form of policing and the policy restrictions rendering their mobility extremely difficult, there is a thriving grey market of irregular migrants in most countries. In fact, in some countries key sectors of the economy depend on undocumented migrants who constitute the much-needed workforce. This arrangement of governments going soft on irregular migrants; employers paying below minimum wages; and the migrants facing exploitation, deprivation, and risks is no longer tenable. Liberalized movement of economic migrants across all skill levels must become the basis for multilateral cooperation. Just as in the case of goods and capital, migration must be governed by a multilateral framework based on the principle of non-discrimination. An appropriate adjustment mechanism to provide for reciprocity and to equalize losses and gains must be provided for. This will require a paradigm shift in the role of the state. It will have to reinvent itself to govern migration in a manner that maximizes welfare. Rather than preventing, it must enable liberalized entry of legal migrants for legitimate economic purposes driven by the policy to increase welfare. This will entail ceding some authority on economic migration to the multilateral process. After all, globalization is yet in its infancy and the integration of more national economies is bound to initially increase migration from the low-income countries to the high-income countries. But as the developing world catches up, competing demands will arise for the same skills sets and will result in a balance between emigration and immigration.

As we move forward in this century, the world will have to learn to cope with the rise of the global citizen with a global culture. Alongside the cross-border movement of goods, services, and capital it will also be compelled to live with the historical inevitability of much greater international migration in the foreseeable future. Reflect on this:

> The inhabitant of London could order by telephone ... the various products of the whole earth ... and reasonably expect their early delivery upon his doorstep; he could ... adventure his wealth in the natural resources and new enterprises of any quarter of the world, and share ... in their prospective fruits and advantages; or he could decide to couple the security of his fortunes with ... any substantial municipality in any continent .... He could secure forthwith, if he wished it, cheap and comfortable means of transit to any country or climate without passport or other formality ... and could then proceed abroad to foreign quarters, without knowledge of their religion, language, customs ... and would consider himself greatly aggrieved and much surprised at the least interference. But, most important of all, he regarded this state of affairs as normal, certain, and permanent, except in the direction of further improvement, and any deviation from it as aberrant, scandalous, and avoidable. (Keynes, 1919: 5)

This was Keynes reflecting on the world nearly a hundred years ago. A world in which there was free movement of not just goods and capital but also free movement of people. Anything less in this century will be a shame.

4

Migration Rhetoric and Reality

The age of migration could be marked by the erosion of nationalism
and the weakening of divisions between peoples. Admittedly there are
countervailing tendencies, such as racism, or the resurgence of nationalism in certain areas ... But the inescapable central trends are the
increasing ethnic and cultural diversity of most countries, the emergence of transnational networks and the growth of cultural interchange
... in tackling the pressing problems that beset our small planet.

—Castles and Miller (2009: 312)

The Idea and the Reality

In the postmodern world getting things done is so much harder
whereas discussing what might be done is so much easier. It is also
fashionable to argue that the world is flat, that the globalization
of today is unprecedented. The truth is that under the surface,
globalization is affecting different countries and peoples rather differently. This is as true of migration. We are certainly far away from
the 'Age of Migration'. The international discourse on migration
is divided between those who see it as a problem, want borders
strengthened and barriers raised, and those who see it as a solution,
want freer mobility across borders and the regime liberalized. In
the animated discourse that follows, both sides are busy mostly

admiring the problem or the solution depending on which side of the divide they are on. Nothing epitomizes the drift in global migration praxis better than T. S. Eliot's immortal lines from 'The Hollow Men' that "between the idea/and the reality/between the motion/and the act/falls the shadow". It is necessary to 'deconstruct' the global discourse on migration to separate rhetoric from reality, situate migration within the wider process of global transformation and move towards decisive action. A good starting point is to understand the movement of people across borders as central to the transformational economic, social and political processes at work across the world. The predominant motivation for the majority of the migrants is simply the search for a better life, an improved income, a better home or simply a safer place to live in where she and her family can aspire to a better quality of life. It is also because man is an itinerant, restless being. Migration is arguably an inevitable and inexorable process. Despite the exertions of destination-country governments to raise barriers and build regional coalitions, committing significant time and resources to prevent it, modern-day migration seriously challenges their ability to regulate the movement of people across borders. International migration policies ironically have proven counterproductive. There are several reasons why migration remains an enduring phenomenon: geographic as well as inter-generational inequalities; asymmetric demographics; uneven development; growing aspirations and the explosion in transport and communications. It is also useful to note that migration is not new nor does it occur in isolation. Alongside the movement of goods and capital, movement of people across borders has shaped societies and at once served as a growth multiplier. What sets it apart today from earlier epochs is that the policy framework in most countries is rendering immigration increasingly difficult. Equally, the international migration discourse, driven largely by the developed countries, is becoming narrow and restrictive. The David of migration is thus in danger of being dwarfed by the Goliath of myths growing around it. This is perhaps intrinsic to the political economy of migration and inherent in the manner in which the process unfolds. The shadow that falls between reality and rhetoric is because of the manner in which the discourse is constructed.

The Right to Mobility

The Universal Declaration of Human Rights adopted by the United Nations General Assembly in December 1948 is considered the definitive charter that commits governments to the recognition and observance of basic human rights for all. The declaration has influenced several national constitutions adopted since and remains the basis for many international laws and treaties. But, not unexpectedly, the declaration falls woefully short on migration. It did not consider it necessary to enshrine the 'Right to Mobility' as a basic human right. Though the right to free movement, as the basis for opportunity, will in the future be seen as a basic right just as right to religion or speech is (Nett, 1971). Article 13 (2) provides that "[e]veryone has the right to leave any country, including his own, and to return to his country". Thus while granting the fundamental right to exit a country the declaration does not provide for a corresponding right to entry to another country. Human rights activists and analysts might consider this simply a case of a halfway house in the right to mobility, even illogical, perhaps. Entry into another country is squarely placed in the domain of sovereign decision-making. Without a right to immigrate the right to emigrate remains only an idea that cannot be applied in practice (Drummett, 1992). The inherent contradiction between emigration and immigration, between the human right to move and the sovereign right to restrict entry, is by design. The right to emigrate was added advisedly and was aimed at helping dissenters and political asylum seekers living behind the Iron Curtain to exit. It was a strategic response to the Cold War and had its ideological basis in the struggle between the so-called open society and its enemies. It was never intended to be a right to mobility with the freedom to enter any country of the migrant's choice. It was not without reason that Eleanor Roosevelt, the first chairperson of the Commission on Human Rights, attributed the abstention from voting by some of the Soviet Bloc countries to Article 13, which provided the right of citizens to leave their countries. The thrust of this article was on the freedom to exit to escape persecution. It is not surprising therefore that the natural corollary to emigration was asylum. Thus it is that Article 14 of the declaration that immediately follows provides that "[e]veryone has the right to seek and to enjoy in other countries asylum from persecution". Grant of asylum was a sovereign decision based on what was described as protected grounds—race, religion, caste, or political persuasions. The intent was less to enable migration and more to provide for political asylum. The result of this construct of emigration and asylum acting in tandem actually limits the fundamental human right to mobility. While perhaps it was relevant to the times immediately following the Second World War and was a political and ideological tool germane to the Cold War decades, today it must be seen as falling well short of the world's migration needs. If anything, it has fragmented the migration process. Asylum seekers, refugees, and those under family reunification constitute the greater part of the flows and hence the stock of migrants world wide. Admission in these cases is a sovereign decision enabling countries to regulate admission. Yet there is an international framework that provides for a degree of coherence in the praxis of most of the developed world. In contrast, economic migrants are fewer, and in the absence of a multilateral framework or an international covenant the decisions to allow immigration are far more unilateral and arbitrary and far less rational. This makes it especially vulnerable to populist right wing politics and xenophobia. The global community must wake up to the fact that the rhetoric of the 'right to emigrate' must now be revisited and action initiated towards a universal 'right to mobility'. While matters of granting admission on 'protected grounds' should remain in the sovereign domain, international economic migration must become a multilateral concern governed by a rule-based framework. This would be reasonable because the international law and practice on refugee- and asylum-related matters is fairly well established. In contrast there is no multilateral framework that can even guide, let alone govern, transnational migration of economic migrants. In the absence of opportunities to migrate, the other universal human rights such as the right to a free choice of employment and the right to an adequate standard of living will remain mere platitudes. Quite simply, this is axiomatic. To paraphrase Thomas Piketty, the grand dynamics of the historical patterns of the accumulation of capital have shaped the evolution of global inequality (Piketty, 2014). Failure to address the primary driver of inequality—the tendency of returns on capital to exceed the rate of economic growth—today threatens to stir discontent and generate conflict of an order that will likely jeopardize the future trajectory of human civilization.

The Sense of a Crisis

The sense of a crisis about migration amongst countries of destination is wholly misplaced. It arises from a combination of factors. First, the unfounded fear of hordes of the poor and the huddled masses pouring in through their gates. Simply put, this is counterfactual. Consider the facts. Of the world's population of over 6.7 billion, as of the first decade of this century just about 214 million people live and work outside the countries of their birth constituting about 3 per cent of the world population. By any standards, whether in absolute terms or as a percentage of the population, this is minuscule. The figure below makes it clear that the trend line for international migrants as a percentage of world population has remained more or less flat over the past three decades. Statistics can be deceptive especially if they are not read in context. The sharp rise in the number of migrants worldwide from 1985 to 1990 was the direct result of the break-up of the Soviet Union. It was really a case of borders crossing people rather than people crossing borders (Wickramasekara, 2011).

The unfounded fear of being inundated by migrants from the Third World is also constructed on the myth that most migration occurs along the South–North axis. This is counterfactual. The intra-region flows of migrants in Asia for instance are as high as the South–North flows. As a matter of fact, the foreign-born population as a percentage of the total population has remained at the same levels for most developed countries despite declining population due to ageing. Besides the flows we might also consider the stock of migrants in different regions. Again, Asia is a big player. It has the second-largest migrant stock at 61 million relative to Europe's 68 million. In the first decade—2000 to 2010—of the twenty-first century, Europe added 12 million migrants while Asia added 10 million (Wickramasekara, 2011). Figure 4.1 shows that Asia is ahead of even North America in the total stock of migrants. It should be clear on an empirical basis that few people actually migrate because migration still entails considerable expense and risks and only those with the wherewithal can embark on the journey. Historically, migration has also created disparities between people and regions. "Mobility is a privilege that is unevenly

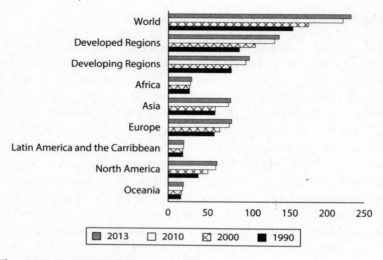

Figure 4.1   International Migrant Stock (in Millions)
Source: Constructed on the basis of data from the UN (2013a), *Trends in International Migration Stock: The 2013 Revision—Migrants by Destination and Origin.*

distributed among human beings: citizens from developed countries may travel and settle down almost anywhere in the world, while their fellow human beings from less developed countries depend upon the uncertain issuance of visas and residence permits to migrate" (Pe'coud and Guchteneire, 2007: 13).

Demography, democracy, and development are rapidly changing Third World countries and their societies. Many countries in the region are already well into their migration transitions and are beginning to see a deceleration of emigration rates. The dominant literature on migration as well as media reporting tends to take an exaggerated and one-dimensional, country-of-destination perspective or the view from the Global North perspective. This view would have the world believe that the developing world has an unending supply of labour and hence migration will continue unabated. The facts are quite the contrary. The labour demand in emerging economies like China and India are huge, to say the least. Besides, relative to their populations the migration flows from these countries are minuscule. It will require considerable effort and much more than progressive policies, which at the present seem far-fetched, to attract skills and talent from the developed world. It would serve the countries of destination in the developed world as also the global discourse better if movement of workers is studied from the perspective of the growth projections and the needs of the countries of origin. Recent data suggests that the numbers of people wanting to emigrate from countries in the South is declining largely because of greater opportunities in their home economies, higher education levels, and declining wage differentials. There is in fact a pattern of reverse migration discernible by which the more entrepreneurial migrants in North America are beginning to return home to China and India to set up new enterprises. While this is still a small number, it points to the fact that countries in the South are emerging as important poles for migration. In the not-too-distant future it is reasonable to expect significant migration in the North–South direction.

Notwithstanding the hoopla over the 'right to emigrate' in Article 13 (2) of the Universal Declaration of Human Rights, the International Conference on Population and Development held at Cairo in September 1994 made an interesting contrarian recommendation on international migration. It said, "The long term manageability of international migration hinges on making the option to remain in one's country a viable one for all people" (ICPD, 1994). The emphasis is on encouraging people to stay home rather than migrate in search of new opportunities. The rhetoric of the migration discourse has been so one-sided and shrill that it has drowned out the voices of reason and realism. The reality of migration seems to miss most policymakers and many governments amongst destination countries. In 2008, Sweden liberalized its immigration regime to enable easier labour immigration and to encourage companies to recruit from outside Europe. The immigration minister of Sweden at the time wrote to the ambassadors of several important countries of origin informing them of the radical immigration reform. He said that his fear was not that the liberalization of the immigration rules might result in Sweden being inundated with immigrants. Indeed, his fear was that despite the liberal immigration policy nobody might want to come to Sweden. This is true for several other countries of destination. Far from hordes of people coming many ageing economies might actually have to incentivize immigration even to attract low-skilled workers who will have better opportunities elsewhere.

Borders, Fences, and Cultures

For much of the nineteenth and the twentieth centuries, with the exception of the years between the beginning of the Great Depression and the Second World War, the world had witnessed significant mass migrations. The first major post-War recession in the early 1970s, however, ushered in the era of border controls and visa restrictions. Countries across the developed world were furiously pursuing 'the quest for control' (Castles and Miller, 2009). Addressing the very first Global Forum on Migration and Development held at Brussels in 2007, the prime minister of Belgium spoke passionately of the futility of the border control and surveillance efforts: erecting higher fences or enhancing patrolling of the land and sea borders will not stem the rising tide of would be migrants—it will only give cause to the networks of smugglers and traffickers who will flourish even as migrants will die along the way. Those who do make it will simply vanish into the dark (Verhofstadt, 2007). Thus the quest for control that has dominated policy action by which several countries seek to 'select' the migrants they want to admit and those that they want to exclude has little to show by way of success. It has in recent years severely strained the credibility of governments and caused great tragedies.

Over the past two decades, and especially after the 2001 terrorist strikes on the World Trade Center, there has been a growing securitization of migration. Borders have become like war zones, heavily policed; border management institutions have grown in power and influence and culturally there has been a narrowing of the liberal mind. Migration is seen as resulting in conflict and sometimes associated with violence and, worse still, extremism. Nothing can be further from the truth. On the contrary, there are rather serious human rights concerns regarding migrants all over the world. Besides hostility towards migrants it has resulted in a rising tide of xenophobia and an undercurrent of racism to perceptions about migrants. Some of the attacks on Indian students in Melbourne in 2009 had racial overtones, the violent migrant workers' demonstrations at the Burj Khalifa construction site in Dubai in 2006 were triggered by deplorable working and living conditions similar to indentured servitude, the widespread riots in France in 2005 were set off by police brutality, and the extensive protests for immigrant rights in the United States in 2006 were the anguished cry for immigration reform. All of these had one thing in common: in the quest for immigration control, "the line between preferences and discrimination ... is a morally thin one that is easily crossed" (Weiner, 1996). The recent action in the United Kingdom to carry out spot checks at railway stations and the streets of London under the campaign titled 'Go Home or Face Arrest', though aimed at irregular immigrants has been variously described as vile and discriminatory. There has been widespread outrage that there is an element of racial profiling in the campaign. At the other end of the world in Saudi Arabia, the Nitaqat policy of preferential treatment to the locals or the sons of the soil has led to a new kind of discrimination against migrants. This, combined with the Kafala system of having an in-country sponsor for the visa, has seriously undermined the human rights of migrant workers.

The quest for control has resulted in several countries in the developed world resorting to protectionist measures, raising tariff and non-tariff barriers against economic migrants. This has also in recent years taken the form of using international instruments as a means of extending hegemony or the sphere of influence to try and secure the policy objective of restricting migration or at the least to be selective about immigration. A striking example is the policy design of the European Union (EU) and its member states linking the signing of 'Return and Resettlement' agreements to the progress of other bilateral cooperation initiatives. Couched as part of the 'Mobility Partnership' under the 'Global Approach' to migration and mobility, under which combating irregular migration is one of the four pillars and, doubtless, for the EU member states, the most important pillar, return and resettlement agreements tend to be positioned as subtle preconditions in bilateral engagement. These agreements compel countries of origin to accept the return not just of their own nationals but also third-country nationals who might have transited through that country or were apprehended on board a vessel that had embarked from or flies the flag of that country. This flies in the face of reason. India is a case in point of why such an agreement would be unacceptable. In South Asia with its porous borders and, as a consequence, where geopolitical security-related issues are paramount, 'return and resettlement agreements' create more problems than they solve. Simply put, for India, ethnicity is not nationality. There can be a Tamil-speaking person from Sri Lanka, a Bengali-speaking person from Bangladesh or a Punjabi-speaking person from Pakistan, all of whom might look like Indians and even claim that they are from India when apprehended as undocumented migrants. A return agreement would commit India to take back these third-country nationals. What is more, several of them might have boarded the vessel clandestinely on the high seas and not at the port of embarkation. A moot point that needs empirical validation is whether at all mandatory return has the effect of reducing the flows of undocumented migrants. Thus far at least the evidence is to the contrary. In practice, border control and regulation has emerged as the central theme around which migration policies are designed and articulated. Despite this emphasis and the surveillance through sophisticated technology applications one fact that has stood out in recent times is that they have been less than successful in preventing transnational movement of people. This is especially true of irregular migration. With the legal avenues for migration progressively narrowing because of policy myopia, irregular networks have flourished in an atypical case of the bad chasing away the good.

Dealing with Irregular Migration

A striking feature of the international discourse on migration is that it has been dominated by the world view of the Global North and the multiplicity of international organizations that they dominate. The developing world is at best at the margins of this discourse. It is an inequitable engagement but one that does disservice to the developed world more than the poorer countries. Quite simply, the ageing world will need young migrant workers much more than the compulsions for the poorer countries to send their workers overseas. The western world view is that migration poses a serious challenge to welfare states, citizenship rights, democratic institutions, and cultural capital. The transnational mobility of people and the solidarity principle on which their societies are based are seen as incompatible. The result of the narrow confines of this narrative has been that the formulation and execution of policy, the institutional and operational interventions and the emphasis of multilateralism has, with single-minded focus, been on undocumented migrants. The typology of state policy instruments deployed to address this problem is truly mind-boggling, covering the entire gamut of pre-frontier, border management and post-entry measures. The increasing application of technology and raising of barriers; innovative campaigns, even if tinged with racial overtones; growing securitization of migration and new actors to control migration have been the marked features of border and entry controls. There have also been controls on employers, through inspections; control of access of undocumented workers to social security; restrictions on access to public institutions, the labour market and welfare services based on immigration status; and upon identification, the detention and expulsion rather routinely of undocumented workers. This is a far cry from the hard fact that for citizens of the newly independent countries in the post-colonial world, free movement to the metropolitan centres of the erstwhile empire was the norm. The anxiety to control irregular movement has induced some countries to use development aid as a tool by linking it to readmission and return agreements and others to outlaw undocumented migrants. Despite these draconian measures the shadow economy has been growing steadily but in the face of policy restrictions has significantly diminished the contributions of the employers and the workers alike. If this be the praxis universe of international migration, the right to migrate will necessarily be claimed clandestinely. Clandestine migration generates high human costs—deaths, deprivation, exploitation and socio-economic vulnerability. It has also meant humungous costs on building fences, raising barriers, restrictions on travel, on study abroad and even on tourism. All this has happened only in the last three decades. The policy discourse underpinning the approach to undocumented migrants has been prescriptive, proposing 'solutions' to the 'problem' based on the varying degrees of success or failure of the enforcement strategies. The approach to irregular migration in all its aspects is thus defined from the standpoint of the state as contrasted with the perspective of free movement. An assessment of the policy fragmentation, the truncated action that follows and the suboptimal outcomes reached give legitimacy to the question: could it be that the problem is the state rather than the people who are mobile? Far greater insight can be gained if a 'bottom up' approach was envisioned and irregularity were to be examined from the perspective of the political and socio-economic processes of irregularity at both the origin and destination ends, rather than just its consequences. In a classic rhetoric on the conception of and the nuanced shifts in legality and illegality, Foucault demonstrates how 'useful delinquency' becomes perniciously pervasive and explains how "the existence of a legal prohibition creates around it a field of illegal practices, which one manages to supervise, while extracting from it an illicit profit through elements, themselves illegal, but rendered manipulable by their organization in delinquency" (Foucault, 1995: 280). In a trenchant critique of the emergence of the prison and the principle of incarceration that serves as a reminder of the manner in which undocumented migrants are treated today, he goes on to argue persuasively that "it may be, therefore, that crime constitutes a political instrument" (Foucault, 1995: 289). "Replacing the adversary of the sovereign, the social enemy was transformed into a deviant, who brought with him the multiple danger of disorder, crime ..." (Foucault, 1995: 299–300). Undocumented migrants are in the end economic migrants who produce surplus value and provide diverse services to citizens. The 'undocumented migrant' is not a one-dimensional woman. She engages with documented citizens, non-citizens and migrants alike as a co-worker, family, neighbour, even a member of the same congregation. She is not hermetically separated and is indeed for much of the time undifferentiated from the others. This socio-economic reality is all too often 'unseen' by governments and policymakers. The unholy trinity of coercion, consent, and immigration restrictions produces and reproduces undocumented migration. This pattern is constituted not to physically exclude the irregular migrants but instead to socially include them under conditions of forced and protracted vulnerability. This specific characteristic of undocumented migration within the broader process of globalization can only be understood when states recognize that labour and capital are the two poles of the same, even if contradictory, social relations. This has not been the case either in bilateral engagements or in the multilateralism of international trade. The continuing challenge that undocumented migratory circuits pose defines the limits of the states in controlling borders. It also defines the autonomy of migration as an economic process, and highlights the urgency for states to ratify and implement the international conventions that provide basic rights to all migrants.

Trade, Investment, and the Movement of Natural Persons

The rationale for the World Trade Organization (WTO) established in 1995 was efficiency and equity in international trade in goods and services. It is axiomatic that the same principles ought to have applied to the mobility of the producers of these goods and the providers of these services. By design, however, the international trading system has not considered the movement of people as an integral part of transnational movement. Historically, since the years of the General Agreement on Tariffs and Trade (GATT) little attention has been paid to the movement of professionals and workers. Similarly, scarcely any work at the multilateral level has been done on the portability of skills across borders. In its preamble the WTO agreement aspires to 'reciprocal and mutually advantageous arrange-ments directed to the substantial reduction of tariffs and other barriers to trade and to the elimination of discriminatory treatment in international trade relations' amongst its members. This is not the case with regard to the movement of natural persons under Mode 4 of the General Agreement on Trade in Services (GATS). Though it has been at the centre of trade negotiations, the attention on GATS Mode 4 has been more because of the promise that it held rather than its actual achievements which have fallen far short of its potential. In fact, it is universally acknowledged that even by modest standards little has been achieved in terms of mobility of natural persons under GATS. The design and structure of the trade in services under mode 4 itself undermines the objective of enabling the presence of suppliers of services in the receiving country. It is discretionary, predicated upon the commitments a member state is willing to undertake, subject to the various schedules that it specifies and reserves the right to states to impose any restrictions on the movement of natural persons that they consider necessary. The temporary movement of natural persons is not subjected to the same rigour of discipline as the other obligations under the WTO as goods, capital, and technology are. Thus, trade in services under Mode 4 or the cross-border movement of natural persons is the chimera of the world trading system. The estimate that Mode 4 currently accounts for just about 1 per cent of the trade in services is a reflection of the restrictions imposed and the barriers raised to mobility. If mobility of people under GATS has to gain momentum and benefit from the principles of equity and efficiency three key non-tariff barriers need to be addressed: first, the Economic Needs Test (ENT), which is discretionary, not clearly defined and creates uncertainty, must be done away with. A beginning can be made at least for certain sectors and skills. Second, a multilateral framework for recognition of qualifications must be put in place; else in the absence of this countries raise regulatory barriers. And third, if national visas and work permits are not to remain the enormous barriers they are today, states must agree to separate Mode 4 movement from other migration. Perhaps, the concept of a GATS visa is an idea whose time has come. The movement of natural persons under Mode 4 of trade is, however, no substitute to a multilateral agreement on migration or to coherent global action that is rule-based and non-discriminatory.

In the close to two decades since the formation of the WTO in 1995 there has been a proliferation of Free Trade Agreements and Bilateral Investment Treaties. These agreements are often between countries with historical ties and strong economic relations. Hence they provide a more promising arena for realizing the gains of temporary movement of workers by going beyond the relatively limited scope of the GATS Mode 4 provisions. Free trade agreements seek to liberalize the trade in goods and services by dismantling tariff and non-tariff barriers and are often presented as a market-driven alternative route for cross-border movement of people. Free trade agreements and bilateral investment treaties in themselves neither promote trade nor enhance foreign investment unless labour mobility forms an integral part of these instruments. Investment and intellectual property have the potential to enhance incomes and spur development; however, a key component of this potential relates to substantially widened market access for the temporary movement of labour. Ironically, despite a proliferation of free trade agreements and bilateral investment treaties along the North–South (or indeed North–North) axis the development potential has remained largely unproven in the absence of appropriate provisions that enhance labour mobility and enable social security coordination. The investment provisions that enhance investor rights have not been shown to increase the flow of investments. Nor have stronger Intellectual Property Rights (IPR) provisions in these agreements (in the case of the United States, even the TRIPS-Plus) been shown to accelerate technology flow. Empirical evidence on such agreements and their impact on the trade and capital flows amongst signatory countries (Hallward-Dreimeier Study, 2003) have demonstrated that controlling for a time-trend and other factors they had virtually no independent effect in increasing either to a signatory country. Simply put, countries signing these agreements were no more likely to benefit from enhanced trade flows or receive additional investment than countries without such an agreement. Two important caveats to this conclusion are worth noting: First, an investment protection treaty cannot compensate for an inadequate labour mobility arrangement. Both of these are necessary conditions to enhance competitiveness of investing firms. Second, a free trade agreement will have a limited effect on trade flows and volumes for either country if restrictions on labour market access are severe, remain unchanged, and/or are fragmented by preferential treatment to segmented labour supply.

Regional integration processes have also been projected as an option to foster intra-region mobility. The EU represents the best example of a relatively advanced, even if troubled, regional integration process, despite its disparate membership and the geographic asymmetry in its development. Yet, in the context of EU enlargement, envisaging a common European migration policy would seemingly indicate a mixed metaphor in its political discourse. A discerning scholar would, however, see that it represents a split metaphor by policy design. 'Europe without Borders' was clearly meant as an objective for intra-EU mobility while 'Fortress Europe' was a reference to mobility of third-country labour into Europe. Historically, enlargement of what is now the EU has not led to major influxes of workers from the new member states (NMS). Typically, capital mobility appears to have substituted labour mobility at all stages. Was 2004 any different (with the exception of the major influx of Poles to the United Kingdom and Ireland)? Apparently not, since workers from the NMS represented less than 1 per cent of the working-age population in all member states except Austria and Ireland (OECD, 2006: 107–8). In contrast, on the 'immigration of Non-EU nationals', the EU has strived towards a common approach manifested in restricting/selective entry of third-country nationals and its one-dimensional focus on preventing 'irregular migration'. This has only served to widen the chasm between market needs and employer demands, on the one hand, and the political discourse and policy on an EU-wide basis on the other. These restrictions, which have become progressively prohibitive since 2007, have served as barriers to mobility of talent and skills to the EU. It has also spawned a 'shadow' labour market that thrives on irregular migratory labour flows from 'third countries'. Read together, despite enlargement, the labour market problems of the EU remain structural and not cyclical. This raises different questions on the ability of the largest economy (as a regional formation) to sustain growth rates over the medium to long term. The global comity of states needs to rethink the role of multilateralism with regard to the free movement of people. State interventions must be judged, as with goods and capital, by whether they catalyse growth and enhance welfare. It is time to recognize that in matters of mobility, bridges are better than fences.

5

Coming of Age

Governance for the Globe

Throughout the twentieth century, there has been an underlying tension between two logically incompatible sets of ideas; the sovereignty of states, on the one hand, and the creation of a supranational order through international law and organization on the other. Sovereignty implies the right of each state to have its own rules and institutions. International law and organization, especially when covering the vast range of matters which they now encompass, imply a serious limitation of sovereignty ... neither can triumph over its opponent.

—Roberts (2002: 317)

The Sum of Its Parts

The attention that state intervention received following the Great Depression of 1929 and the rise of the nation states post-1945 shaped the governance paradigm in the twentieth century. Along with this, the idea of citizenship was cleverly woven into what was considered essential in the new discourse of political advancement, prosperity, and modernization (Castles and Davidson, 2000). It also set the context for the apparent conflict between national interests and international concerns; between nation states and the world at large.

Yet, the events of the last three decades suggest that these are not mutually exclusive categories. It is becoming increasingly clear that governance for the globe is necessary to secure our collective future while nation states will continue to thrive and grow. Indeed, they will grow inevitably in a symbiotic relationship. We need to ask whether governance can serve the interests of the globe and not just parts of it and whether the international institutional architecture extant can meet the grand societal challenges that the world increasingly faces. We must also create conditions that will encourage countries, based on some guiding principles, to willingly cede some of their sovereign authority to a governance body for international economic migration. Our world is exceedingly more complex, interconnected, and faces societal challenges many of which are of a scale and spread that is unprecedented. The complexity arises from the fact that the world today is more than the sum of its parts. Despite the fact that it is more interconnected than ever before, it is becoming increasingly difficult to deal with challenges that affect most countries—be they political, social, or economic. The levels of interconnectivity are demonstrated through a high level of interdependence. It is a classic case of a 'sneeze–fever syndrome' where a sneeze in one part of the world causes a fever in another. For instance, sudden rising interest rates in Argentina in 1998 were the result of what happened in Russia, and Argentina could not be blamed for Russia's crisis (Stiglitz, 2002: 202). The Asian Crisis of 1997 shook the international monetary governance structure and seriously questioned the legitimacy of the International Monetary Fund (IMF). Other catastrophes have followed. Poverty, malnutrition, climate change, conflict, the Great Recession, the resource crunch, to name a few. The common thread that binds all of these problems together is that all of them have been triggered in one part by the actions of a few and went on to spread like a contagion and affect the many. They went well beyond the realms of national boundaries and beyond ideologies. We are in a world that has grown out of ideology simply because the grand societal problems are beyond ideology. They affect humanity as a whole. The twenty-first-century world is very different from the world of yesteryear. *We face a governance deficit.* Our governance framework has not been able to keep pace with the remarkable changes that the world is going through. There is a widening gap between how and where problems occur and how they are dealt with. *We have to bridge this gap by revisiting the role of global governance.*

The Governance Deficit

How did we reach this governance deficit? The dominant ideologies that were the organizing principles of societies in the past underwent multiple changes. The world view that emerged as the twentieth century drew to a close tended towards convergence with the propensities and aspirations of people, irrespective of the ideologies that had shaped their lives, making them more similar rather than different. The sharp lines of political economy that had carved the world into its parts—the First World that was capitalist and representative of an open society; the Second World bound by the egalitarian idea of socialism and perceived as a closed society; and the Third World that comprised the newly independent states and was 'non-aligned'—were gradually erased. With the end of the Cold War and the collapse of the Soviet Union, there is no Second World anymore. The economic division between the rich and poor countries has taken on the label North and South (Desai, 2002). It is safe to say that the dominant ideology that exists in most parts is capitalism, in its many forms. The most popular, however, is the school of thought that has come to be known as 'neo-liberalism'. This was strengthened and crystallized by a set of policies that came to be known as the 'Washington Consensus'. A strong state and a free economy are the chief 'hallmarks' or requirements for a neo-liberal system to function. Neo-liberalism may be understood in different ways (Gamble, 2009) as there has never been 'one neo-liberalism'. What exist as neo-liberal 'dogmas' are actually different strands of neo-liberalism. Neo-liberalism in its different forms was especially valuable in helping to articulate the new financial growth model, identifying what was wrong with Keynesianism and the extended State, and finding a new policy direction in the form of privatization, liberalization, and deregulation. The different definitions of neo-liberalism also arise from the fact that there is no agreement upon this issue. "One thing distinguishes neo-liberals—they believe in the importance of maintaining a minimal state and acknowledge that without certain functions which the state discharges, the market order could not exist at all. This is the Hobbesian side of their dilemma" (Gamble, 2009: 81). It is not counter-intuitive then that 'nation-states' are a construct of the neo-liberal paradigm.

Neo-liberalism has continued to survive and, in fact, thrive. A key feature of the neo-liberal doctrine was that it was deployed as the 'reform package' in the developing world. Asia and later Africa constituted the theatre of reform led by the World Bank and the IMF. Under the guise of reforms, newly independent countries seeking to find their economic feet were drawn into opening up their markets, deregulating core sectors of the economy and privatizing the commanding heights of their economies. Besides enabling the developed world and their transnational corporations to gain access to developing markets, the developed world was able to extend its hegemony over economic governance in their pursuit of market access and capital accumulation. This was new imperialism at work through the international institutions established to legitimize governance by the elite. *Good governance* emerged as a buzzword around the last decade of the twentieth century. The structural adjustment programmes were not working as anticipated. There were discussions of human development and the need to give a human face to the impact of neo-liberal reforms and counteract its effects. Non-government organizations advocating human rights together with social movements that demanded democratization were becoming more prominent in the developing world. The World Bank issued a report in 1989 in which it identified the failure of public institutions as the root cause of weak economic performance. The Bank was keen not on moving away from the Washington Consensus but beyond it. It admitted that the root cause of the poor economic performance was the failure of public institutions. The president of the World Bank at the time, Barber B. Conable, defined *good* governance as "public service that is efficient, a judicial system that is reliable, and an administration that is accountable to its public" (World Bank, 1989: xii). The progress that we have made in purely conventional economic terms *seems* to have been abetted by the inception and acceptance of the neo-liberal system (notwithstanding the fact that it is now fashionably being referred to as an 'intellectual swear word') since the second half of the twentieth century. The world gross domestic product (GDP) has experienced tremendous growth in the past half century. However, contrary to claims of a paradigm shift towards a more 'Keynesian world', at least in the invocation of ideology (due to evident failures of the system, especially signified by the global recession), we have never completely stepped out of the 'neo-liberal paradigm' that our world was brought to in the Thatcher–Reagan era.

Neo-liberalism also meant an excessive emphasis on expanding international trade in goods and services and the expansion of international capital. The rise of transnational corporations deterritorialized production of goods and the provision of services; gave rise to global manufacturing supply chains, and led to the capture of valuable natural resources. The General Agreement on Tariffs and Trade after the protracted Uruguay Round gave birth to the World Trade Organization (WTO). Contemporary globalization now demanded that nation states co-operate. This 'multilateralism' has been deployed selectively to expand international trade, facilitate the movement of international capital, and to protect intellectual property. Capital and manufacturing were taken to where low-wage surplus labour was available, restricting labour mobility. Factor mobility was no more an essential economic principle. Labour did not follow capital. New bilateral instruments for investment protection came to be crafted, and regional and bilateral free trade agreements proliferated. None of them contained any provisions relating to mobility of labour or portability of skills, or dealt with the free movement of natural persons. This obsession with material progress through trade in goods and expansion of markets was to the near-complete exclusion of human development, geographic inclusion, or evenhanded distribution of its benefits. As the large corporations with deep pockets grew in spread and depth, they destroyed in their wake livelihoods of traditional occupations. Even as countries were forced to embrace neoliberal programmes funded by the Bank and the IMF, they became that much more vulnerable to external pressures and their economies more fragile.

In the developed world, meanwhile, countries were raising barriers to entry. While trade and services were governed through the WTO, immigration was squarely placed within the sovereign rights of countries. They thus raised innovative (and sometimes not-so-innovative) tariff and non-tariff barriers to restrict the mobility of people. Liberalizing the policy regime on the mobility of people has been left out of the bucket list for creation of institutions. While the transnational movement of goods and capital is seen to be in the realm of global governance requiring states to submit to a rule-based multilateral regime administered by a supranational body, the transnational movement of people is still seen to vest decidedly in the realm of nation-state sovereignty. Most recently (with effect from November 2013) India, which is seen as a potential supplier of high-skilled migrants (in the form of professionals, students, entrepreneurs) was put on a list of 'high-risk' countries for the issuance of visas of duration of six months or less to visit the United Kingdom. The only way for an individual seeking to travel was to pay a bond of GBP 3,000 to be refunded if the individual were to return without overstaying the visa period. Introduced with the intention of preventing illegal migration, this policy measure was counter-intuitive and has since been withdrawn after widespread protests and perhaps the realization that it will harass legitimate visitors to the United Kingdom more than help stop irregular migrants. It was clear to all that the consular policy at least in this case was barking up the wrong tree. It had struck an odd note following Prime Minister David Cameron's visit to India with one of the biggest business delegations abroad. "The UK is open for business," he had said just a few months before. Such restrictive policies have repercussions. There is evidence to suggest that the outcomes are often counterproductive and result in adverse selection. They also cause discontent. The discontent is real and unless this is addressed, multilateral platitudes like the 'Millennium Development Goals' will not help eradicate deep-rooted economic and social inequity. We need to seriously question the relevance of the international institutions available for global governance and revisit their mandate, composition, and modes of engagement. Doing so will enable us to measure the governance deficit and perhaps help define first principles for global governance that are essential in our old, new world.

The Imperatives of Global Governance

Robert Cox, drawing on Polanyi, argued that neo-liberalism as a political and ideological project should be understood as the successor to the economic liberalism of the 19th century, the ideological and political projects which had been responsible for the free markets experiments of the time ... Much of the deregulation that occurred in the neo-liberal era, as Michael Moran has pointed out also involved re-regulation, the establishment of different kinds of agencies and regulatory bodies overseeing a freer market.

—Gamble (2009: 86–7, 90)

Whether you are a hyperglobalist/globalization enthusiast or an anti-globalist, it is important to keep in mind that globalization is not a 'new' phenomenon. The late nineteenth century and the early twentieth centuries also experienced globalization albeit with some differences. The obvious differences are the ones seen in trade. Trade then was inter-sectoral. Trade now is mostly intra-firm. The biggest difference that plays an important role in shaping societies is in the mobility of people. Mobility of people was unrestricted in the late nineteenth and early twentieth century. Barriers are recent phenomena. It has never been harder to migrate in the history of humankind (Nayyar, 2008). This is ironic, considering how easy it is to travel across time and space now. Capitalism, globalization and global governance are inter-woven processes. For example, *Globalization* has reduced barriers in trade but this has had an impact on the mobility of workers. It has enhanced mobility for the privileged and skilled workers but increased the elasticity of demand for semi-skilled and unskilled workers (Rodrik, 1997). This means that the *governance* for semi-skilled and unskilled workers is left to the uncertainties of the market. Global governance without a global government is the dilemma that has become real for this century. Our governance system exists in the form of institutions that were built in the middle of the twentieth century. They represented the rule of the elite in which a trans-Atlantic conceptualization provided for 'de jure' political equality to all countries and 'de facto' control to a select few. As already noted in the first chapter, the United Nations General Assembly represents the Westphalia ideology of sovereignty of 'nation-states' whereas the United Nations Security Council represents the 'Concert of Europe' (Desai, 2002). The world has transformed dramatically from the time the 'Bretton Woods' institutions were conceptualized. That construct is outdated, the ideologies archaic, and the underlying principles that formed the rationale for those institutions obsolete. More important, the balance of power in the world is changing. In the rebalancing, the Global South is no more the subaltern. The international organizations themselves appear to be stuck in a time warp, ill-equipped to respond to the new demands of a multipolar world. What we face now is a classic case of 'governance deficit'. There is a wide and glaring gap between our problems and the instruments that we have as a world community to cope with these problems. Our challenges are *spatial* and *intergenerational*. Spatial because we are unable to deal with the world as a whole and are still prisoners to categories that are no more relevant. We still speak for the 'north' or the 'south', the 'developed' or the 'developing' regions, the countries of destination or of origin. We are still deeply suspicious of foreigners and still ring-fence our communities based on a monocultural identity. We still believe in the 'cultural capital' argument and find ways to exclude the 'other'. We are not one people but many communities within communities defined not just by geographic borders but also by colour, ethnicity, and material wealth. Very obvious examples are the unsuccessful and inconclusive Doha Round. Climate change is constantly being spoken of, concern is being expressed, effects are being felt—intergenerational because we tend to take a short-term view of the world and its resources—and yet there is very little consensus on what we might be able to do as a community. Long-term problems cannot have short-term solutions. We stop not to pause and ask whether we have a longer-term vision of the world and a sustainable development path that will help us give to the next generation a better world than that we inherited. It also gains a profoundly inter-generational poignancy because of the inequality of today's world. Not only is the Gini Coefficient between countries as bad as never before, the intra-country Gini Coefficient also shows disturbing asymmetry. Several generations will pass, millions will perish with no access whatever even to basic amenities—education, health, and economic opportunities—while the global elite will continue to aggrandize themselves. Some of the governance deficit comes from the severe limitations of the policy frame and the institutional architecture extant but the greater part of it comes from the lacunae—inherent and instrumental—in the exercise of hegemony that uses all its powers to prevent the democratization of development. "International institutions like the WTO, the IMF, the WB and others provide an ad hoc system of global governance, but it is a far cry from global government and lacks democratic accountability.

Although it is perhaps better than not having any system of global governance, this system is structured not to serve general interests or assure equitable results ..." (Stiglitz 2002: 204).

Keynes' counsel to the world at a point of crisis is supposed to have given birth to the IMF. It has, however, completely turned his advice on its head. The IMF was set up with the objective of overseeing international monetary cooperation and promoting the growth of world trade. The International Bank for Reconstruction and Development, which later became the World Bank, is the international institution for providing capital to developing countries. Both the IMF and the World Bank are Bretton Woods institutions. Since these bodies were created in the year 1945, they have been a part of an interstate system (now called international). As mentioned earlier, these are institutions that belong to a different time, a different world. The voting rights in the IMF and the World Bank were allocated not on a one-country, one-vote basis, but on the basis of the quotas subscribed to by countries to the capital of the IMF and the World Bank. These organizations have been rendered less than optimal by the current state of affairs and have come to be associated with First World institutions, run in the interests of the First World (Desai, 2002). The international financial institutions have been accused of advancing a particular ideology. According to critics like Stiglitz (2002), the market fundamentalism that is doggedly pursued makes for bad economics as well as bad politics.

These institutions were built on the idea that markets exist and in some ways assuming that they work fully well. This is obviously not true and much less for developing countries. The 'paternalism' demonstrated by the insistence of the IMF on discipline provided by capital markets is reminiscent of a colonial mentality (Stiglitz, 2002). The role of economies within societies has been ignored and implementation of policies without a broader vision of societies has undermined the organic development of newly emerging democracies (Stiglitz, 2002). The United Nations has singularly failed in its objective of preventing war. It has also been in a state of paralysis when prompt action needs to be taken. Who can forget Rwanda or Kosovo? More recently it has failed in its attempts to be a representative of the comity of nations for the prevention of conflict. Again, who can forget Iraq or the current situation in Syria? It is in many ways an ineffective body and no greater than a high-profile talk shop. The General Assembly has come to be associated with the Third World and the Security Council is an expression of the Concert of Europe.

Governance and Social Transformation

Karl Polanyi's immense contribution to institutional econom-ics and the social sciences in general and his theory of 'The Great Transformation' (1944) have resonance in our discussion on global governance. There are numerous ways of interpreting Polanyi's the-ory. We attempt to showcase the strength of the need for governance by highlighting some of his ideas that transcend the context, space, and time they were originally used in (i.e., nineteenth-century indus-trializing England and tribal economies). Polanyi concluded that institutions were essential for *maximizing* the functions of the mar-kets. In his eloquent words, "The origins of the catastrophe lay in the Utopian endeavour of economic liberalism to set up a self-regulating market system. A self-regulating market is an artificial disruption of society" (Polanyi, 2001: 31). The market is also an institution, unlike the conception that it is a 'natural phenomena'. Markets have to be developed. They have to be 'deliberately constructed' (Chang, 2003: 120). Markets do not exist outside of societies. They are 'embedded' in the social life of human beings. "[I]n no case can we assume the functioning of the market laws unless a self-regulating market is shown to exist. Only in the *institutional setting* of market economy are market laws relevant ..." (Polanyi, 2001: 46, empha-sis added). Borrowing from this strong argument, we argue for the 'deliberate construction' of a market for labour, that is liberalization of the labour market for, 'economic migrants' and that this market needs a strong organization to govern it.

It has been argued by Gray (1998) that the WTO (and other similar) 'governance' bodies have adopted and advanced Polanyi's prescriptions. Increasingly, economic globalization, which has out-paced political globalization (Nayyar, 2003), seeks to undermine and not strengthen the current regime of laissez-faire. It has been widely accepted that if there is to be a free market on a 'wider scale' we need a legal framework that entails the sacrifice of the absolute sovereignty of nation states. The rules of this new game need to be placed in a sacred unchangeable domain (Gray, 1998). Hence the need to establish a rule-based democratic body for the governance of migration that serves to 'mutualize' the interests of all countries of the world and not to serve as another instrument for the maintenance of the status quo. The idea of 'pure' market capitalism removed from any social institution does not and cannot exist (Brown, 1990: 46). The second arm of the 'double movement' that Polanyi talks about is self-protection. This also finds a parallel in light of the economic inequality and insecurity that a majority of people encounter. Movements—whether populist and xenophobic, fundamentalist or neo-communist—have raised their heads all over the world. Easier movement of 'economic migrants' addresses the question of inequality to a great extent—after all, it will present migrants with the ability and willingness to migrate to explore better employment opportunities.

The importance of Polanyi's theory of social transformation in understanding the acceleration of neo-liberal globalization since the mid-1970s has been acknowledged in the research by Dr Stephen Castles and his colleagues at the University of Sydney (Castles et al., 2011). They do not rely exclusively on Polanyi's theory but consider it a starting point because of the relevance of his theory. However, the views of Polanyi and his other supporters have been strongly contested and called out to the battlefield. Among Polanyi's contemporaries, Hayek is his challenger. Hayek's book was published around the same time as Polanyi's. Hayek took off from where other liberal thinkers left. He argued that society was a self-organizing organic process and not a result of human action (Desai, 2002). Desai offers a rather caustic challenge to the spirit of Polanyi's contribution. His interpretation marks Polanyi's theory as anti-market. He argues that Polanyi's theory would be against even a well-functioning market as it is inconsistent with the 'democratic, humanist polity'. He critiques it for being temporally and spatially specific because it was based in industrializing England (Desai, 2002). Even with this well-thought-out critique, the spirit of Polanyi's theory is not lost. If Polanyi's theory is to be applied to the contemporary context, its most important implication would be the justification for the governance of the markets. Governance institutions for international monetary cooperation like the IMF and the World Bank are based on the assumption that markets work, that markets are benevolent.

While the liberalization of the market for the mobility of people is a must, we must also recognize that migration has its downsides. These need to be ironed out. There needs to be a global policy harmonization to mutualize the gains and losses through a supranational governance institution. The concept of governance gained popularity (and later notoriety) with the failure of structural adjustment programmes that were being carried out in the developing world. The worst of its effects were in sub-Saharan Africa. The cry for 'human development' led to the Bank's insistence on 'good governance'. This meant reforms for the already 'slim' governments. There was an attempt to impose governance through certain indices. For some time it was believed that we had stepped into a new paradigm—that neo-liberalism was history. However, the 'good governance' agenda seemed to be the same bitter tonic in a new bottle. Conditionality for 'good governance' became the order of the day especially for borrowing from the Bank. Mushtaq Khan (2007) differentiated between 'Market enhancing governance' and 'growth enhancing governance'. *Do as we say and not as we have done (or have done historically)' seemed to become the dictum.* The tenets of the Washington Consensus were never blindly accepted by the 'most successful globalizing countries'. They determined their own pace of development (Stiglitz, 2002). Market fundamentalism has become the mistaken child of the paradigm that we live in. The 'East Asian miracle' is not an example of a blind acceptance of policies propagated by the international monetary institutions. The very successful economic transition has been at their own pace, on the terms and conditions set by their governments (Wade, 1990; Chang, 2006). Let us extend the argument for governance to a global level. Polanyi's theory helps us establish the *need for governance* of markets for they do not exist independently or outside of societies. That idea is dystopian. This is important to understand in the light of governance structures that we currently have in place internationally. Current imperatives demand governance that *does no harm; is democratic, neutral, effective, representative, fair and beneficial to the world as a whole.* The guiding principle for governance should certainly not be the evocation of a colonial mentality, an accusation that rings through the corridors of the current institutions.

Now let's narrow this down to migration. We need a genuine coalition of interests. The Global North or the Global South cannot stand alone. It is becoming increasingly tempting, though, to suggest that the Global South (especially the BRICS [Brazil, Russia, India, China, and South Africa]) should take the leadership role in fostering a consensus for governance. We live in an interdependent world in every sense—economically, demographically, and in terms of levels of development. If democratic capitalism is our future (without leaning on either side, that is not conforming to the ideas of market fundamentalism, ideas of doing away with the state or heavily leaning on a 'welfare state' concept) as it has proved to be the most successful organizing principle for modern society, we need better governance.

The dilemma remains. Is it possible to have a democratic institution to 'govern' migration? Is it possible to seriously challenge the current status quo on migration, and to challenge the categories of convenience that have been created and established as 'win–win' situations for 'countries of origin' and 'countries of destination'. These categories are becoming increasingly irrelevant. We have seen that existing structures for 'global governance' serve narrow interests. Is it then possible to imagine governance for an issue like migration? "The overall picture of global migration governance remains incoherent, poorly understood and lacks an overarching vision" (Betts, 2010: 1). What exists as global migration governance is a disparate set of attempts at 'managing migration'. As Newland (2005) rightly points out, the use of the term, 'migration management' suggests a slightly old-fashioned and pre-globalization assumption of state control over migration processes. It took several years for migration to even figure on the agendas in global policy discussions. Borders have been accepted as sacrosanct and entry controls seem so natural. There seems to be no option for global governance of migration that has not been proposed/discussed/debated/critiqued/ridiculed. The idea of a 'World Migration Organization' analogous to the WTO for a consensus on global migration policy (Bhagwati, 1992 and Helton, 2003) has been suggested and calls for a New International Regime for Orderly Movement of People (NIROMP) (Migration News, 2002) have been made. There are recommendations for bodies like the International Organization for Migration (IOM), International Labour Organization (ILO) or the WTO to become 'lead organizations' for the coordination of governance efforts for international migration (Newland, 2005). There have been proposals for 'bilateral deals' between rich and poor countries that set up ingenious arrangements for labour mobility (especially for the unskilled), which would benefit the migrants as well as the sending and receiving countries (Pritchett, 2006). Going beyond how global governance is traditionally defined, Anne-Marie Slaughter introduces the idea that governance exists through a complex set of 'government networks'. Despite questions of democratic accountability, this new world order cannot be one in which some 'world government' enforces global diktats. The governments we already have at home are our best hope for tackling the problems we face abroad, in a networked world order (Slaughter, 2009). Given imperatives such as differing demographic futures in the rich and poor countries, the widening gap between countries of the world, the rising number of in situ services, also termed 'hardcore non-tradables' (Pritchett, 2006) and the 'globalization of everything but labour' will lead to an increased number of migrants. Formalizing 'governance of migration' and making it more coherent, straightforward, and fair is an opportunity. The question really is whether we are ready for a global mobility consensus and a one world, one people paradigm. What is at stake is whether we want to bridge the gap between the world's rich and privileged and the world's poorest and disadvantaged. We need to act with speed for inclusive growth in the future.

6

A Global Mobility Compact

> A realistic approach to multilateralization must first recognize that its
> principles ... exist only as ideals.
>
> —Dadush (2010: 4)

In Search of a Global Framework

The economic history of the last three decades has demonstrated that
economic development is far too important to be left to the markets
alone simply because a perfect market mechanism is a utopian idea.
Governance is a prerequisite for the efficient functioning of markets,
for maximizing growth, to widen access and to democratize welfare.
Economic migration must be market-driven and calibrated by the
demand for and the supply of labour and skills. This cannot be a 'self-
regulating' market, though. There is need for a multilateral framework
and an impartial, independent body to govern international migration. There are many international conventions that have sought to
provide such a multilateral framework. Notable among these are the
'International Convention on the Protection of the Rights of All
Migrant Workers and Members of Their Families, 1990' and the
'ILO Multilateral Framework on Labour Migration, 2005'. The first
establishes normative standards from a 'rights'-based perspective but

is yet to be ratified by most countries and hence remains a paper tiger. The second seeks to provide principles for guidance and action to maximize the benefits of migration for all parties, but is non-binding and hence a toothless tiger.

The mandate on migration is currently fragmented across different institutions like the International Organization for Migration (IOM), United Nations High Commissioner for Refugees (UNHCR), International Labour Organization (ILO), and so on, which deal with different types of migration and therefore different types of migrants. However, serious discussion on migration governance has not figured in the mainstream agenda in the UN system. There have been a few feeble attempts like the International Conference for Population and Development (ICPD), the Global Commission on International Migration (GCIM) and the Global Forum on Migration and Development (GFMD) which have not been able to bring about any substantive change and have often worked towards the maintenance of the status quo in international migration. Within the United Nations system, migration governance is fragmented across several organizations, though efforts have been made, but with little result, to infuse some degree of coherence through what has come to be termed as the Global Migration Group (GMG). The GMG is an inter-agency group seeking to promote the wider application of all international and regional instruments and norms relating to migration, and to encourage the adoption of more coherent, comprehensive, and better-coordinated approaches to the issue of international migration.

It is essential that there is a consensus on the imperatives for the international mobility of people. Countries have barely just agreed at the global level (GFMD, 2010) to not 'criminalize' irregular migrants but there has not been much movement forward otherwise. The need for a rule-based multilateral framework for migration has been voiced from time to time. In reality, though, the platforms that discuss migration have always been in the nature of 'voluntary, informal, non-binding bodies for the management of migration.' It is indeed time that the international community moves decisively towards 'a global migration compact' that will constitute an agreement among countries to govern the international mobility of economic migrants and the portability of skills. Such a compact must be based on a minimum set of universally accepted principles of international migration. It should also be binding.

We live in a world that is constantly changing. It is worth recalling that demographic transition is a natural force that creates structural changes in population. Economic transition creates aspirations. These forces are compelling. One of the great concerns of a majority of the world's population in the century gone by and the century that we live in is the search for better opportunities. This drives people from villages to towns and then to cities. This is the 'supply' side of labour—demography creating huge youth dividends or bulges (according to how these are or are not reaped) and economic growth catalysing aspirations to a 'better life'. The demand side is characterized by population ageing and high dependency ratios. The demand for labour is also driven by certain types of jobs being non-transferable. Besides, higher educational attainment has also meant lower labour market participation rates. Even in young countries like India in some ageing states with a declining working-age population, young people are unwilling to do low-paying work. A case in point is the state of Kerala in India where it is difficult to find agricultural labour from amongst the locals because they have either migrated to the Gulf or are unwilling to work at the market wage. The state is now served by a considerable number of farm workers from other Indian states. What is clear is that demographic deficits are structural and cause endemic labour shortages. Another important factor is that technology is rapidly changing the way work is done resulting in the demand for a higher order of skills while the demand for unskilled and low-skilled jobs is steadily declining. All of this has created severe skills shortages in several geographies and across diverse sectors. A key intervention to develop a robust skills market where the demand for and the supply of skills will be need-based is to liberalize the transnational movement of economic migrants.

A World of the Future

In the year 2013, the number of migrants worldwide was 232 million (UN-DESA, 2013), which roughly makes up 3 per cent of the world population. However, this large number includes different groups of people—refugees, asylum seekers, migrants for family reunification, and economic migrants. The category of 'economic migrants' is defined vaguely and quite grudgingly in existing literature on migration. It consists of all those people who emigrate from one region to another for the purpose of seeking employment and who are not refugees. While there cannot be a mutually exclusive distinction, it is important that a distinction be made between non-economic and economic migrants. The category of economic migrants includes students, workers, professionals, entrepreneurs, scientists, technologists, business people, and independent service providers.

The Universal Declaration of Human Rights (1948) as well as the International Covenant on Civil and Political Rights (ICCPR, 1966) recognize the importance of freedom of movement, that is, nationals have the right to leave their country of origin. The 2009 Human Development Report, 'Overcoming Barriers: Human Mobility and Development' defined mobility as "the ability of individuals, families or groups of people to choose their place of residence" (UNDP, 2009: 15). Ironically, a rapidly globalizing world is also increasingly imposing restrictions on the movement of people. Huntington in his *Clash of Civilizations* had argued that nation states would remain the most powerful actors in world affairs (Huntington, 1993). This is not exaggerated. The right to freedom of movement is recognized but it is within the sovereign authority of each state to accept or reject an immigrant. Hyper-globalists like Ohmae claim that 'the nation state is increasingly a nostalgic fiction' (Ohmae, 1995). It is not. It is fiction to assume that we are close to such a day. The governance of the mobility of refugees and asylum seekers must remain within the realm of sovereign states (or at least until such a time as a better solution is found) as these have implications for national security, diplomatic relations, and national policy. Economic migration must, however, be placed in the global governance realm. Governance of international migration is strongly resisted because it is seen as a threat to national sovereignty. This sense of trepidation is misplaced. Global governance seeks to improve coordination and cooperation between states and therefore in no way limits national sovereignty. In fact, sovereignty is only limited by insufficient global governance (UN, 2013). Also, highly politicized as the issue is, there is evidence to suggest that better-governed economic migration (or, to use the more politically correct term, mobility) can catalyse global economic growth rates.

The idea of a borderless world is fascinating but romantic and far-fetched. It is also impractical. On the other hand, the current policy regimes in many countries of stringent restrictions to entry, severe visa regimes, and growing barriers to transnational movement of people are both counter-intuitive and counterproductive. The current phase of globalization has seen processes that have restricted mobility of labour and in fact has been seeking ways to substitute labour mobility in the production of goods or in the provision of services. One explanation for this is that due to reasons found in economic theory there may have been a belief among public and policymakers that reducing trade barriers is a substitute for international migration (Rodrik, 1997).

However, to state the truth rather bluntly, trade is seen as beneficial to the North and hence there are attempts to liberalize trade whereas international migration is seen to benefit countries in the South and therefore liberalization of mobility is restricted. There is mounting evidence though that the benefits of expansion in international trade have not been even; in fact it is indeed the developed world that has gained more from international trade than countries of the developing world. Equally, the benefits that flow from transnational capital have been skewed in favour of the rich. Vast masses of people in the developing world live in abject poverty with no means of improving their lives. The world will of necessity require a liberal regime for international migration as it has for trade and capital flows. On a multilateral basis countries will have to agree upon a minimum set of rules and be governed by them. Unilateral barriers or measures that violate the minimum agreed principles of international migration must attract penalties. There must be as much traction between countries to enter into human resource mobility partnerships as there is to enter into investment protection agreements or free trade agreements.

It is now widely recognized that owing to the large differences in average income between countries and wide wage differentials both the incentive for and the potential gains from greater migration remain large. The association between openness to migration and growth is much stronger, especially in the long run, than the associations with openness to trade (Rodrik, 1997). Empirical studies carried out comparing the results of trade and investment liberalization with the gains from freeing up human mobility estimate that by removing all the barriers to migration, world GDP could be more than double (Hamilton and Whalley, 1984). This study was later updated. The authors compared developments over time with the aim of producing more reasonable and politically relevant scenarios. The updated results suggest that the estimated gains from the liberalization of global immigration controls have increased substantially (Moses and Letnes, 2004). For an idea of what they are proposing, the estimate is that a 10 per cent increase in international migration corresponds to an efficiency gain of about USD 774 billion (1998) (Ortega and Giovanni, 2012). There are other studies that challenge the assumption that "gains from migration accrue solely from factor price equalization arising from movements of people between countries" (Rosso et al., 2012: 2). Other studies prove that the benefits from migration have a wider impact. For example, a cross-country analysis confirms that an increase in the foreign-born population is associated with an increase in income per person (Ortega and Giovanni, 2012).

The period between 1870 and 1914 was that of laissez-faire and the period between these years was witness to a globalized world. This can be compared to what has come to be known as 'contemporary globalization'. There are marked differences. For example, differences in how finance is liberalized—there is much more global banking now than there was in what may be known as the 'first phase of globalization'. Another marked difference is in labour mobility. In the so-called First Globalization era, international migration (along with international trade and capital flows) was high relative to the population. Some economic historians have argued that migration was an important vehicle for economic convergence in terms of factor prices and income levels during that period (Taylor and Williamson, 1997). The analysis of the role of immigration in accounting for cross-country differences in income has been neglected because of the relatively low levels of immigration (and trade) in many countries for several decades.

However, since the 1980s, a second era of globalization has begun rekindling interest in the question. Putterman and Weil (2010) have argued that migration played an important role in the early economic development of many countries and its effects have been sustained. According to Hall and Jones (1999) and Acemoglu et al.

(2001, 2002), the main reason why geography appears to be a crucial determinant of cross-country differences in income per capita is that geography was decisive in determining a country's history of colonization which, in turn, laid the foundations for the existing institutional arrangements in many countries. A recent study by the World Bank suggests that trade can have poverty-reducing effects only if it is accompanied with removal of barriers in labour mobility. The authors discuss trade in Africa and its results on poverty reduction (Le Goff and Singh, 2013). "For comparative advantage to increase the incomes of unskilled workers, workers need to be able to move out of shrinking sectors and into expanding ones. If there are too many barriers to labor mobility and the entry and exit for firms, the potential for poverty-reducing impacts of trade may remain untapped" (Le Goff and Singh, 2013: 2). A contra view about trade and mobility is expressed by Rodrik (1997). He suggests that the liberalization of trade and investment deepens the divide between the groups that have the ability to migrate and those that have not. In other words, liberalization of trade increases the mobility of high-skilled migrants and professionals who are free to move to a place of deficit—where there is a high demand for them while for unskilled and semiskilled workers, it is a great disadvantage. Putting the same point in more technical terms, globalization makes the demand for the services of unskilled and semiskilled workers more elastic—that is, the services of large segments of the working population can be more easily substituted by the services of other people across national boundaries. The grey markets will continue to exist unless labour restrictions are eased by governments.

The Story So Far

Let us now briefly turn to the attempts made hitherto towards a global view on migration. The International Conference for Population and Development held in 1994 was touted as the first Global Conference on Population and Development. The participation in the conference was unprecedented. The Programme of Action was signed by 179 states amongst which one was to "address the individual, social and economic impact of urbanization and migration". In a review of the ICPD achievements in the year 2003, it was reported that around

73 per cent of countries reported action on international migration. "Measures included plans, programmes and strategies on international migrants and/or refugees, laws or legislation on international migrants and migrant workers ..." (UNFPA, 2004). The ICPD is known as a milestone in the history of population and development and in the history of women's rights (UNFPA, 2004) but it made less than a significant impact on the discourse of migration and development. It did not break away from the 'sedentary bias' of development and was more or less ignored in practice.

The next important milestone was the Global Commission on International Migration (GCIM) established in December 2003 by Sweden and Switzerland together with the governments of Brazil, Morocco, and the Philippines with a view to providing a framework for the formulation of a coherent, comprehensive, and global response to migration issues. Its mandate was to place international migration on the global agenda, analyse gaps in migration policy, and examine linkages with other issues and present recommendations to the UN Secretary General, governments, and other stakeholders. As part of its work, the GCIM undertook research and analysis, consultations with stakeholders, regional hearings in different regions of the world and information sharing. It submitted a final report to the United Nations Secretary General (UNSG) in October 2005. The GCIM proposed some principles for action: that people should be able to migrate out of choice rather than necessity; international migration should become an integral part of the national, regional, and global strategies for economic growth; addressing irregular migration; protecting the rights of all migrants; strengthening social cohesion and cultural diversity through integration, and enhancing governance through coherence, cooperation, and capacity building. This could have served as a good template to start with but little has been done to build on them.

The process mandated by the UNSG through the mechanism of a Special Representative supported by a clutch of ad hoc groups—the Friends of the Forum and the Troika—to continue the high-level dialogue was the Global Forum on Migration and Development (GFMD). The GMFD describes itself as the "largest and the most comprehensive global platform for dialogue and cooperation on migration and development". It has been called the most 'inclusive' forum for dialogue on migration available to states. The drawback is that it is not inclusive, either in terms of its participants (both state and non-state actors) or in terms of the range of migration topics that it covers (Betts, 2010). The expectations from the GFMD, to begin with, were modest since it was meant to be a non-binding forum for the free and frank exchange of views. Hence its performance, unsurprisingly, is less than modest. This can best be judged from the assessment of the GFMD carried out by the GFMD itself through a survey of the participating governments. It says:

> A number of governments regret a lack of practical policy outcomes and a certain bias towards migration issues in contrast to develop-ment issues …. The main impacts of the GFMD are its contribution to the international debate on migration and development and the fostering of exchange of policies and practices at the international level. In comparison, its impact at the national level is considered to be weaker. (GFMD, 2011)

In the absence of a global 'institution' for migration, scholars like Dr Stephen Castles have argued for a conceptual framework for migration and an institutional framework which would provide for membership like the UN. Professor Jagdish Bhagwati famously put forth the idea of a 'World Migration Organisation' on economic grounds, an organization analogous to the World Trade Organization (WTO) (Bhagwati, 2003). Late legal scholar Arthur Helton also sug-gested something similar but on normative grounds. Arguing for a multilateral framework, he suggested that the current incoherent policy framework feeds into 'friction and fears' (Helton in Newland, 2005). He argued that a comprehensive global migration policy may not be achieved without appropriate institutional arrangements at an international level (Helton in Newland, 2005).

Bimal Ghosh offered the outline for a New International Regime for Orderly Movements of People (NIROMP) aimed at managing the increasing number of international migrants. His vision is that of "regulated openness" for a migration policy that is "politically achiev-able and operationally viable" (Ghosh, 2000). However, sweeping statements like "huge waves of emigrants from poor and weak states" suggest that his position does not break free from the discourse that international migration is mired in—one that focuses on entry controls. His argument that extremely poor people migrate runs counter to years of established empirical work on migration transition. The poorest are never the ones that leave home. His approach may be radical at face value but is rather conservative and serves more as an apologist's view.

The Barcelona Development Agenda of the year 2005 discussed international migration. It bagged the sixth spot in the seven issues on its agenda. The authors agreed that there was a need for 'rules' to govern international migration and that freer international mobility would reap more benefits for the global economy—much more than international trade does. Building on this point, the development economist Deepak Nayyar (2008) points to the need for a multilateral framework for free international mobility—something akin to what global trade has achieved—this suggestion is remarkable. He, however, does this with a regular dose of skepticism attached. There is hope but not without a 'this may be a thing of the future' disclaimer.

There have been suggestions for the management or governance of migration. The opposition to these are mostly from policymakers, academics, and 'citizens' who would actually go for the jugular of the ones who suggest that migration should be governed because they firmly believe that 'immigration' lies in the sacred realm of the 'sovereign' nation states. This 'sovereignty' is only compromised for nobler causes—like the freer mobility of goods and services but not for those who are the producers of these goods, the providers of these services or those who consume these goods and services.

Where Do We Stand?

No, migration is not a 'problem'. And it is certainly not going away! Migration is a truly global phenomenon. There is no country in the world that is unaffected by migration. Countries always feature in one or more than one categories (origin, destination, transit) at some point in time. The neoliberal system has rendered the nation states as its strongest actors. However, migration cannot be in the realm of national sovereignty forever. The behaviour of the comity of nation states in relation to a global response to international migration is akin to ostriches burying their heads in the sand. Migration will take place with or without a consensus on migration and it will take place with or without a multilateral organization. However, we have an opportunity to build a consensus to embed the international market for labour and skills in an organization that will mutualize the benefits from migration.

Migration has shaped the societies we live in and will continue to do so. The stocks and flows are becoming increasingly complex. The participation of women as active migrant workers is only increasing. The United Nations General Assembly met in 2014 to review the progress of the ICPD, 1994. Twenty years after the first global conference on population and development, how different is our approach? The migration discourse in various forums has been discussed above. Apart from these efforts, there have also been regional initiatives. These have helped ease migration in the regions concerned. For example, the Southern Common Market (MERCOSUR) helped increase mobility of people in Latin America. The European Union achieved a 'Europe without borders' for its population but it resulted in 'Fortress Europe' for the rest of the world. Artificial constructs such as 'temporary migration' and 'circular migration' in effect undermine the very nature of migration but are extolled in global discussions on migration such as at the GFMD. These categories are also reflective of the level of commitment or the lack of it to issues of mobility. These categories are essentially meant to deter movement. The demographic dynamic, the growing inequality, the unequal distribution of opportunity, the deceleration of growth rates all over the world and the growing divide between the economics and politics of mobility are all compelling factors for mobility of people. We need to wake up from our deep slumber and smell the coffee. A Global Compact is essential and so is a multilateral institution for migration.

The Way Ahead

The post-2015 development agenda perhaps sets the context for a global compact on migration. The Universal Agenda, as it has been termed, envisages five big transformative shifts: First, leave no one behind—move from reducing to ending extreme poverty, in all its forms. We should ensure that no person—regardless of ethnicity, gender, geography, disability, race, or other status—is denied universal human rights and basic economic opportunities. Second, put sustainable development at the core—act now to halt the alarming pace of climate change and environmental degradation, which pose unprecedented threats to humanity. We must bring about more social inclusion. Third, transform economies for jobs and inclusive growth—for a quantum leap forward in economic opportunities and a profound economic transformation to end extreme poverty and improve livelihoods. Fourth, build peace and effective, open, and accountable institutions for all—freedom from fear, conflict, and violence is the most fundamental human right, and the essential foundation for building peaceful and prosperous societies. Fifth, forge a new global partnership—towards a new spirit of solidarity, cooperation, and mutual accountability that must underpin the post-2015 agenda. A new partnership should be based on a common understanding of our shared humanity, underpinning mutual respect and mutual benefit in a shrinking world.

The post-2015 development agenda constitutes both a challenge and an opportunity. While doubtless these five transformative shifts are necessary conditions in the vision to end poverty and bring prosperity to all, the global community will have to take responsibility for action on the ground to ensure that national governments act if the sufficient condition to achieve these goals is to be met. Establishing a sustainable, symbiotic, and mutually beneficial framework to facilitate liberalized mobility of economic migrants, thus enabling democratization of development, will be central to the post-2015 development agenda.

What might constitute a global compact on migration that would best serve the needs of the global economy, ensure equitable engagement between the countries involved, provide for a fair distribution of its benefits and best mitigate its negative effects? At a rather basic level, we might consider the Universal Declaration of Human Rights as a global expression of human rights. It is important as a reference point in international law. How might the rights articulated in this noble declaration be realized? Are there actions that the global community can catalyse and sustain to establish a more humane world? The Millennium Development Goals, popularly known as the MDGs, were adopted at the Millennium Summit of the United Nations in the year 2000. These goals provide a direction to national governments. They are motivating and inspiring, but non-binding.

Governments cannot be held to account for failing to drastically cut child and maternal mortality. As the 15-year time frame envisioned draws to a close, the progress is at best modest. The UN Economic and Social Council (ECOSOC, 2013) notes that

> the eight Millennium Development Goals (MDGs)—which range from halving extreme poverty to halting the spread of HIV/AIDS and providing universal primary education—have been a milestone in global and national development efforts. The framework has helped to galvanize development efforts and guide global and national development priorities. While three of the eight goals have been achieved prior to the final deadline of 2015 progress has been uneven within and across countries.

The ILO Conventions on Migrant Workers were adopted by the UN in 1990 and they finally came into force 2003 as the United Nations International Convention on the Protection of the Rights of All Migrant Workers and Members of Their Families. This is a non-binding international agreement/comprehensive international treaty which sets a moral standard, and serves as a guide and a stimulus for countries to respect migrant rights. However, the voluntary, non-binding nature of this international treaty makes it quite ineffective and not much more than a lengthy document.

Time and again, it has been argued that the European Union serves as the most 'successful' form of regional integration relative to other regional integration processes. The EU's attempts to free the movement of people, goods, services, and capital have borne fruit. The Norwegian Nobel Committee awarded the 8 million krone (USD 1.2 million) prize to the European Union in October 2012 purportedly because the EU for "six decades contributed to the advancement of peace and reconciliation, democracy and human rights in Europe" (Pearson, 2012). However, even a Nobel Prize for Peace in 2012 could not prevent the severe challenge both to its territorial integrity as also to its economic and social future. The execution of its governance has fallen into disrepute and its long-term existence has been challenged time and again. The model of the EU kind of governance entails member states ceding their sovereignty. It is a highly evolved "government network" (Slaughter, 2009). Imagining this kind of governance would be akin to imagining a 'borderless' world. Political support and will for such an organization will be next to impossible, considering how 'naturally' different we have accepted we are and how 'real' our boundaries are.

The WTO has been called the "plank of globalisation" (Dadush, 2009); "the first institution of the new phase of globalisation" (Desai, 2002); a "premier institution for global governance" that has broken away from the inter-state system of yesteryear like the UN, the IMF and the World Bank where inequality of power is codified in their operations (Desai, 2002) The WTO is a democratic body governed by certain principles. The basic principles of the WTO are non-discrimination through the national treatment and the most-favoured nation principles, freer trade through negotiation, predictability, competition, encouragement of reform, and so on (Messerlin, 2010). Since the WTO follows the one country, one vote principle, it is the most egalitarian of the global institutions. Reciprocity and symmetry are at the heart of all WTO processes (Desai, 2002).

Among the drawbacks that critics have pointed out, the WTO has been called a forum that is, "increasingly fragmented, irrational, chaotic and ultimately unjust" (Messerlin, 2010: 80). It is also said that its flexibility is being hindered by the single undertaking principle according to which every member should sign all the agreements negotiated during a round. To get around this, WTO members are induced to form coalitions pre-empting commitments (Messerlin, 2010). The WTO has also been called ineffective. It is believed that it is living off the gains of its predecessor, the General Agreement on Tariffs and Trade (GATT), and that no new lowering of bound tariffs have been agreed since the Uruguay Round concluded in 1994 (Dadush, 2009).

Two lessons that emerge from the failings of the WTO are that a body like it needs flexibility and that it cannot remain in splendid isolation, removed from reality.

Each experiment in governance is imperfect. Governance is essential, especially in a globalizing world. We have established that 'economic migration' as we envisage it needs global governance. Contrary to the developed world's 'worst fears', ease in economic migration will not lead to a drastic increase in the number of people migrating for work; it will only make it more orderly and mitigate irregular mobility.

There are many opportunities before the international community to put in place a robust, fair global governance regime for international migration. For instance, it could use the model of a body like the WTO—a body that breaks out of the current binding discourse of migration—a body that is democratic and neutral and has all the good practices that are followed by the WTO. Another option could be using the WTO itself. It has the structure, the rules. The dimension of liberalization of mobility could be added to its mandate.

Alternatively, a body like the IOM that deals exclusively with migration, has the domain expertise (broadest mandate for migration issues of any international institution), wide membership (151 member states and 12 observer states), and is democratic, could be designated. It suffers because it is outside of the UN system. Also, it does not have a comprehensive mandate on migration. Its mandate includes providing services to states, and many a time for return migration (UN, 2013). It is project-based and donor-driven and therefore its agenda is set by member states. It recognizes the importance of humane migration but it has been held to a 'zero net growth' standard in recent years, even as its programmes and ambitions have grown (2001, 'International Dialogue on Migration' for better understanding of migration and strengthening of cooperative mechanisms between governments and articulation of broader objectives in the year 2004). The first step to even consider the IOM as a lead organization for coordinating governance efforts in migration will be to bring it under the UN system. The GCIM recommended that the IOM be brought under the UN system to bring coherence and consistency in the multilateral process (GCIM, 2005; UN, 2013). It already works very closely with the UN system; bringing it inside the UN system will lead to a more positive role being played by the IOM. This would require considerable revision of its mandate (UN, 2013). This is not easy as it touches on highly contentious issues among bodies whose mandate it might overstep (Newland, 2005).

However, these are matters of detail. What is important is to have a regime that is based on some broad principles. The key is to arrive at a multilateral agreement. For instance, the UNGA must discuss a global, multilateral regime for migration and this regime must be based on some basic principles of non-discrimination, reciprocity, and symmetry and should be binding on the member states. The sooner the world arrives at such a compact, the better it would be for global economic growth and human development. Also, there is a need for leadership that will drive the course of events. This leadership needs to be an enlightened, sagacious, visionary leadership. In the current scenario, the countries which today represent multicultural open societies and democratic polities such as the United States, India, the United Kingdom, and Brazil need to take the lead. The time is now—the next UNGA presents itself as an opportunity before the comity of nations. The issue of a multilateral framework needs to be raised, discussed, debated, and converted into praxis.

There is already recognition of the broad tenets that can constitute the framework for a global compact on migration: the need to widen access to legal migration; the urgency of addressing the problem of irregular migration; the potential for bilateral engagement to calibrate migration flows based on the labour supply gaps; the importance of well-designed instruments (human resource mobility partnerships, for instance) to facilitate mobility; harmonization of skills standards to facilitate universal recognition of skills; facilitating the mobility of students; enhancing capacities amongst countries for governance of migration; and ensuring the safety and security of migrants and facilitating their integration. These principles would be a good starting point for a dialogue and hold promise for minimum policy harmonization at the international level.

Though it is difficult to mark a clear distinction between different kinds of migrants, by economic migrants we mean all those migrants who move to offer their skills from a place of surplus to a place of deficit. There have been some attempts to govern migration and these have been discussed and critiqued in this chapter. We have discussed how these bodies remain ineffective in easing the restrictions on the mobility of economic migrants and continue to stay within the established paradigm of migration discourse. Currently, the interpretation of the development impact of migration is biased. Even when the importance of migration is recognized, it is almost always to extol its virtues in the development of the countries of origin.

The focus is mostly on how the migrant or her country of origin benefits as a result of migration. The migrant is better off because she is provided with an opportunity to make a better living and the country of origin is better off because of the remittances it receives. There is rarely an acknowledgement of the gains for the destination country. Migration continues to be perceived as a 'problem'. It is time to recognize the significant economic, social, and cultural benefits that the countries of destination receive from migration. Even so, liberalized movement of people continues to be resisted because of ill-informed and populist perceptions that it results in gains only for the developing part of the world. This perception needs to be challenged and the results of empirical work on how destination countries benefit from migration need to be disseminated widely. There has to be a concerted, well-articulated and extensive effort to dispel populist myths about migration if we have to reverse the uninformed anti-immigrant sentiments that right-wing politics whip up to stop progressive and inclusive policy reforms. Migration will happen with or without a multilateral framework—but it will be so much better for the world if it happens under a global mobility compact. It is an opportune time to build a consensus on international migration. The review by the UNGA of the ICPD in 2014 and the launch of the post-2015 Development Agenda were missed opportunities to move towards such a Global Mobility Compact. Typically, development experts regard migration as a sign of failure: if development policies work, people should not want to move. Accordingly, migration has been viewed as a problem to be solved—not as a solution to a problem. But migration should not be considered good or bad; it is simply natural to the human condition. People migrate from poor countries, from middle-income countries, and from rich countries. They go from north to south, south to north, south to south, and north to north. The overarching goal must be to design a roadmap that can take us from today's poorly managed, exploitative system of human mobility to one that is well-managed, protects migrant rights, and plans for the consequences and opportunities of migration (Sutherland, 2014).

7

The Skills Paradigm
When Geography Is History

> The world is flat for goods, downhill for capital, but a steep uphill climb for workers, especially unskilled workers with the misfortune of not having been born with the right nationality.
>
> —Nancy Birdsall in Pritchett (2006: xiv)

The Emerging Skills Paradigm

> The real barrier to the movement of people across national boundaries is coercion—people with guns stop them. The fact that coercion is civilized, legal and even polite should not prevent us from naming it 'coercion' ...
>
> —Pritchett (2006: 7–8)

The world of the twenty-first century needs firm and unapologetic advocates for the democratization of development through a transformative shift to an international regime for skills. It is in the interests of the world—including those in advanced stages of development—to recognize that liberalized mobility of skills across borders will soon become an essential objective condition for productivity and profitability. The compelling forces of demographics, technological advancement, and the growing importance of in situ services together make the efficient and competitive transnational portability of skills a challenge that industry and government alike will have to address. 'Skills' should include the entire spectrum from those provided by high-skilled migrants through those seen as middle-skilled to those considered low-skilled migrants. Labour market segmentation on the basis of skills or preferential policies that seek to include *high skills* while excluding *low skills* are inimical to economic progress and have the effect of fragmenting the productive process. The real economy needs skills at all levels, if only because it includes sectors and jobs that span the entire skills spectrum and constitute essential parts of a robust process of the production of goods and services. In the increasingly competitive world of manufacture and service delivery, the demand for and the supply of skills is more a function of the market and less of state policy. Quite simply, technological advances, innovations in production and delivery techniques, and the compulsions of achieving higher total factor productivity will determine the skills mix. Competitiveness while eliminating redundancies will command freer portability of the *relevant and useful* skills and raise a premium on them. Any policy construct that attempts cherry picking of the so-called high skills to the exclusion of the so-called low skills is by definition artificial and far removed from the economic processes at work. Whether the butcher, the baker, the fruit-picker, the janitor or the home caregiver, they perform tasks that are as important and with skills as much in need as do the high-skilled workers. Given the skewed distribution of the demand for and the supply of skills across space, the skills market of the future will by definition be deterritorialized. Yet, there are several barriers to an integrated and composite international skills market on an economy-wide basis. Not least is the resistance to the democratization of development through the shift to an international regime for skills.

Human skills have shaped societies. It does not take much to reveal the importance of skills—just a quick look at history of human progress! Skills have always been closely linked to the great discoveries and pioneering inventions. The discovery of fire and the invention of iron resulted in transforming man from being a nomad and food-gatherer to becoming pastoral and taking to settled agriculture. This was also the beginning of family, community, and private property. The invention of the wheel revolutionized transportation in unprecedented ways and with it the pace of human progress. The invention of the steam locomotive led to the Industrial Revolution, the emergence of the factory system and the process of urbanization. The discovery of new continents and the invention of seafaring ships led to colonialism and empire. The invention of guns and gunpowder led to unprecedented death and destruction especially during the Great Wars. Each of these epochs in history gave rise to demands for new skills. In the last few decades, the advance of information technology and the internet has transformed the world—brought a host of new skills that are difficult to find. At the same time, the innovations in the production and distribution of goods and in the provision of services have given rise to newer skills that are necessary for the success of businesses.

The Knowledge Economy

The twenty-first century will truly be the age of the *knowledge society* in which the knowledge economy will dominate. This will imply that, in the future, skills will be at a premium. While it was relatively easy to accelerate the transnational movement of capital to where cheap labour resided as a substitute for the migration of labour to where the demand was, skills shortages are a different matter altogether. Unlike the availability of cheap labour which was in abundance, skills are scarce. The higher up the value chain, the scarcer they get. This situation is compounded by the fact that several workaday jobs in different sectors of the economy cannot be ported or outsourced. In many countries such sectors as forestry, agriculture, construction, healthcare, hospitality, fisheries, and civic services like water and sanitation are already facing a severe skills shortage and some of them are facing closure. These are also jobs that the local workforce considers dirty, difficult or demeaning. The rise in tertiary education has meant lower labour market participation in blue- or even grey-collar jobs in the developed world. This, combined with the sharp decline in the working-age population, has meant that several sectors face serious skills shortages. The challenges that employers face in sourcing a young, productive, and skilled workforce could still be addressed effectively were it not for immigration policies that are both short-sighted as well as fragmented. Policies that build in a sedentary bias towards temporary migration and high-skilled migrants in a rigidly segmented manner represent poor politics and poorer economics. The policy frame of restricting legal avenues for the immigration of lower-order skills and focusing exclusively on high-skilled migrants have proved counterproductive. Europe is a good example of how not to deal with structural labour supply gaps and chronic skills shortages. Despite its emphasis on attracting high-skilled workers and announcing the 'Blue Card', all that it has managed is to attract a disproportionate number of irregular workers while the best and the brightest continue to seek their fortunes in North America. Mobility of *skills* essentially implies the transnational movement of economic migrants on a market-driven basis across the 'skills spectrum'. With technological advancement, innovations and rapid strides in higher education, most processes will get automated, thereby leading to very specialized skills. This is at the higher end of the skills market. However, there will also be a great shortage of workers at the lower end as a result of the demographic dynamic, unequal access, upward professional mobility and inter-country wage differentials for unskilled and semi-skilled workers. Most countries have relaxed the barriers for high-skilled migration with 'welcome mats' for a few (Pritchett, 2006) but cherry-picking or market segmentation cannot meet economywide needs and the imperatives of demographic transitions.

Local versus Global

There are two opposing views in play. One that argues for an international *market for skills* where there is a movement from the areas of surplus skills to areas with skills deficits and the other opposing force emphasizing greater *localization*. This is when a large number of jobs are reserved for nationals or specific ethnicities for fear of the immigrant taking away jobs in situations with high levels of unemployment. The most recent example of this is the 'Nitaqat' being enforced in Saudi Arabia. This new law makes it mandatory for all establishments from small shops to larger commercial entities in Saudi Arabia to employ a fixed percentage of nationals. For a country that has been predominantly dependent on migrant labour and has a significant stock of migrant workers, this policy decision has serious long-term implications. Besides the fact that there is inadequate capacity and skills in the local population, most locals are unwilling to do the work that is being done by the contractual migrant workers from a diverse group of countries in Asia. It also has significant financial consequences for employers since it is mandatory now to pay the locals nearly two or three times the wages that they pay to the temporary contractual migrant workers. The Nitaqat law has also meant that a large number of immigrants have to return home. Immigrants with middle-level skills are most affected by this policy. Many of these are from the state of Kerala in India (Balaji, 2013).

The preference for skills available locally, even if not the most competitive or drawing upon skills based on geographic proximity and cultural affinity, is not unique to Asia alone. This has been true even for Europe. Consider the 'Europe without Borders' policy aimed at encouraging intra-regional mobility. Despite this policy preference, the mobility of skills within Europe is less than optimal because of 'invisible' borders—linguistic, social, cultural—that seriously challenge the 'cultural capital' argument that the European Union (EU) policy for closing its external borders to third countries makes. The asymmetric financial 'borders' has only served to exacerbate the Eurozone crisis, especially with reference to labour mobility. Family reunion is the main reason for immigration in Europe unlike the 'economic migration' rhetoric (Castles and Miller, 2009). There are thus several barriers to portability of skills and the emergence of an integrated skills market even within the EU. Competition is what the EU faces for attracting talent, the challenge it needs to address is to source skills across labour market segments and the opportunity is to partner with a young, knowledge-based, and globalizing world. How it will do this is a question worth asking from the perspective of its common approach to migration and asylum. Portability of skills is not easy. Absence of standardization of skills; language barriers; cultural and nationalist chauvinism; and the anti-immigration sentiment are all hurdles to the mobility of skills. Some other problems include the perception of the effect on wages and the effect on businesses that employ irregular migrants. The world faces a development deficit. There is a need to provide access to skills to a wider population and to economic opportunity on a more inclusive basis in developing countries. It is incontrovertible that *the democratization of*

development based on the principles of non-discrimination will be key to
stay on the path of further human progress.

Defining the Problem

The world needs to pay attention to the central concern that requires
to be addressed in *international* migration praxis: how long can
labour market segmentation by policy design continue without seriously impairing economic progress for all? Quite simply, economic
opportunity and finding jobs must not be determined by origin,
gender, race, ethnicity or legal status. It should be based on merit
and a function of education and skills. The reality, however, is different and raises the question whether in a globalizing world protection of the domestic workforce, policies aimed at 'localization',
and tariff and non-tariff barriers to mobility of skills have a place
at all in the modern economy without distorting macroeconomic
outcomes and adversely impacting the productivity of firms? There
are three important arguments to support the case for freer mobility
of economic migrants: First, across the board are labour shortages as
a result of demographic futures. As we have discussed in an earlier
chapter, the compelling forces of the *different demographic futures and*
their interaction with different stages of economic transition will impact
the demand for and the supply of labour. This will perhaps be the
defining feature of the aggregate labour shortages in both the developed
and developing parts of the world. Demographic futures differ due
to the different pace of the demographic transition around the world.
When faced with an ageing population and a sharp decline in the
working-age population the labour shortages are going to be endemic
and structural. Even though causality may not be established, there
is a very strong correlation between the two. Shortages will not ease
with the passage of time. The labour shortages will be felt in several
core sectors but will get exacerbated in the health care sector owing
to the enhanced health care needs of an ageing population. But
more generally it will create severe gaps in the labour market across
the board. The shortage of skills as a result will be significant in the
international labour market. The second argument is the limits to
outsourcing as a result of some services being terrestrial and hence
on-site. There are limits to capital mobility substituting for labour

mobility. There are also limits to outsourcing manufacture. Despite the strategy of moving capital to where the surplus labour is through multinational corporations and global supply chains there remain significant sectors of the economy that cannot be outsourced. Health care, hospitality and agriculture are sectors that are not just crucial but need workers. Typically, there will be a rise of employment in 'low-skill, hard-core non-tradables'—the result of increased productivity, rising incomes, ageing populations, and the globalization of manufacturing (Pritchett, 2006). It must also be recognized that as societies move to a higher stage of development, the local population because of higher standards of living, better educational attainments, and higher aspirations is no longer willing to do low-skilled jobs. This may be due to a variety of reasons, one of which is that post the Second World War, certain jobs came to be associated with a lower status, as jobs performed only by immigrants. There is a social stigma attached to these jobs. They may not offer the desired amount of wages for the domestic workers or the working conditions may be unacceptable (Boswell et al., 2004). According to the projections of growth in demand for specific occupations made by the United States Department of Labour, more than half the labour demand growth in the top 25 occupations (5 million jobs) will occur in this category. Though modern economies will need more computer engineers and postsecondary teachers, they will also need more health aides, housekeepers, janitors, cashiers and fast-food workers. Along with every wealthy settlement, there is a shanty town full of people willing to do the 3D (dirty, dangerous, and demeaning) jobs. Third, technology bites as economies progress resulting in newer skills gaps. As economies are driven by aspirations to becoming 'knowledge-based', there are certain *skills gaps* that arise due to rapid transformations in technology and innovation. These are *qualitative mismatches* in the labour market that cannot be filled with domestic workers in the short/medium term. The dynamic developments especially in innovation and the use of information and communication technologies cannot always be met by the local workforce or skills pool. Even if education reforms are introduced to address these gaps, there will be a lag before this is reflected in the skills of the workers. *These are likely to persist despite presence of unemployment.* A number of surveys and studies have also pointed out that there will be gaps at the very high end of the skills level. These projections are supposed to serve pre-scient policy for mobility of people. Solutions include overhauling education systems, increasing retirement ages, increasing participation of women in the workforce and inviting temporary migration for these specific skills gaps. However, an immigration policy based on labour market segmentation on the basis of skills is both specious and short-sighted. Countries must also understand that full employment is an illusion. Most times there will be shortages of skills in some sectors while facing high rates of unemployment in others. The Beveridge Curve is a tool to depict the inverse relationship of unemployment and job vacancies (Boswell et al., 2004). Even though it is not possible to ascertain the nature of the mismatch on the basis of the Beveridge curve (that is, whether they are aggregate labour shortages or qualitative mismatches), it is quite useful in studying the simultaneous levels of unemployment and vacancies in an economy over a period of time. Very simply put, developed economies face both labour shortages (aggregate shortages) and skills gaps (qualitative mismatches). If projections across the board are to be believed, this will continue. The problem is when these exist along with high unemployment rates. Migration is the most politically sensitive issue of our time. Even though it may seem the most 'feasible' solution to certain gaps and shortages, it is resisted due to the apprehensions locals have of alien people, their alien language, and the fear of the pressure they bring on public services along with the issues of security. Yet, it is quite obvious that in order to keep up economic growth rates, the aggregate labour shortages and skills gaps need to be filled. How best this can be done is what must engage economic multilateralism.

It Is Not Going to Be Easy

Even though there is great merit in advocating mobility of skills, some 'immovable ideas' such as anti-immigration sentiment (Pritchett, 2006), 'the cultural argument', and migrant-integration difficulties come in the way and have come to be perceived as real problems in the mobility of economic migrants. Matching of employers and skills is not easy. One of the most important hindrances in the movement of people is the lack of universalization of the concept of 'skills'—the universal recognition of qualifications, integrity of standards judged through certification, and the lack of a standard curricula and training.

Language

Language constitutes a major challenge to the portability of skills. Teaching and learning in what is not their first language places migrants at a disadvantage. As alien language learners they are routinely subjected to low expectations, discrimination, and lack of cultural peers. A major concern for countries in Europe is that mobility of skilled migrants may fill gaps temporarily in the labour market but it is no panacea because of the 'language barrier' (Hemme, 2006). Often, migrants are considered inept at integration in the host societies because they do not speak the language of the natives. This is especially problematic in the European countries where there is a very special attachment to their native tongue and a growing intolerance of 'foreign tongues'. When the leader of the opposition in the UK, Ed Miliband, announced in December 2012 that every Briton will have to speak English under a Labour government (Watt, 2012) to enable *social integration*, it spurred a huge debate. The emphasis on language was considered a cover for the 'irresponsibility' shown by the Labour governments in allowing two million migrants to enter.

The 'Migrant' Will Not Understand/Appreciate 'Our' Culture

A central theme of the resistance to migration has been the concept of *community and culture* and therefore *nationality*. There is a history of cultural capital that makes each group unique and therefore lends itself to the formation of communities which then is welded into the concept of nationality and citizenship. Nationality then becomes a 'morally legitimate' basis for discrimination (Pritchett, 2006). What resonates through these constructs is 'homogeneity'. When an individual migrates into a new environment, he/she is perceived as the alien or the 'other' as opposed to the 'self'. This perception then takes expression culturally, socially, and economically. Therefore, even if there is freeing up of the mobility of migrants, there can be barriers to access to social welfare and economic opportunity—all based on the cultural issues of the 'other'. Just as capitalism grows through 'creative destruction', migration also causes creative destruction of homogenous societies and builds new cultural narratives. It has through many centuries. Social transformation is in the nature of societies. Emergence of culturally and racially diverse populations is a result of processes of globalization, that is, through the growing interconnectedness of ideas, economies, societies, and cultures. Migration is a force that can result in the emergence of a more robust, new culture. More importantly, the movement of economic migrants goes beyond their cultural identity.

Anti-immigration Sentiment (Pressure on Social Security and Public Services, Possible Security Risks)

Pritchett (2006) refers to ubiquitous anti-immigration sentiment as an 'immovable idea'. The general rhetoric and discourse in particular is against the 'immigrant', portraying her/him as an alien who puts pressure on the social welfare system and on the public services and infrastructure in general. Too many opinion polls show how little support there is for migration. It is almost a story of one in twenty in favour of migration. The existence of unemployment along with substantial vacancy rates shows that there is a qualitative mismatch between the skills of the domestic workers and the skills required to fill the vacancies. However, immigrants are looked at as the cause of scarcity in jobs and high rates of unemployment. At a more nuanced level, they are blamed for the delay caused in the reforms for training and expanding the current labour force (Boswell et al., 2004). This is not to imply that there is a high level of acceptability in developing countries of 'outsiders' or immigrants. India receives a lot of immigrants from its neighbours in the subcontinent. Many of these immigrants are illegal. Anti-immigration sentiment runs high in India. The fear of the 'other' is not only of the immigrants from outside of its borders but also from within. Regional political parties in the state of Maharashtra first made villains out of 'South Indians', accusing them of 'stealing' all the government jobs and received widespread support for the politically driven campaign. Once this fire died down, another regional party in the same state targeted another group of people. This time it was the 'North Indians' who were accused of stealing jobs from the 'natives'. A majority of the taxi drivers, construction workers and so on come from the north Indian states of Bihar and Uttar Pradesh. The call to drive them out received support even from the 'educated middle class' that Indians are so proud of. Despite the fact that the events of 9/11 had little to do with migration, public perceptions about migrants changed decisively in America and the rest of the world in its aftermath. The change in the world post-9/11 has been discussed ad nauseam. It has made life more difficult for migrants. The USA Patriot Act 2002 was one of the most drastic of all measures. The movement of people now automatically in a stereotyped manner leads to concerns about security.

Effect on Wages?

A popular perception and a contentious issue in the populist rhetoric on migration is that the immigrants from impoverished developing countries push down the wage rate below the standard market rate as they distort the equilibrium, provide a cheaper source of workers, and are willing to work for much lower wages. This has been widely studied and debated. Figure 7.1 sums up the two major opposing

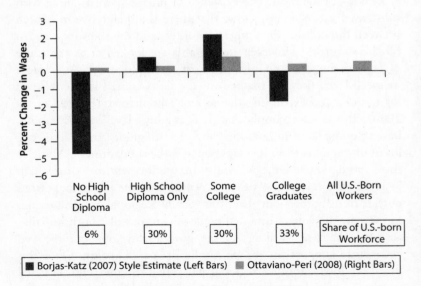

Figure 7.1   Effect of Immigration on Wages of US-Born Workers
Source: Greenstone and Looney (2012).

arguments on the issue. It has been argued that in the long run, the impact on wages of natives is next to nil. The economic impact of immigration has been studied extensively. It was found that there is a very slight reduction in the wages in the developed countries but the impact on the immigrant is quite drastic. The wages received by the immigrant are much greater than what she/he would receive in her/his country of origin.

The Business of Irregular Migration

There are close to 11 million irregular migrants in the United States. The major reason for a proliferation in the number of irregular migrants is the fact that they benefit businesses immensely. These incoming irregular migrants are employed by businesses at wages below the market rate. They are exploited and have almost no recourse to social welfare/security systems. Since they are on the wrong side of the law due to their status as irregular migrants, they lead invisible lives. It is therefore in the interests of these businesses to let irregular migration continue, to let the 'grey market' flourish. It has been widely argued that removal of restrictions on movement and easy access to economic opportunities will reduce the incidence of irregular migration. In many cases, migrants become irregular/illegal because they are unable to procure the legal access to be in the host country. In a majority of cases they overstay their visit/tourist visas. There is a lobby that prevents ease in mobility of migrants. This is the lobby of businesses that benefit from illegal labour and indirectly by restrictions on labour mobility.

Effect on Countries of Origin

Conventional wisdom dictates that the drivers of migration are lack of development in the country of origin of the immigrant. People chose to migrate or were 'forced' to migrate due to a lack of development in the country of origin. This is because of the sedentary bias in development, that is, development necessarily takes place within the borders of a country. The proliferation of aid and development assistance was in part due to the fear of people from developing countries 'flooding' the developed countries. Soon, studies started to show that economic migrants actually had a beneficial impact on development in both the country of destination as also the country of origin. There is evidence that migrants spur growth, provide for diversity at the workplace and catalyse innovation and higher productivity. The remittances they send home benefit the migrants' families and the economies of the sending countries. It was even shown that the remittances sent home are very often greater than the aid received by these developing countries. Traditionally, in colonies the movement of people was restricted and, if it took place, it was mostly towards the metropolis. The debate that emerged from this kind of movement was that of 'brain drain', 'brain gain', and the more optimistic sounding 'brain circulation'. These along with 'push and pull factors' summed up the discourse on migration and development. *Brain drain* and *brain gain* were discussed for years as important economic consequences of international migration of the skilled. It was argued (and endorsed by international organizations) that countries of origin (read developing countries) were worse off once their skilled personnel moved out in search of greener pastures. This idea is based on the fact that development is often seen as that of the country, the 'nation', and not of the 'national'. They claimed that the high costs of training these cohorts who were leaving, the social ramifications of their flight, and the impact they had on the other skilled migrants were all too much to bear. These claims were often given 'empirical backing' by organizations. They concurred with facts on how 'brain drain' in one part of the world was leading to 'brain gain' in the others. This was termed extremely problematic especially in the field of healthcare from countries of origin with inadequate number of health care workers and inadequate health systems. This was directly related to the way development practitioners viewed migration—it was as a result of lack of development that skilled migrants left the country of origin in a lurch. Figures were bandied about. A study showed vacancy levels in countries to demonstrate the point (Stilwell et al., 2003, cited in UNFPA, 2004). It seemed for a while that all this was true. Recent research, however, differs. Clemens studied the impact of emigration of skilled personnel on the prospects for their countries of origin. His initial research has suggested that there is no measurable impact of emigration on the health indicators of the sending countries. In fact, his study suggests that the reasons for the understaffing and poor public health conditions are almost entirely unrelated to the emigration of health care workers from Africa. It goes further to suggest that emigration has caused an increase in the number of health care workers in Africa (Clemens, 2007). The migration of health care workers is a symptom and not the cause of the disease. To blame the country's poor health care on the doctors who have the ability and the willingness to migrate is grave injustice to the freedom to live and work in the country that they wish to migrate to. The inability of a country's health care system to retain their health care workers shows the lacuna in the system altogether. Unfortunately, this movement of health care workers gave birth to the controversial term, 'ethical recruitment', which meant that as a developed country, hiring doctors or nurses from developing countries was 'unethical'.

India, in the recent past, has made some rather absurd attempts to 'retain' doctors; these seem to border on coercion. Most health care workers leave for a better standard of living; to practise in a country with better work ethics. Coercion to stay back in the country of origin or a ban on the immigration of health care workers in the country of destination cannot be a solution to the shortage of skills, especially in health care.

Democratization of Development through Mobility

Human progress is closely linked with the democratization of development and, ideally, this is the goal we must seek in the twenty-first century. There is a development deficit in a large part of the world. In countries with a large young population, there is both a resource deficit and capacity constraint to train the burgeoning numbers or absorb them in productive employment opportunities. Many countries in Africa, Asia, and Latin America boast huge populations but if they do not have access to human development (education and skills), it will jeopardize the process of development. The millennium development goals and the interest in development aid to assist poor countries emerged because these countries are perceived to be a severe drag on global growth prospects. The rationale for development aid was to spur development within countries to provide economic opportunities and thereby reduce the pressure on migration.

While laudable, this strategy fails to acknowledge that people are essentially itinerant and they migrate in search of greater opportunity.

However, even if they are provided with skills, it is improbable that they will all be absorbed productively in the economies of the developing countries. In India, a large majority (over 60 per cent of the population) depends on agriculture but the contribution to the GDP is only 17 to 18 per cent. There is a need to give access to economic opportunities to all to improve their incomes. Similarly, there is also a deficit for skills in the developed part of the world as we have discussed. The creation of a market that responds to the surplus/deficit of skills allows both these problems to be addressed. Going beyond these concerns, there is a *need to reformulate the concept of skills*. Skills are not just the ability to use technology. Skills should mean something more fundamental. It can be safely stated that human creativity and ingenuity are the drivers of human progress. Material progress can be attributed to: (*a*) scientific discoveries and inventions, (*b*) application of technology to production, and (*c*) innovation to improve productivity and reduce costs. It is not so much a specific job-related skill that will in any way in the future enhance human material progress. It will be the skills that lead to discoveries, inventions, and innovations. *A constant supply of new ideas is absolutely necessary*. These will be in great shortage. A global hunt for talent is already on. There is scope for a strong 'business case for migration'. Migration and migrants generate profit and therefore the private sector is more forthcoming about the benefits of migration than most governments (Koser, 2013). Moving beyond benefiting from mobility for their own sake, businesses are also capable of building creative alliances, especially with governments; investing in skills development, facilitating bilateral agreements on mobility, and advocacy for well-designed programmes for addressing labour shortages are just some of the areas where businesses can contribute.

What we are looking for is skilling the world, that is, raising the supply of skills. The world is faced with grand societal challenges—those fundamental problems that affect the world at large and at a pace that might be faster than the potential solutions. Therefore, if we have to address these in a sustainable and equitable manner, we will need skills of a high order. Increasingly, in developed and ageing societies, fewer and fewer people will be able to acquire these skills because of the lack of numbers. In developing societies and the post-colonial world, these skills are mostly lacking because they do not have the wherewithal yet. Currently, the supply side of skills is inelastic and the demand side of skills is elastic. There is a demand for skills of this nature; the demand for enhancing the size of the cake itself—*the challenge is to see if migration can catalyse this*. For a long time, the argument was that the creation of 'cool cities' will attract high-skilled migrants and this will in turn cause economic growth (Florida, 2004). This was a study based largely on some qualitative data and has come under a lot of criticism. It has been proved empirically through a study of graduates in Canada that a large number of skilled migrants actually move to areas of high economic growth (this may seem almost intuitive too, because this is where they are most likely to find job opportunities) and, obviously, there is some feedback involved (Shearmur, 2006). The British government recently 'celebrated' a reduction in the number of immigrants to the United Kingdom. After all, David Cameron had promised the people of the United Kingdom that he would systematically reduce the number of immigrants to the 'tens of thousands' and he did. A large reduction in the numbers is because of a drop in the number of international students (de Haas, 2013). As de Haas succinctly points out, "Thriving economies attract migrants, stagnant economies deter migrants. Rising nations attract migrants; declining nations try to keep them out. Anti-immigration politics reflect a culture of fear and an overall lack of confidence and political courage. Rather than a cause for celebration, declining immigration therefore signals a more general state of crisis."

It has been empirically proved that the most educated, the ones with the highest levels of skills are the ones who are able to recognize the areas with skills deficits (Cousineau and Vaillancourt, 1987; Antolin and Bover, 1997, cited in Shearmur, 2006). They move to areas they recognize as 'high-growth economies'. They recognize where their skills will be best paid and best utilized. Are they, then, the ones likely to be most mobile? Why is it that we have plans to make our systems even more segmented and only welcome *high-skilled migrants*? It has widely come to be accepted that when immigration does not follow a 'plan', that is, when it is non-selective, it can exacerbate problems of mismatch. Therefore, creating a segmented approach towards migration unilaterally by countries will do more harm than good. There is clearly a need for a more comprehensive skills paradigm based on the demand for and the supply of skills.

8

Access
Who Gets What and Why?

Western European countries have ... tended to write immigration out of their histories because it contradicted myths of national homogeneity.

—Noiriel (1988), cited in Castles and Davidson (2000: 60)

Defining Access in a Mobile World

In all societies, *who gets what and why* is determined by the social relations and the world view that the socially dominant group holds, including shared beliefs that rationalize particular attitudes, social practices, and the patterns of resource allocation. The behaviour of people supports inequality when they rely on ideologies that give preference to one group over another. The enacting of social roles further supports these learned ideologies (Pratto et al., 1999). Perceptions about migrants and their entitlements are similarly influenced by the cultural milieu in which these exchanges occur. In the previous chapters we have argued the case for the governance of migration and the need for a global mobility compact leading up to a multilateral framework for the liberalization of the mobility of economic migrants. Along with the liberalization of mobility, it is important to provide economic migrants access to basic entitlements to be able to benefit from and contribute to the host society. This chapter seeks to answer the question of who gets what and why from freer transnational mobility or the lack of it, that is, the gains for an individual and the state in the presence or the absence of a global mobility compact.

The question of 'access' for migrants broadly includes: (*a*) safety and security, (*b*) social welfare and social security benefits, (*c*) civic amenities, and (*d*) economic opportunities for advancement. The often insurmountable difficulties and sometimes the denial of access for a significant proportion of economic migrants is a problem the world is struggling to address. Access is not just a matter of entitlement to benefits or to rights by virtue of being human or meaningfully contributing to society. It is indivisible from being part of a community and—even if it is often a diverse, pluralistic, and sometimes disparate population—of sharing the same geography, resources, and concerns. It is about 'belonging'. Belonging tends to be defined more often from a nativity perspective. But belonging is as objective and real a condition for a migrant. The need to belong is as much a felt need for migrants as for the native populations. Belonging, simply put, is the sense of being part of a larger group, of feeling at home, of feeling safe. In the context of migration, though, the idea is caught up in the politics of belonging and of identity. The politics of belonging seeks to construct belonging in particular ways for particular collectivities (Yuval-Davis, 2006). At the heart of this divisive politics is the complex and often controversial relationship between nationality, race, and migration within the confines of citizenship and the state. Who you are and where you come from, the colour of your skin, the social class you belong to, your religion; all of these in part or together determine what you get or cannot get. Despite the empirical evidence pointing to the obvious benefits of the liberalized mobility of people, populist politics and xenophobic elements thrive. The question of belonging and hence of access to basic human rights for migrants centres around the question—just what must constitute a nation? Must it contain as full members only those who are seen as their own? Anti-immigrant sentiment against the 'alien' or the 'other' finds natural resonance amongst groups that see themselves as unitary and homogeneous. This is especially so when that homogeneity or social order appears to be threatened by the 'other'. Recent and not-so-recent stories show malice towards people and policymakers who dare to advocate making life for immigrants easier (Curtis, 2013). It is not surprising, therefore, that public opinion often reflects racist attitudes. There is also the *cultural capital* argument of the western way of life and how the *occidental* is so different from the *oriental*. This again is a construct that serves a particular purpose "… not that it is a misrepresentation of some Oriental essence—in which I do not for a moment believe—but that it operates, as representations usually do, for a purpose, according to a tendency, in a specific historical, intellectual, and even economic setting" (Said, 1978: 273). The pervasiveness of populist stereotyping of the migrants from the South as uncultured and uneducated and in ways less than the natives of the North remains a conscious historical misrepresentation.

Nationality, Citizenship, and Migration

Citizenship as a construct arises from the dynamic between sovereignty of states and the rights of individuals. In fact, its primary function is to define the rights and duties of a state towards its members. Citizenship also determines the rights and responsibilities of individuals and communities. Simply put, it provides the basis for a symbiotic relationship between a state and the people who are its members. Nationality is a larger construct based on the principle of identity circumscribed by ethnicity, culture, language, and religion among other shared features, usually but not necessarily located within a defined territorial space. International law has little to say on these two ideas though customary international law, from the Westphalia era, leaves it largely in the domain of the states. Thus granting of citizenship is rather discretionary. Hence, who gets what in the case of non-citizens also becomes discretionary. The challenge in a world that has significant mobility of people is to strike a balance between the legitimate interests of individuals residing within the territory of a state and the exercise of sovereign discretion. With greater transnational movement of people, both the flows and the stocks of migrants have grown. States are becoming multicultural and individuals are increasingly transnational. In the face of ethnic and cultural diversity countries are reimagining the idea of national cohesion. It is now widely recognized that states need to be inclusive in determining who gets what. This has led to review and reform of both immigration laws as also citizenship laws with regard to immigrants, their families, and their children. The distinctions between Jus Soli—citizenship by birth, and Jus Sanguinis—citizenship by naturalization, are getting blurred and a number of governments are now keeping pace with the trends in migration by modifying who qualifies for citizenship even though traditionally they may not have been considered eligible (IOM, 2005). The path to citizenship for migrants generally requires a specified period of residence. The challenge for most states is really determining the manner in which to deal with the growing temporariness of migration, the mobility of individuals across multiple borders and their residence in more than one state for considerable lengths of time. Most obligations of individuals towards the community and the state—taxes, social security payments, and welfare contributions, are based on residence and commence with the fact of entry and residence if the period of stay is longer than one year. The rights of individuals to entitlements from the state, in contrast, are in most countries predicated on completion of a specified mandatory period of residence to qualify. This dichotomy is the policy expression of the underlying conflict between citizenship and the legitimate interests of migrants. The rise of the global citizen, of individuals who are connected to and maintain substantive links with both the country of origin as well as the country of destination has necessitated recognition of significant diasporas and hence compelled states to recognize the need for multiple citizenship. However, there is no consensus on the merits of providing multiple citizenship, culturally or politically, although in some cases multiple citizenships may give rise to situations of perceived disloyalty (IOM, 2005). Most countries therefore see immigration as a problem that needs to be addressed and the solution that populist politics dictates is to simply restrict it. Enhanced mobility has seriously challenged hitherto monocultural societies. It has created ethnic, cultural, and socio-economic tensions that sometimes tend to result in conflict, especially during economic downturns. A creative policy prescription that has been pushed is to emphasize and give impetus to intra-regional rather than inter-region migration.

Regional Integration Processes

A direct consequence of this has been a proliferation of regional integration processes aimed at ensuring greater intra-regional cooperation
across a wide gamut of areas but principally in political economy. Freer
mobility of people between countries within the region is expected
as a result. What is perhaps also hoped for is that it would reduce
migration pressures and hence reduce immigration to countries in
the North. Similarly, such agreements among countries enjoying
'geographic proximity and similar levels of development' have a more
liberal approach to labour mobility (Nielson, 2003). There are two
important caveats though: First, the degree of regional integration
is a direct function of the geopolitical security environment. South
Asia is a case in point. The South Asian Association for Regional
Cooperation (SAARC), for instance, is a cauldron that is constantly
simmering. Porous borders, irregular movement, and considerable
conflict pose serious security challenges. Hence, SAARC has been a
non-starter. Second, evidence abounds that the most active mobility corridors with significant multidirectional flows occur outside
the regional integration processes. The International Organization
for Migration (IOM) classifies integration into four different levels.
The lowest of these is a free trade area of which a common example
is the North American Free Trade Agreement (NAFTA). The next
level is that of a customs union wherein there is deepened integration
through equalizing of trade advantages to third country exports. The
Caribbean Community (CARICOM) is an example. Next is the level
of a common market of which the Southern Common Market
(MERCOSUR) is an example where there is mobility of all factors
of production, including labour, and finally the highest level of such
integration is an economic union of which the European Union
(EU) is an example (IOM, 2007). The European Union's policy of
a borderless Europe for EU nationals and Fortress Europe for third-
country nationals is a reflection of the dilemmas that continue to
dog the question of access. Similar is the case with the regional
trade agreements which treat movement of persons as secondary.
While some like the EU provide for the 'right to mobility', though
one might add that this has not in any significant way changed
the mobility pattern, others provide for a General Agreement on

Trade in Services (GATS) Mode 4 type of movement and yet others merely facilitate entry and do not assure market access. Evidence suggests that these agreements have done little to foster liberalized movement of people within the region. It is quite clear that a push towards liberalizing labour mobility within the regions is also aimed, conversely, at restricting freer mobility between regions. South–South movements, after all, are more widely acceptable and seen to be less disruptive than South–North movements. But the newsflash is that the largest-organized and orderly free movement of persons is occurring outside of regional processes. In September 2013, the United Nations Population Division reported that the number of international migrants had reached 232 million in 2013. What is noteworthy is that since 2000, the migrant stock in the South has been growing more rapidly than in the North. Between 2000 and 2010, the average annual growth rate for migrants in the South was 2.5 per cent per annum. In the North, the annual growth rate was around 2.3 per cent. Since 2010, the annual growth rate has slowed to 1.5 per cent in the developed regions and 1.8 per cent in the developing regions. The *Top ten country-specific corridors, 2013*, given in Figure 8.1, makes for interesting reading and demonstrates the migration reality that the international migration processes are finally the function of the market and the forces of demand and supply. The demographic futures, the great disparities of income, the systemic labour and skills shortages have all posed problems to regional integration. Relying only on intra-regional movement will only exacerbate the demographic distortions. Our problem is that regional integration processes have resulted in barriers to entry being raised to prevent non-member nationals from gaining access to the region (Gollerkeri, 2007).

In 1965, President Lyndon Johnson signed a bill that dramatically changed the method by which immigrants were admitted to America. This was the Immigration Act of 1965, also known as the Hart–Cellar Act (Graham Jr., 1995). It allowed more individuals from Third World countries to enter the United States, including Asians, who traditionally had been hindered from entering America (Kutler, 2003). The significance of this bill was that future immigrants were to be welcomed because of their skills/professions, and not for their countries of origin (Reimers, 1985). The prime

Destination: South		
Origin	Destination	2013
Bangladesh	India	3.2
India	United Arab Emirates	2.9
Russian Federation	Kazakhstan	2.4
Afghanistan	Pakistan	2.3
Afghanistan	Iran (Islamic Republic of)	2.3
China	China, Hong Kong, SAR	2.3
State of Palestine	Jordan	2.1
Myanmar	Thailand	1.9
India	Saudi Arabia	1.8
Burkina Faso	Côte d'Ivoire	1.5
Destination: North		
Mexico	United States	13.0
Russian Federation	Ukraine	3.5
Ukraine	Russian Federation	2.9
Kazakhstan	Russian Federation	2.5
China	United States	2.2
India	United States	2.1
Philippines	United States	2.0
Puerto Rico	United States	1.7
Turkey	Germany	1.5
Algeria	France	1.5

Figure 8.1   Top Ten Country-Specific Corridors, 2013
Source: United Nations, Population Facts 2013/3, September 2013.
Note: 'United States' stands for United States of America and 'China, Hong Kong, SAR' stands for China, Hong Kong Special Administrative Region.

driver for the Immigration Act was the Civil Rights Movement that sought to rid America of racial/ethnic discrimination. Two earlier laws reflecting this discrimination were the National Origin Act of 1924 and the McCarran-Walter Act of 1952 (Kutler, 2003). Both of these granted residency on the basis of national origin, and were particularly discriminatory against Asians. For instance, under the McCarran-Walter Act, while the quota for European immigrants was 149,667, that for Asian immigrants was 2,990, and for Africans 1,400 (Shih, cited in Koeller, 2003). How does one human being have more of a right to access basics like safety, security, education, housing, and health care than another? *Life, liberty, freedom and opportunity* are the *mantras* of what forms the bedrock of human rights. However, the degree of *access* to these or the *absence* of access is mostly a function of entitlements—access based on an individual's social, political, and economic position. We explore this concept in the case of migrants. Despite over half a century of material progress, inequality has widened within and across countries. It is axiomatic that where people have been denied opportunities, indeed because they have no access, they might choose to emigrate from their country of birth to another in search of a better life. The right to emigrate is enshrined in Article 13(2) of the Universal Declaration of Human Rights. But a migrant is placed in a unique conundrum. Because migration is a highly regulated space, the role of the state becomes very important in denying/giving access. Economic migrants leave their homes in search of better opportunities. However, in their new homes they are denied access to the basics because they represent the 'other'. They are expected to contribute towards taxes, towards community, and comply with the rules of the society even before they are granted citizenship, but their access is based on their status as a migrant. This affects the lives of millions of people. *Access, especially for the mobile economic migrants, should be based on residence and not nationality or 'national identity'.*

Why Should Access Be Based on Residence?

The simplest but by far the most compelling arguments for residence as the basis for access are that *if obligations are based on residence, then rights of access should be too.*

The Ethical Perspective

Access to security, social welfare, to civic amenities and to economic opportunities is a basic human right. There is no justification for basic rights to be caught up and denied in the politics of belonging or unbelonging. It is an irony of international law that the grounds on which asylum seekers are granted protection, that is, race, religion, nationality and so on (albeit in steadily fewer numbers) are the very grounds on which access is denied to migrants. There is an international law that protects the rights of asylum seekers but none that protects economic migrants on the basis of their residence. They come and go without any entitlements but not without obligations. Since the world is in favour of privileging the privileged, it is worth mentioning that there is an element of universality in mobility. It is not just the nationals of the poor countries who leave their homes in search of better opportunities. Everyone in search of better opportunities does. Also, migrants are not just economic actors. They are also co-workers, community members, members of the local congregation, and members of the local borough and the neighbourhood. Denying them access on the basis of their being the 'outsider' is discriminatory and unfair. It risks making a fairly large number of people vulnerable. It also constitutes a challenge to national cohesion.

The Migrant Perspective

This is an opportunity to address racism. It gives minorities a chance to break out of the vicious circle of poverty and lack of opportunity. Besides being occupationally immobile, the opportunities for a good education or vocational training are woefully inadequate in isolated housing where the migrants may reside. This means that the *misfortune* of being a migrant is carried forward to the second and third generations. (Castles and Davidson, 2000). This puts migrants at grave disadvantage. They are termed as threats to society without giving them the opportunity to prove otherwise. They are caught in a vicious cycle of being a part of the *ghettoes* or the *underclass*. However, this is a direct consequence of the lack of access that the migrants face.

The State Perspective

Migration is good for business so it is a good practice to make your cities globally 'fluent'. Migration has important economic benefits. It increases the profitability of business. An important trait of a globally fluent, metropolitan area is "opportunity and appeal to the world" (Singer and Wilson, 2013). A region that is viewed as appealing and has opportunities to prosper attracts immigrants. It is a sign of the economy being healthy, of its doing well (Singer and Wilson, 2013).

Significant economic migration happens when migrant networks are successfully established. It is a no-brainer that the more access a city, region, or country provides, the more attractive it is.

Increasing the solidarity base

Many societies are based on the solidarity principle, which means that every citizen must contribute to the state. This solidarity principle works well if there is some symmetry in the dependency ratios. However, the demographic futures of all nations are undergoing fundamental changes. In ageing societies, the dependency ratios are higher. There are fewer earning members supporting a larger number of older people. If residents are granted access and integrated into this system of welfare, the solidarity base will become stronger. By our growing interconnectedness, we are quickly marching towards irrelevance of state boundaries that are considered so sacrosanct at the moment. Access based on citizenship and not residence will simply become untenable. If access continues to be based on the intertwined ideas of nationality and citizenship and not residence, fewer people in the world will have access. We will be beating the ideal of human progress.

Problems with the Idea of Access Based on Residence

The Muckiness of the Politics of Belonging: Nationality and Citizenship

When a third generation non-white British citizen is asked, 'But where are you *really* from?' we can be absolutely sure that the concept of citizenship is closely linked to the concept of nationality. Nationality is defined as the idea of being one people with common cultural characteristics whereas citizenship is a political concept. Ideally, the two concepts should be separated. The reality is that they are not. In fact, there is a great tension between these two concepts. Citizenship is universalistic whereas nationality is particularistic because of its bond to a culture. Naturally, the conflict between the two is palpable and quite unmanageable (Castles and Davidson, 2000).

Compelling arguments have been made for the right of migrants to citizenship (Castles and Davidson, 2000) which will then make them eligible to gaining access. However, these stem from the perceived

importance of territoriality; from the importance of artificial boundaries of nation states which are considered sacrosanct. In the age of
mobility every migrant need not become a citizen in his/her country
of residence. Very simply, just as obligations to the state are on the
basis of residence, access—especially to the basics, must also become
an entitlement on the basis of residence. It is not impossible to fore-
see this as a solution to the politics of belonging. Migrants only need
economic opportunity and equal treatment—socially and legally.
Few would be interested in participating in political life.

The idea of citizenship of a nation state is dated. *Transnationalism
will not allow this to last beyond its expiry date.* This leads us to the
contradiction or the dialectic of citizens versus aliens and from there
entitlements based on residence. We are an increasingly interconnected and integrated world driven by the very complex movement
of people between borders, transnational corporations, global supply
chains, and cross-border movement of goods, capital and services.
Migration must be seen as one of the historical processes of globalization.
It is not just the policies of the nation state that have an impact on
its people. Our economies are global. It will not be long before our
states will be too.

Racial Shadow on Migration Discourse?

The binary of the national and the 'outsider/alien/non-national' has
resulted in xenophobia and a racial shadow on the migration discourse. Populist right-wing politics and xenophobic fringe elements
exploit any fear and/or insecurity that citizens may have. Usually,
the visible 'effects' of migration are pressure on infrastructure, new
languages, culture, multiple ethnicities, the fear of 'losing jobs' to
the 'ethnics' and so on. It has been famously said, "As the global
expansion of Indian and Chinese restaurants suggests, xenophobia
is directed against foreign people, not foreign cultural imports"
(Hobsbawm and Kertzer, 1992: 6–7). There are three main aspects
emerging from this that have an impact on access: First, *resistance
to the outsider/foreigner essentially because s/he is seen as taking away
what is one's right.* Competition for space, for limited opportunities
and for access has led to conflict in many parts of the world. Even
though the United States of America is a country of immigrants,

the resistance to Hispanics in Afro-American dominated areas can be seen as a challenge to access. Especially in times of economic down-turns it is easiest for populist politics to direct popular discontent and dissent towards vulnerable immigrants. In India, in the state of Maharashtra, 'North Indian workers' from the states of Bihar and Uttar Pradesh were blamed for the negative influence on language and culture, loss of jobs and pressures on infrastructure. The 2012 clash of 'Bodos' and Muslim immigrants in Assam and its subsequent effects also assumed racist overtones (Dutta, 2012). Not very long ago, a spate of attacks on Indian students in Australia was portrayed as 'racially motivated' by the Indian media. There were accusations and warnings: a substantial decline in the number of Indian students choosing to study in Australia and much speculation and a great deal of resentment. In fact, the city of Melbourne, which is supposed to be a melting pot of immigrants, was soon perceived as 'racist' (Biswas, 2010). Second, the issue of access has become a lot more complicated as a result of the process of securitization—national concerns about the safety and security of citizens—of migration. Incidents of attacks and violence against people of the Sikh faith in the United States post 9/11 (McGreal, 2012) is a classic example not just of mistaken identity but of insecurities due to misunderstandings—an expression of misdirected anti-Islamic sentiment. Sikhs have mostly been attacked physically or tauntingly referred to as 'Bin Laden' because their appearance is similar to Muslims. The populist perception is that migrants pose a threat. Third is the *economics of distribution/sharing*. The Nitaqat Movement in Saudi Arabia has at its heart the internal contradictions that arise from the political economy of surplus accu-mulation and who gets what. Intolerance seems more likely to rear its ugly head when the economy goes through rough passages, especially downturns. We believe that the answer to making an economy more robust is more migration, not less. As de Haas puts it, 'The only way to reduce immigration is to wreck the economy' (de Haas, 2011).

Social Protection Based on Residence

There are gains and costs in any process and mobility of people is no exception. Migration is seen as beneficial to the countries and nationals of the Global South. Very simply put, it appears that the biggest gains from freer migration and access based on residence will accrue to developing countries and the citizens of developing countries and the most burdensome costs will be borne by the developed countries. There is no evidence to suggest that this is the case. The Global North, if it dares to be prescient, has much to gain from providing access and making their cities attractive to migrants. The misconception of the poor flooding the gates of the North needs to go. Migration is an inevitable, value-neutral process. In fact, apart from being intrinsic to the process, migration lends modernity to globalism (Castles and Davidson, 2000). A multilateral framework that eases mobility will be in a position to establish a compensatory mechanism that addresses the various costs of migration. Perhaps the future is in Asia. Many have said that this is the 'Asian Century' and it might well be in pioneering robust migration reform and good practices. One of these is the idea of *social protection based on residence.*

India has recently launched a mammoth and revolutionary programme of providing a unique identity to every one of its residents. This programme is *mammoth* because it seeks to cover over 1.27 billion people and *revolutionary*, because it signals a paradigm shift in the idea of 'access'. It provides national treatment to all residents in the country—national and non-national, citizens and foreigners, natives and migrants—and is based on the principle of non-discrimination in so far as access to social security, social welfare, safety and security, and economic opportunity are concerned. The 'Aadhaar' programme in India is unprecedented in its scope and scale and profoundly alters how the state delivers on its responsibilities. The world can surely learn from this the importance of the residence principle as the basis for access. India has the largest number of absolute poor in the world. A substantial number of these are irregular migrants from the neighbouring states in search of a livelihood. In 2013, persons from Bangladesh residing in India constituted the single-largest 'bilateral stock' of international migrants in the South (3.2 million) (UN-DESA, 2013). One of the biggest problems that the government faces is in the 'identification' of the poor— recognition of families that are eligible for various social welfare programmes. There are a large number of people who are virtually invisible (Nilekani, 2009). Inclusiveness as an intrinsic democratic principle and the acknowledgement of residence, or counting all residents as done in census operations globally, as the basis for extending access and identity to people in India gave birth to the Unique Identification Number (UID) or the Aadhaar scheme. It is an initiative that anticipates the future to leverage technology to improve delivery systems. It tries in some ways to emulate the successful models of Brazil's 'Central Registry' that is used to track families for its successful cash transfer programme, Bolsa Familia or the Social Security Number (SSN), for which every resident of the United States is eligible. Without going into the merits of Aadhaar—since it has come under the scanner of civil society which believes that the UID poses several uncomfortable questions for civil liberties; that it is wasteful and unnecessary; that its real aim is national security—it must be said that it is a programme that treats citizens and non-citizens equally (Dreze, 2010; Menon, 2010). The idea of Aadhaar is based on providing an identity to every resident thereby making every resident (and not citizen) eligible for benefits under the various schemes of the government. The importance and the uniqueness of Aadhar centres on this fact. The idea or the concept of social welfare based on residence and not citizenship is in practice and has to date covered nearly half the residents. That it is actually being implemented gives hope for the rest of the migration world.

Is 'Multiculturalism' the Answer?

Global mobility will greatly increase in the coming years and the idea of 'Global citizenship' is certainly not utopian.

The shadow of race looms heavily on the migration discourse. As we have seen, it affects access for migrants to a great extent. In our policy, institutions, and instruments of engagement, we need to consciously foster multiculturalism. *Consciously fostering multiculturalism* encourages migrants from different nationalities to coexist, that is, belonging nationally is not a requirement or a prerequisite for citizen rights (Castles and Davidson, 2000). Australia and Canada have done the most in their institutions and policies to foster multiculturalism but even in a country like Australia, which emerged from the principles of *Jus Soli* and adopted multiculturalism, its 'ethnic minorities' are not truly empowered and more needs to be done

(Castles and Davidson, 2000). The idea of citizenship is predicated upon the idea of territoriality, on the idea of the absoluteness of the nation state. However, this idea will not last too long in the face of change that globalization is bringing, the change that is intrinsic to the 'modernity of globalization.' Is there a solution to this problem of lack of access? Is it possible for residents to get the same basic rights as citizens? Or will they have to acquire citizenship of that nation? Is not this a tiresome process in a world that will certainly be more mobile in the years to come? With some countries allowing dual citizenship and others refusing it, is it really prudent to wait until all immigrants are granted citizenship before they can assert their right to access? True, there are costs to migration; there is a strong misplaced anti-immigrant sentiment often on specious grounds. But it is also true that there are compelling reasons to aspire to access based on residence in humanity's eternal quest for progress. In a world that aspires to progress, it is entirely unacceptable to proactively discourage the right to dream, the right to move to fulfil that dream and then the right to the basics. Migration is the *original* strategy for people seeking to escape poverty, mitigate risk, and build a better life. It has been with us since the dawn of mankind, and its economic impact today is massive. Migrant remittances exceed the value of all overseas development aid combined, to say nothing of the taxes that migrants pay, the investments they make, and the trade they stimulate (Sutherland, 2014). Migration has to be an inseparable part of the world's development strategy.

9

The Current State of Play

State of the Global Discourse on Migration

The first decade of the twenty-first century has reiterated in no small measure the fact that countries need to work together; and that at heart there is a common future for all of humankind. The grand societal challenges that we face, especially climate change, global poverty, and international conflict need to be tackled together as a global community. Failure to build an equitable, reciprocal, and mutually beneficial international agenda of action will result in dissonance of a high order. A strong correlation can also be found between these grand societal challenges and the discourse on international migration. An objective analysis of the current state of play on international migration and the convergence and divergence in praxis catalysing or constraining action would provide the basis for what might be a possible pathway to the future. We must hasten to recognize, however, that the policy approach to international migration at the global or national level is dynamic and therefore constantly changing. We do not therefore propose to elaborate on specific policy frames. Rather, we attempt a broad overview of the current approach shared by a wide group of countries.

The discussions on international migration at a global level really began about twenty years ago with the first International Conference on Population and Development (ICPD) in the year 1994 culminating in the High-Level Dialogue (HLD) on Migration at the United Nations in New York in early October of 2013. In 2014, the twenty-year review of the ICPD was held in a Special Session of the United Nations General Assembly. In parallel, the global community adopted the Millennium Development Goals in the year 2000 and the curtains came down on this initiative in 2015. All emphasis now is on what has been described as the 'Post 2015 Development Agenda', the Sustainable Development Goals (SDGs). A brief overview of the progress made in the last twenty years marked by important milestones would help. For a brief overview of the policies at the global level see Box 9.1.

International Conference on Population and Development, Cairo, 1994

Though this was the first time migration was being discussed at an international conference, a large number of participants from all over the world discussed subjects related to international migration and a whole chapter (Chapter 10) was dedicated to the issues of international migration, the consensus that emerged was rather disappointing. The conference came up with a twenty-year Plan of Action to be followed and 179 countries signed it. Its progress was evaluated in 2014. In 1994, migration was looked at as a negative phenomenon that needed to be dealt with. There was an emphasis on promoting development so that emigration is rendered less necessary. There was a clear 'Stay home' message embedded in its outlook on international migration, treating it more as a problem to be solved and also as unnecessary if development policies were pursued effectively in the countries of origin. With grudging optimism, it was believed that international migration could only be reduced in the long term with effective interventions like addressing poverty in the countries of origin. The 'economic situation' of these countries cannot be changed in the short- to medium-term and, therefore, the migration flows have to be 'dealt' with through transparent migration policies and international co-operation. It failed to recognize that mobility of people was a necessary condition for development and that it was both the cause, as also the consequence, of globalization.

The Berne Initiative, 2001

Launched by the Swiss Government at the International Symposium on Migration in 2001, it was an attempt to reach a consensus through its 'International Agenda for Migration Management'. It tried to fill the gap for inter-state dialogue and cooperation at the global level and in doing so involved the International Labour Organization (ILO), the United Nations High Commissioner for Refugees (UNHCR), and the International Centre for Migration Policy Development (ICMPD). It recognized that there may be common interests in international migration at a global level and therefore tried to deal with all major aspects of migration management comprehensively. Its main recommendations included capacity building, and stronger cooperation and dialogue at a global level. Through its 'Common Understandings' and 'Effective Practices', it sought to serve a myriad roles—as a reference document; planning and evaluation tool; training instrument and the basis for inter-state cooperation at every level of dialogue. The Berne Initiative was given a pat on its back for creating a spirit of 'open and constructive dialogue' to be carried forward. Though it concluded on a self-congratulatory note of a 'path breaking initiative', the fact was that nothing 'path breaking' emerged. This document was to be widely disseminated among governments and also presented to the Global Commission on International Migration (GCIM). While acknowledging the commonality of interests on international migration among countries especially because no country can be categorized exclusively as of origin, transit, or destination it failed to identify an actionable agenda even on a rudimentary set of principles that constituted common ground.

The Global Commission on International Migration (GCIM), 2005

An independent body comprising 19 experts responsible for drafting a coherent, comprehensive and global response to the issues of international migration was constituted at the turn of the century in the year 2000. The GCIM report presented in 2005 formed the basis for the HLD of the United Nations in 2006. The GCIM acknowledged the disparities created in the process of globalization as among the main causes of why migration occurs. The commission claimed to have travelled far and wide and to have met people with an interest in, involved with, and affected by migration. It purportedly "heard about the lives, the achievements and hardships of the world's 200 million migrants, as well as the complex issues that confront states and societies when people move in significant numbers ..." (GCIM, 2005). It is a shame then that despite all this it remained captive to an agnostic and doctrinaire approach as of the past ('migration out of choice' as the first of its principles) and continued to articulate the sedentary bias or the 'hordes' of migrants tone (comparing the number of migrants to the population of Brazil—the fifth-most-populous country in the world) in its analysis. The GCIM belied the expectations of a wide array of stakeholders. Its report therefore truly disappoints. It argues that 'best/good practices' of a country that deals with issues of international migration successfully may be adopted by others but hastens to add the caveat that ultimately every experience is unique and there is no model that can be followed. It attempts to set out principles that would serve many purposes and to serve different ends, that is, it may be employed by States and the international community for formulation of policies; it may be used to monitor and evaluate these policies and also to provide a framework for action (GCIM, 2005). Apart from this, for the short term, it insisted on the need for enhanced cooperation and coordination between the different multilateral organizations in the field of international migration; the immediate establishment of a high-level inter-institutional group paving the way for an inter-agency global migration facility which led to the formation of the Global Migration Group (GMG) (Martin et al., 2007). For the long term, it advocated a single organization but without recommendations of what it might look like and its functions (Martin et al., 2007). It did acknowledge the link between international trade and migration and that GATS (Mode 4) should be brought to a successful conclusion. The GCIM could have been visionary, sagacious, and decisive. It could have anticipated the future and set a progressive agenda. On balance, it would be fair to say that the GCIM raised expectations but fell well short of its potential. It was a lost opportunity and did not achieve very much.

United Nations General Assembly (UNGA) High-Level Dialogue (HLD), 2006

This was the first major event of the United Nations focusing exclusively on issues of migration. It held great promise and could well have galvanized a global concert for action. It was built around a theme that had dominated international discussions in the last decade of the twentieth century—'Migration and Development'. The issues dealt with were also not very different. Traditional ways of thinking about international migration such as 'addressing' the causes of migration; promoting circular migration to address 'brain drain'; pledging to reap benefits from the growing volume of remittances but hardly reaching a consensus on how to reduce costs (Martin and Cross, 2007); pleas were made to increase safe and legal avenues for migration to curb irregular migration. There was no consensus on a way forward except the formation of a voluntary, non-binding body with no powers of execution of policy. Many member states were of the view that there are enough structures within the gamut of existing institutions to take care of all the issues of international migration; others were of the opinion that bodies such as the GMG and the International Organization for Migration (IOM) should be better utilized. The concluding remarks of the Secretary General are quite telling. He said: "Clearly, there is no consensus on making international migration the subject of formal, norm-setting negotiations. There is little appetite for any norm-setting intergovernmental commission on migration" (UN-DESA, 2006; Martin and Cross, 2007). Thus, it was that the Global Forum on Migration and Development (GFMD) was born out of the HLD in 2006.

The Global Forum on Migration and Development (GFMD), 2007–14

The GFMD was born out of demand; a demand by member states to have a forum for maximizing the development impact of migration and minimizing its negatives. Consensus for it emerged because of its design. It was intended to be a voluntary, informal, non-binding and state-led forum. It was meant to exchange free and frank views and discuss good practices, but was not meant to set normative standards, be outcome driven, set an actionable binding agenda or provide for negotiations. The GFMD's umbilical cord was linked to the United Nations through the United Nations Special Representative for Migration, Peter Sutherland. The first GFMD was held in Belgium in the year 2007 followed by one in 2008 hosted by Manila; the one that came after was held in Athens in the year 2009–10; in Mexico in 2010–11; Switzerland in 2011–12; and Mauritius in 2012–13; Sweden in 2013–14; and in Turkey in 2014–15. Thus the GFMDs have alternated between the developed and the developing world. The agenda for all the GFMDs was more or less fixed by the different clusters that were considered most relevant; these were mainly labour migration, addressing irregular migration, remittances and other diaspora resources, and institutional structures for greater policy coherence. In the GFMD held in Athens, participants expressed an interest in the development of a multi-year agenda for the sake of continuity and for the need for flexibility and innovation with due respect to the 'thematic' priorities of successive chairs (GFMD, 2009). Of all the GFMDs held in different parts of the world, the one held in Mexico in 2010 stood out owing to its new ideas. Of course, most of these were unworkable. The GMG issued a landmark statement on the human rights of irregular migrants in the year 2013 (UN, 2013). There was a call to end the 'criminalization' and 'demonization' of irregular migrants. Another new idea was the proposal to carry out an assessment of the GFMDs to take stock of whether the forum was able to achieve or was close to achieving what it was supposed to. The assessment was to be carried out in two parts. The result of the first part of the assessment was carried out through a survey of the participating governments and announced in the GFMD held in the following year, that is, in 2011 under the Swiss chair. However, instead of the self-introspection (critiquing national policies) and failure to adhere to what was spoken of for three years, most governments agreed that the GFMD was a success. Of the sixty-six participating countries, 80 per cent in fact voted that the GFMD was a success (GFMD, 2011). The reason for this 'roaring success' is quite straightforward. Everyone had agreed at the outset that any multilateral framework should be voluntary and non-binding and that is exactly what the GFMD was. In a way, countries found that they could salve their collective conscience and perhaps fulfil their ethical duty towards issues of international migration by making lofty speeches and agreeing to do very many things to improve the lives of migrants. It was a different matter altogether that none of this translates to action on home ground. Political will is shaped by popular opinion that invariably sways against the migrant. The result of Phase II of the assessment revealed that the GFMD does not monitor whether or how the governments fulfil the pledge/outcomes made in the forum (UN, 2013).

The other innovation of the Mexico GFMD was the creation of the 'Common Space'. In all the GFMDs, the civil society and the government officials met on separate days. This particular idea sought to bring them together for at least some discussions. However, it was deemed a flop at the Swiss GFMD the following year due to its lack of structure that was too open-ended but lauded for its innovativeness. According to the report by the Special Rapporteur, this is an idea worth pursuing as the contribution by civil society is invaluable (UN, 2013). The GFMD held in Sweden (2013–14) was commended for being dynamic and reaching out to more stakeholders including the Civil Society and the Private Sector. Indeed, many of the good ideas that were mentioned in the GFMD report came from civil society. One such idea in the 'Common Space' was in the opening remarks of a BBC journalist, Zeinab Badawi, and they clearly stood out. She reminded everyone that in the discussion on irregular migrants, the principles of anti-racism were clearly forgotten. The negative attitudes towards migrants were responsible for negative attitudes and prejudice towards people of colour regardless of their status (GFMD, 2011). The GFMD in 2010 affirmed that the United Nations Secretary General provide continuity and institutional memory to the GFMD (GFMD, 2010) but a report to the Secretary General by the special rapporteur confirms that the lack of transparency of what was discussed in the forum—the absence of a secretariat and the rotation of the chair every year—served to wipe out the institutional memory of the GFMD (GFMD, 2010). The GFMD held in Sweden (2013–14) was deemed significant; it had the potential to contribute towards the then 'Post-2015 Development Agenda' and it coincided with the UN HLD on migration of 2013. This particular chairmanship was congratulated for contributing towards a better, more sustainable financing model as well as more transparency and predictability. The GFMD held in Turkey 2014–2015 endorsed the idea of private sector participation in migration policy and had follow-up action for the inclusion of migration in the 2030 Development Agenda.

However, being toothless is one reason why the GFMD is termed a 'success'; it is also the reason why it has brought no substantive change at all (see Table 9.1). Even if one were not to expect actionable outcomes from the GFMD since it was meant to serve as a forum to enhance international cooperation, what was disappointing was that it achieved no movement forward even towards building a consensus on positive governance for international migrants.

UNGA HLD, 2013

The HLD on International Migration in the United Nations General Assembly was held on 3 and 4 October in 2013 in New York. Among other things, it was supposed to have strengthened the GFMD process.

> **Box 9.1**   Précis of the Policies at the Global Level
>
> *Exploring Commonalities*
>
> - *Management of migration*: there is an emphasis on nation states developing their own capacity to better 'manage' migration. Assumption: If developing countries or countries of origin do this more effectively, then there will be lower volumes of migration.
> - *Migration out of choice, not necessity*: hinting towards development within the countries of destination and therefore supporting the 'sedentary bias'. Assumption: If employment is provided in the country of origin there will be no need to leave the country in search of better opportunities/livelihood.
> - *Irregular migration*: Statements have been made to not criminalize migration and to find better ways than just building more walls and spending more money on border control to fight/combat irregular migration. Even though there have been agreements for more 'legal' channels to migration, these are almost always only for high-skilled migrants. None of the national policies recognize the need for liberalization of policies for migrants who belong to the low-skilled category. Assumption: Low-skilled or unskilled migrants do not fit the image of a 'benign' migrant and therefore public opinion will always swing against welcoming them.
> - *Migration and development nexus*: This has been the overarching theme for almost all discussions regarding migration. However, the 'development' in question is always of the countries of origin with

very little acknowledgement of the contribution of migrants towards countries of destination.

- *Remittances*: Most discussions at the global level referred reverentially to remittances; it being the most 'tangible of all benefits of migration' (UNGA HLD, 2006). Even though the volume of remittance exceeds the level of Overseas Development Assistance, there is a plea to not treat the two equally. Whereas one is for the personal development of the migrant and her family, the other is aimed towards a whole nation.
- Emphasis on *temporary and circular migration; return migration* to fight brain drain and yet the only policies that facilitate freer migration are aimed towards high-skilled migration.
- Emphasis on *South–North migration*.
- *Unprecedented migration/Large volume of migrants*: GCIM compares the number of migrants to the population of Brazil which is the fifth-most-populous country in the world rather than comparing it to what a small percentage it constitutes with respect to the world population.
- Consensus on a forum like the *GFMD* for international migration; a body that is essentially toothless—because of differing interests, there is an emphasis on forming a body that is *voluntary, non-binding and state-led*. The problem with this is that even if there is a lot of discussion and important issues are raised, there is absolutely nothing to follow it up, no framework to implement these decisions—everybody is happy with the meet, greet, eat and retreat and then meet again policy. That's the only consensus.
- Agreement over *demographics* but no action to follow it up. Talk of labour shortages and supply gaps in the labour economy but it is acknowledged only for the top end of the market; not for in-situ services where semi-skilled and low-skilled migrants are needed.
- Almost every country agrees on the issues of *security in* the face of rising migration.
- Everyone wants to fight *racism and xenophobia* through better integration of the migrants in the host society and yet acts of racism continue to shock.
- *Access to portability of pensions and health care* have been advocated as an incentive for the 'regulars'/temporary workers to move back to their own societies and invest/save/contribute, and so on.

Sources: Matrix prepared on the basis of the Compendium of Recommendations on International Migration and Development, 2006; Chapter X of the ICPD Report, 1994; GCIM Official Report 2005; Martin et al., 2007; UNGA HLD 2006 official summary; GFMD Reports since 2007 up to 2012; Report of the Special Rapporteur to the Secretary General, 2013; and UNGA HLD 2013.

Table 9.1 A Bird's-Eye View of the Global Discussions on Migration

Issues	ICPD (1994)	GCIM (2004)	HLD (2006)	GFMD(s) (2007–12)
1. Causes of Migration	Enumerated the causes (poverty: root cause; other causes: conflict, environmental degradation) so that they may be effectively addressed	Development and demographic disparities and also due to differences in governance	Poverty, conflict, human rights violations, poor governance, or lack of employment; the need to search for livelihood and security	Economic, demographic and social disparities and, in particular, poverty, political instability, conflict, non-respect of human rights, climatic and environmental degradation (2007)
2. Migration and Development	Better development (sustainable economic growth with equity and development) will lead to less migration—inverse relationship	Migration contributes to development in both developing and developed countries. This fact should be acknowledged and be made a part of global and national economic growth strategies	It set out to explore different aspects of the relationship in order to maximize the good and minimize the negative impacts	The first GFMD in Brussels claimed to have a new approach to migration with a shift in paradigm; legal migration should be treated as an opportunity for development for both countries of origin and destination but it is in no way an alternative to national development strategies or ODA (2007)

(Cont'd)

Table 9.1 (Cont'd)

Issues	ICPD (1994)	GCIM (2004)	HLD (2006)	GFMD(s) (2007–12)
3. Management of Migration	May have negative impacts in countries of origin and destination and therefore long-term manageability is on the basis of making the option to remain in one's country viable for all people	National migration policies should be supported by efforts of the international community through contribution of resources and appropriate expertise and training	National strategies to address international migration should be supplemented by bilateral, regional, and multilateral cooperation	Bilateral agreements are most helpful (2007)
4. Irregular Migration	The countries have their sovereign right to determine who can enter; expected to increase due to the rising numbers in labour force in developing countries	Active cooperation among states; should uphold rights of the migrants; should consult employers, trade unions and civil society; objective debate about the negative consequences and its prevention; border control policies should be a part of long term approach; improve opportunities for regular migration	Increase in irregular migration and exploitation due to restrictive policies; against criminalization of irregular migrants; call for migration policies that would produce a better balance between unmet labour demand and inflows of workers from abroad	Acknowledgement of the human rights of irregular migrants and the remarkable recognition of 'human rights' of irregular migrants (2010); continued plea of no criminalization of irregular migrants and reallocation of resources from border controls to enforcement of labour standards and address exploitation of irregular migrants (2011)

| 5. Migration Out of Choice | Necessarily but migration can be addressed if economic situation of countries of origin is improved | The first among the six principles of action; to this end greater efforts must be made to create jobs and sustainable livelihood so that people are not compelled to migrate | Addressing the root causes of migration will ensure that people move out of choice rather than necessity | Addressing the root causes of migration targeting development; providing information to migrants; right migration policies that address the fulfilment of the MDGs can ensure this (2007) |
| 6. Addressing Brain Drain: Temporary and Circular Migration | The individuals from developing countries should be trained in developed countries so that they can carry these skills back | Both states and the private sector should choose carefully designed policies for temporary migration to address the economic needs of both countries of origin and destination | Essential for high-skilled migrants for addressing 'brain drain', especially in health and education sectors | Temporary migration is a flexible way of meeting labour shortage across countries; circular and return migration will favour the source countries and reinforce the development efforts (2007); the Civil Society called upon governments to reconsider circular migration, assess its pitfalls and stop overestimating its advantages (2010); circular migration schemes should not replace permanent migration and pathways to citizenship (2011) |

(Contd)

Table 9.1 (*Contd*)

Issues	ICPD (1994)	GCIM (2004)	HLD (2006)	GFMD(s) (2007–12)
7. Return Migration	Developing countries should aim to reintegrate these migrants and make use of their newly acquired skills	State and international organization policies should enhance the impact of circular and return migration; one way to deal with irregular migration	Return of high-skilled migrants, especially entrepreneurs, to successfully contribute towards development of country of origin; return of illegal migrants to country of origin	
8. Governance of Migration	Co-operation and dialogue to maximize the positive effects of migration and development	Advocates coherence, capacity building at national levels; cohesion, cooperation and dialogue at the regional and global levels	No consensus; a few members argued that adequate means to address international migration issues already existed in different structures including in the UN system; very many were in favour of using existing institutions like the IOM and GMG	Recommendation of institutionalized framework for government coordination, interstate cooperation as well as informed consultative processes (2007); need for a new form of global governance due to the complexity of migration and to balance national sovereignty with the right to migrate (2010); the ILO should show new energy in developing a new approach to labour migration (2011)

9. Access to portability of pensions and health care	The documented migrants who acquire citizenship should have access to all the rights as other citizens	Equal rights to long term documented migrants	Bilateral agreements are most important in securing rights such as portability of pensions	Migrant health as a key determinant of empowerment and protection of migrants; access should be equal and not just for some migrants; critical to the well-being of migrants and their families but can be pursued more effectively at the bilateral and/or regional levels (2010)
10. Migration and Security	Pre-9/11 world!	No mention	Illegal migration is considered one of the main threats to security	Moved away from portrayal of migrants as a 'threat' to host society
11. Demographics	Migrants may change the demographics in countries of destination	Important cause for migration	Not acknowledged as a potential 'cause' for increase in migration in the coming years	Cause of migration (2007) acknowledged widely in almost all the years

(Cont'd)

Table 9.1 (Cont'd)

Issues	ICPD (1994)	GCIM (2004)	HLD (2006)	GFMD(s) (2007–12)
12. Labour Shortages and Skills Gaps	Not acknowledged	Need for realistic and flexible approaches to international migration to fill gaps; cooperation among labour-rich and labour-poor countries to create a global pool of professionals	Migrants may be essential in meeting labour shortages but international migration cannot be a long-term development strategy; also, some countries had adopted or were about to implement the ban on active recruitment of health workers from developing countries affected by labour shortages in the health and education sectors	High-skilled migration to developed countries will grow but this will adversely impact the vulnerable sectors such as health and education in developing countries (2007)

13. Xenophobia and Racism	Governments are responsible for instituting policies to protect migrants against negative attitudes. Should be avoided even in case of undocumented migrants	For long-term migrants—States should value social diversity, foster social cohesion and avert marginalization of migrant communities	There is a need for concerted efforts on the part of the governments to combat xenophobia, discrimination and social exclusion of the migrant population; social consequences of migration need urgent attention–integration through combating of intolerance and awareness of the positive contribution of migration	Integration of migrants in host countries is one important element of implementation of relevant instruments (2007); racist discourse on irregular migrants and the usage of incorrect terminology like 'illegal migrants' and negative media coverage need to be challenged (2011)
14. High-Skilled Migration	States should recognize the talent of the migrants so that they may fully contribute to their new States of residence	Governments and private sector should review barriers to improve economic competitiveness	High-skilled migration in the South–North direction is adversely affecting development	High-skilled migration will grow to the developed parts of the world and this will adversely impact development efforts in the source countries (2007)

Almost all attempts at reaching consensus globally have unfortunately only remained 'attempts'. They are fancy talk shops at the end
of the day that might make some useful suggestions but remain in the
realm of the undoable because of the nature of these bodies. How much
can dialogue achieve, after all, if it is not followed up by appropriate
action? What stands out in all these attempts is the absence of the
'how to' even within the narrow confines of 'migration management'.
While many agree that it is important to diligently pursue an agenda
of action on international migration, few actually support even baby
steps towards decisive action. A look at the policies at the national level
shows that we are far behind on a consensus on global migration. One
clear shortcoming has been the absence of leadership to champion the
cause of shaping a progressive, inclusive, and actionable agenda.

Country Perspectives on Migration

It's easy for this discussion (on immigration reform) ... to assume
a feeling of 'us' versus 'them' but what we may be forgetting is that
most of 'us' used to be 'them' before we became 'us' .

—President Barack Obama, 2013

This section has a two-fold objective. It highlights the fact that whatever is considered to be a 'consensus' at a global level is not necessarily
translated into national policies. In doing so, it highlights where the
roads meet and where they separate, that is, the convergence and
divergence between the global and national levels. In highlighting
the migration policies of some of the most important global economic actors, it draws attention to the search for leadership within
the global community. Leadership by one or a small group of progressive countries could take responsibility to articulate the need
for, shape the contours of, and help build a multilateral framework
for freer economic migration. Such leadership could emerge from
amongst the G-20.

Competition is fierce for high-skilled migration and many of the
old restrictive policies are making way for a new competitive, mar-
ket-oriented approach (Shachar, 2006: 139). However, at the lower
end of the skills spectrum, most countries of destination are still
trying to limit immigration because of their perceived inability to

absorb labour. This perception is often a function of the state of the economy—the levels of unemployment extant or the political economy of immigration, the anti-immigrant public opinion, for instance. But this is very often at the cost of unrecognized and unacknowledged labour needs in their markets. Along with this, a majority of the decisions on immigration policy are driven by considerations of security even though most migrants are harmless (UN, 2013). The Eurobarometer recently recorded in a survey that immigration was second on the list of concerns—occupying a spot higher than terrorism which is ranked third. Security and unemployment are, therefore, the new enemies of international migration and, unfortunately, the migrant is the new category of criminal (Rekacewicz, 2013).

The following are highlights of the policies of some of the G-20 countries, some or all of whom we think can lead from the front. Some like the United Kingdom and Brazil have been discussed in earlier chapters. Following is an overview of immigration policies of some countries of the Global North and the Global South in order to understand the imperatives at a national level.

The United States of America

Illegal immigration is a bellwether of economic conditions, growing substantially in a strong economy with high demand for low-skilled labour (the 1990s and early 2000s) and tapering off with economic contraction (since 2008).

—Hipsman and Meissner (2013)

The Immigration Reform Act in the United States has generated a lot of heat and dust. Analysts have been busy at work trying to generate numbers for what the effects of the new policy may look like. Students are dreaming and so are the millions of illegal immigrants who will be granted pathways to become citizens of the most sought-after country in the world. The underlying principles are simple: increasing border enforcement to keep out illegal migrants but at the same time opening up avenues for low-skilled and unskilled migration (through the W visas); giving illegal immigrants a chance to earn United States citizenship; and providing better opportunities to high-skilled economic migrants to enable the country to achieve a more competitive edge in the global economy. The refrain has been 'for our economy and our security'. What is more, the immigration reform is driven by popular demand as well as bipartisan support. The problem, however, is that the support does not exist uniformly for all three principles.

However, the public acknowledgement of the history of the United States of America—of it being a country of immigrants and the recognition of their contribution to its economic, social, cultural, and political success—is in itself a big step forward.

The United States has come a long way from denying certain ethnicities rights of admission (1882, 1888, 1892, and 1917) to a quota-based system (1924) graduating to a seven-category preference system (1965). However, for a nation of immigrants and immigration, it has rarely adjusted its immigration policies to the economic realities of its times (Hipsman and Meissner, 2013) President Obama has acknowledged that the current system of immigration is outdated for our century. However, post 9/11, the security imperative has been a strong force in driving its migration policy. There are still an estimated 11 million illegal immigrants in the United States but the number is steadily declining. The United States has been missing in most global discussions of migration. Also, the two major attempts at Immigration Reform (the 1986 Immigration Reform and Control Act and the 1990 Immigration Act) before the one in 2013 have been perceived as having failed to achieve their objectives especially to meet labour market needs during the economic boom of the last decade of the twentieth century (Hipsman and Meissner, 2013).

However, immigration reform in the United States is timely and encouraging. The United States remains one of the most important countries in the new century and continues to attract the best and the brightest from around the world. It is a potential leader for a new global migration regime.

Canada

Canada has been credited with being one of the frontrunners in the global hunt for talent, for skilled human capital. Since its inception, it has been a country of net immigration (Challinor, 2011). More than 20 per cent of its population is foreign-born permanent residents (Challinor, 2011).

However, in the recent past, its policies have increasingly focused on high-skilled migration. The Immigration Act of 1976 marked Canada as an official destination for migrants from all countries. In a revised law in 2001, the Immigration and Refugee Protection Act (IRPA), the emphasis for welcoming migrants shifted from humanitarian concerns and family reunification to the skills sets—language ability and education and adaptability of the immigrants (Challinor, 2011). It came into force in June 2002 and is the main piece of legislation on immigration in Canada. By 2003, 60 per cent of the immigrants were admitted on an economic basis (Mayda and Patel, 2004).

Since 2013, there has been pressure to attract only those migrants who are high-skilled as well as fluent in either English or French because public opinion is increasingly against those migrants who do not seem like a 'good fit' in the Canadian society (MacDonald, 2013). There is an attempt to attract the 'right type of migrants' (Challinor, 2011).

One of the biggest concerns in Canada today is the systemic barriers that immigrants face in the labour market. There is a significant amount of 'brain waste' because high-skilled migrants are not able to find employment commensurate with their education and experience (Challinor, 2011). This has resulted in high unemployment among migrants. A part of this may be the inability of the government to engage employers (Myers and Conte, 2013). Questions are being asked about the ability of the Canadian economy to absorb all the foreign-born workers who migrate to a country that emphasizes the importance of human capital (Challinor, 2011). This points to the importance of engaging industry.

However, with the recent change in government (2015), tides seem to be turning. There is a promise of encouraging and facilitating family reunification, better ease of skilled migration, especially for students educated in Canada and health care workers, as well as more ease of mobility in general. It remains to be seen to what extent this promise may be fulfilled.

Australia

Australia is one among the three 'traditional countries of immigration', the other two being the United States and Canada. This is because Australia has had a relatively more open immigration system—27 per cent of Australia's population in 2013 was made up of immigrants (MPI tabulation from UNDESA, 2013). Immigration has been central to nation-building in Australia (Collins, 2013).

In order to build a knowledge-based society, Australia has welcomed high-skilled migrants since the beginning of the new century. Businesses, academia and the hospitality sector have been more forthcoming about the benefits of migration and welcomed easy access to temporary movement for skilled migrants, students and tourists (Inglis, 2004). However, the other huge chunk of migration opinion in Australia is driven by the imperatives of security, culture, and sustainability (Mayda and Patel, 2004). This may be attributed to incidents in the recent past that have increased apprehensions of irregular migrants or 'boat people'. Subsequently, there has been a marked shift in overemphasizing and increasingly prioritizing skilled and highly qualified immigrants over other immigrants in the past few years (Collins, 2013). The Government's aim has been to 'build a stronger Australia' through welcoming the contributions of immigrants to the Australian economy (Australian Department of Immigration and Border Protection).

France

According to the International Migration Outlook (2013), the stock of migrants in France in 2011 was 11.6 per cent. This has grown from 10.5 per cent in the year 2001. However, France seems to be regressing through its immigration policies.

In the post-war period, it was the only country in Europe to welcome permanent immigration, much like the United States. However, like most other countries in Western Europe, the oil price shocks and the consequent high rates of unemployment, resulted in halting of the recruitment of immigrant workers (Guiraudon, 2001). Since then, the efforts of the French government have been in stemming or deterring migrants even though many legislative changes have been introduced in the area of immigration (Guiraudon, 2001).

Critics have looked upon the French immigration system as one that is failing both its people and its industry. The French Government's anti-immigration and anti-migrant rhetoric continues to be highly politicized. The focus has been to restrict immigration based on two issues—concerns of security and curbing immigration through family reunification. In July of 2006, a new law was adopted that was expected to encourage high-skilled migration, combat illegal migration using more effective measures, and restrict family immigration. According to Sarkozy, who was then the interior minister, the new law passed was an expression of France's sovereignty—it would afford France the right to choose which foreigners were to reside in its territory (Murphy, 2006). He emphasized the importance of having neither zero immigration nor total opening up of borders (Attardo, 2003).

Very recently, France has come under the scanner again. The European Union has threatened it with sanctions for carrying out expulsions of the members of the Roma community. The recent case of Leonarda Dibrani garnered widespread criticism for the manner in which a 'legal' deportation was carried out. She was ordered off a school bus while on a school trip and was with other students when she was taken away to be deported with her family who were put on a flight to Kosovo (*The New York Times*, October 2013). Kosovo is not a member of the European Union and therefore the Dibarani status in France was 'illegal' but such expulsions only serve to perpetuate long-held biases. Prejudice against the Roma community is widespread all over Europe but France and Italy have in the recent years carried out many such 'legal' deportations. This is because recent legislative measures seem to target the Roma communities from a 'security-conscious' point of view (Attardo, 2003).

France continues to court the highly skilled and sweep under the carpet even the felt needs for low-skilled or semi-skilled migrants. It continues to hope that these gaps will be filled by mobility within Europe.

Smith (*The New York Times*, 2014) has given us a good idea about the anti-immigration sentiment prevalent in France. He concludes that it is always easiest to blame the migrant for problems such as unemployment because they represent the weakest section of the society.

Though the French Interior Minister, Manuel Valls, had remarked that Sarkozy's immigration policies were 'random and discriminatory', it remains to be seen if France will be able to keep up with the global hunt for talent and, to borrow a phrase from Clemens and Pritchett (2013), keep up its search for low-skilled non-substitutable workers.

China

China is still the fourth-largest 'country of emigration'. However, a unique combination of a large population, an ageing population, along with a dwindling labour force has forced it to acknowledge the importance of immigration. China is now also a 'country of immigration'. It faces shortages in advanced technology and modern manufacturing; cultural and creative industries; finance; and modern agriculture. Until recently, there was no law to govern this but the fact is that China receives a large number of immigrants—both legal and illegal—and the Chinese government has enacted an immigration policy. The new law came into effect on 1 July 2012 (*China Law & Practice*, 2012). This new policy aims to attract talent and fight irregular migration through strict employer sanctions and border controls.

China has also been making efforts to attract its skilled workers. The Communist Party of China introduced in 2008 a programme known as the '1000 Talents Programme' to actively offer incentives to those wishing to return and has been successful in generating what has come to be known as 'reverse brain drain' especially in technology transfer. Chinese return migrants, especially from the United States, are successfully returning as entrepreneurs attracted by the economic opportunities, access to local markets and family ties (Wadhwa et al., 2011).

Japan

Japan can no longer afford to have a homogenous ethnic population. It has to be tolerant of other ethnicities because it faces one of its biggest challenges yet, that is, an ageing population. There are gaps at both ends of the labour market. It does not favour the admission of 'unskilled foreign labour' but instead offers trainee and technical internship programmes (Mayda and Patel, 2004).

Almost all countries are realizing that there is a need to address the question of labour and skills shortages in their economies. However, public opinion only allows the policies to be less restrictive to the 'high-skilled' segment of the society. There are many problems with such an approach.

Convergences and Divergences at the Global and National Levels

1. National policies are still influenced by a *'security' approach* whereas at the global level the discourse is slowly changing to perceive the migrant (even an irregular migrant) as harmless.
2. There is an acknowledgement at the global level of the *demographic future* of the whole world and the role that international migration will play. However, this is not adequately acknowledged at the national-level policies. There is only an attempt to welcome migrants who are deemed 'highly skilled'.
3. It is widely acknowledged in global discussions on migration that one way to address irregular migration is by *increasing the legal channels to migration*. At the national level, however, there is a greater focus on border controls and stricter enforcement of penalties against migrants who try to cross the borders of countries without papers. The recent Lampedusa tragedy is a result of this dissonance between the reality and the policies.
4. There is an attempt to *'criminalize' the irregular migrant* at the global level. Irregular migrants have also come to be perceived as people in search of better livelihoods. However, the criminalization of the irregular migrant at the national level continues quite unabashedly.
5. There is an increasing consensus on *recognizing xenophobia and racism against migrants* at the global level with a push towards better integration, changing negative perceptions of migrants, improving knowledge and databases to educate people, and so on, but at the national level migration continues to be an issue of great concern, even more than international terrorism. There is not much in national policies to actively address the problem of racism against migrants.
6. There is a need felt to provide *for access for migrants* to social security, especially health, at the global discussion level irrespective of their status, that is, not just to permanent residents or

citizens but at present most national policies do not allow this. There is no provision for portability of social security (pensions, health care, and so on) for temporary economic migrants even though there is an increasing push towards increasing 'circular migration'.

Global Economy Needs: How Are These Different from the Convergences and Divergences?

1   There is a close relationship between demography and development (labour shortages, rise in the number of in situ services).
2.   Economic migration is a global public good (significant economic gain from the liberalization of economic migrants).
3.   Technological changes are creating skills gaps.
4.   The importance of low-skilled migration: selective policies for migrants do not address all the needs of the labour market. The tacit approval of the 'shadow economy' increases irregular migration by not addressing the needs at the lower end of the market.

The Counterfactual: Possible Impacts of Carrying On 'Business as Usual'

> As the scope of complexities of migration continues to grow, the alternative to more robust global migration governance is a highly unregulated system, with a range of uncoordinated actors, including from the private sector. More migration governance would also assist states in combating exploitation of migrants by, inter alia, traffickers, smugglers, recruitment agencies and unscrupulous employers.

> —UN (2013: 33–4)

If the governance of migration is never institutionalized; if only recommendations are made without any decisive action, it is possible that the rhetoric of international migration may never change; that we may always prefer to not take 'normative action' and continue to consider movement of people as a problem. It is important to analyse what may happen if we carry on business as usual, if the global community continues to make hollow promises of cooperation; if we keep building our walls higher and preventing the most natural and historical of all phenomena and if we do not acknowledge the changing needs of our changing world.

The first impact of the absence of coordinated governance of international migration might well mean giving an unintended handle to transnational cartels and intermediaries—illegal and others.

The second is that restrictive national policies have changed a great deal post 9/11 but there may be greater security implications for ungoverned international migration because the forces that are at the root of extremist violence will find ways to use irregular pathways.

A dramatic and worse economic crisis may be on the cards—certainly in poorer regions of the world as a consequence of climate change, conflict, and extreme poverty, which will, in turn, create dissonance of a high order. Whether this impacts global stability or not is not important; what is important is that as a society we will be regressing from the higher goals of an equitable and humane world.

10

India in Transition

> Over the past millennium, world population rose 22-fold. Per capita
> income increased 13-fold, world GDP nearly 300-fold ... the
> growth process was uneven in space as well as time ... this gap is still
> widening. Divergence is dominant but not inexorable. In the past
> half a century, resurgent Asian countries have demonstrated that an
> important degree of catch-up is feasible.
>
> —Maddison (2001: 19)

A Work in Progress

The year 1991 was cathartic for India. From the midst of deep economic crisis the country embarked on a path of economic reforms
that changed the course of its development. There was for some years
in its aftermath a widely held sense of triumph: that finally, good
economics had displaced poor politics in the national discourse. There
was also the fond hope that the reforms would open up opportunities
to all and these, in turn, would help overcome the differences of
caste, class, and religion that tended to so divide a young nation,
and that economic prosperity would forge a new national identity. In
some ways it did. India's economy was opened to competition compelling it to raise productivity, improve efficiency, and reduce costs.
Indian industry, and innovation gained impetus. In the twenty-five
years since the reforms, India has changed significantly—economic

opportunities have indeed expanded, Indians within and outside the country have prospered, India is now seen as a big market by foreign investors and there is a new-found confidence that India can aspire to becoming a global economic power. Doubtless, several seemingly intractable problems remain. India still has a large share of the world's poor, infrastructure bottlenecks are constraining growth, and a serious governance deficit is creating a growing mistrust of government. The idea of India is still evolving and India is yet a work in progress. There is no doubt, however, that India is changing rapidly, and for the better.

India is on the threshold of a great transformation that will witness, over the next few decades, two significant historical processes unfolding in tandem—demographic transition and migration transition. It is similar to a social transformation of a scale that will change social relationships so profoundly that it will affect all social interaction, and all individuals and communities simultaneously (Castles, 2010). It will impact the way social and economic relations are organized and will dramatically alter conceptions of identity, community, and society. This paradigm shift will also challenge hitherto-held notions of growth and welfare; of citizenship and community and the basis for access to economic and social opportunity. The prime drivers of this 'step change' will be the twin dynamics of economic growth led by a young population and growing interconnectedness with the world outside resulting from globalization—integrated markets for goods and capital, reduced barriers to trade and investment across the world, and easier migration (Crafts, 2004). With the remarkable advances in transport and communication lowering costs significantly and the emergence of transnational networks enhancing connectivity in unprecedented ways, the world will be a smaller place and societies diverse as never before. Globalization is not an unmixed blessing, though. It generates its own contradictions—making high-skilled migration easier but at the same time displacing unskilled workers in traditional economies (Li, 2008).

There comes a time in the history of nations that is definitive, a time when a country comes of age and joins the ranks of the comity of nations on the world stage. A discerning economic historian would not miss the intimate interplay between the demographic transition of a country and its economic progress. Demographic transition is the movement over several decades from a pattern of high mortality and high fertility rates to low mortality and low fertility. Historically, countries experiencing the first phase of the demographic transition have experienced high rates of emigration (Goldin et al., 2012). All the miracle economies that demonstrated phenomenal growth and prosperity and today rank as major economic powers in the world made that transition when the share of their working-age population was the highest. India will over the next decade, be on that very threshold. It will have a demographic structure that will come but once in its history, when its working-age population will be at its highest. India is a country of young people with 52 per cent of its population in the age-group below twenty-five years (Census of India, 2011). By 2025, India will become the world's youngest nation with the largest workforce projected at over 832 million in the working-age group (18–59) as compared to 658 million today (Census of India, 2011). This will be a time when it will have the potential to dramatically enhance labour supply and productivity and it will have too, the ravenous appetite to maintain high rates of saving and investment that only a 'young' workforce can.

There is a caveat, however. In the ensuing years, in the small window of time before India reaches that definitive period in its history it will have to invest, in considerable measure, in social and human capital, innovation, and institutional infrastructure. Else, the much-hyped 'demographic dividend' can dramatically turn into a 'demographic disaster'. India's young population has often been described as the aspirational generation. For the vast mass of young people in the countryside in India aspiration is not just two square meals. Migration to a big city even if to work only as a daily wager, a security guard, or a lift operator, is aspirational for young people in India's vast and restless rural population. Aspirations and migration are symbiotic. They fuel and feed each other. The younger the population cohort, the more mobile are people and ideas. While aspirations are a prerequisite for, they can also be a consequence of, migration. Migrants generally have higher aspirations than non-migrants mainly driven by being young, well educated, and economically and socially well placed (Czaika and Vothknecht, 2012).

A direct consequence of globalization has been the rapid change in the composition of the gross domestic product (GDP) of many economies around the world with the share of agriculture and industry declining and that of the services sector growing rapidly. India's economy is still a strange mix encompassing traditional farming, modern agriculture, handicrafts, modern industry, and a growing services sector. More than half the workforce is in agriculture, but services contribute about two-thirds of India's output, with less than one-third of its labour force. This is also resulting in rural displacement and large-scale urbanization. Mumbai, Delhi, and Kolkata, for example, are projected to have a combined population of nearly 70 million by the year 2025 and will figure among the top ten most-populous cities in the world. Jobless growth is exerting considerable emigration pressure in several parts of India and this will remain a key challenge in the foreseeable future.

Declining birth rates and increased longevity have together resulted in ageing populations in many other countries. These two processes have coalesced to create structural imbalances in the international labour market. Large labour supply gaps in several key sectors in many countries are constraining future growth prospects. Asymmetry in the demand for and the supply of skills is eroding productivity of firms, driving up the demand for skilled, trained, and productive workers. At the same time, economic progress and greater democratization of the developing world has led to the emergence of a young, educated, skilled and trained workforce. The Global Commission on International Migration succinctly noted that currently the principal forces driving international migration around the world are the differences in development, demography, and democracy and that the number of people seeking to migrate will continue to increase (GCIM, 2005). Thus, the potential for the convergence of the economic interests of countries of destination and of origin is significant. Quite simply, migration in the future is more likely to be propelled by the labour supply gaps of the global market. Movement of people across national boundaries and the matching of demand for and the supply of skills will substantially determine the pace, the direction, and the future growth prospects of the global economy.

Migration and Development

India's experience as a major country of origin, transit, and destination in the Global South places her in a unique position. The scale and spread of the Indian experience in migration as well as development and the intimate interplay of these two complex processes is matchless. While there is an estimated overseas Indian workforce of over five million, what is less known is that India with its rapidly growing economy and its pluralistic society is also host to millions of migrants. The patterns, processes and the pathways of India's migration praxis and often their absence, for the most part, have been a function of the political economy of underdevelopment and more recently of its development divide. Through the epochs of its history of the last two hundred years—mercantilism, colonial rule, emergence as an independent nation state, industrialization and urbanization—the principal characteristics of India's migration experience have remained largely unchanged, arguably with nuanced variations: coercive mobilization of labour; appropriation of surplus through capital accumulation; exploitative practices of intermediaries; the preponderance of the disadvantaged in the flows; the predominance of the contractual nature of employment; the South–South circuit of movement; the upward mobility on the skills ladder and the colonial underpinning that circumscribes its regulatory architecture. Under merchant capital the movement was mainly of traders, mariners, and slaves; the period of colonial capital saw the movement of convicts, indentured labour, and soldiers; the post-colonial period after the mid-twentieth century witnessed 'free migration' not just of workers but of professionals, entrepreneurs, businessmen, and skilled workers to new and, in some cases, hitherto prohibited destinations—Australia for example, which was formerly prohibited till the time of the White Australia policy or before that Canada which, by policy, discriminated against non-Whites. The 'oil boom' in the Gulf and the 'miracle' economies in Southeast and East Asia catalysed the movement of large numbers of workers and the reappearance of temporary contractual mobility.

Migrant workers in more recent times face oppressive conditions similar to that of the indentured labourers of the nineteenth century but, unlike them, are not allowed to take up residence in the countries of destination (Lal, 2007). This, in turn, has meant exploitation and abuse of migrant workers, greater privation, and separation from the family with implications over the long term from a 'life-cycle' perspective. It also has implications for social security for the migrant, interpersonal relations inter se for the family and for the development prospects for the community. All of these are seen at their starkest in the major states of origin, for instance, in Kerala and Andhra Pradesh in south India and in Rajasthan and Uttar Pradesh in north India.

From a simple narrative shorn of doctrinaire theoretical interpretations, the 'India Migration' experience demonstrates in its size, spread and depth and across time and space that migration is integral to society. Migration must be conceptualized as integral to broader development processes (de Haas, 2010). In India it has been a socio-economic process driving and driven by development and change; constantly redefining the logic of identity, family, and community, and steadily emerging as one of the dominant modes of India's engagement with the outside world. It has also demonstrated the complex, disparate, and multiple sets of endogenous and exogenous factors that influence the decisions that an individual or a family make on migration: to migrate or not to migrate, the preferred mode of migration, the choice of destination, the nature and period of migration, and the coping mechanism to deal with the dramatic changes that leaving home and family as well as return entail. India exemplifies the strengths of a large, tolerant, secular, live democracy with a pluralistic society in which people of different faiths, languages, ethnicities, nationalities and political persuasions co-exist and thrive. Indeed, this milieu is the 'sine qua non' of a society that can foster: (*a*) conditions for positive migratory movements as part of the human development process and (*b*) demand-based labour mobility as a natural corollary to the liberalized movement of goods and capital. In fact, the continental proportions of internal migration in India best epitomize the migration dynamic, with its benefits as well as all its ills in full display. Internal migration can and does strengthen the propensity for international migration. It also serves to demonstrate migration as an increasingly important influence on social, economic, and political relations. The lived migration experience of India in its myriad dimensions represents a microcosm of the migration universe and holds many lessons for future policy, strategy, and modes of engagement.

The forces of rapid development characterized by growing urbanization, a sharp rise in labour-market participation, considerable internal migration, higher education and skills and the steady, even if slow, democratization of economic opportunity will catalyse greater mobility of people from and to India. The combination of intra-country migration, international migration and the diversity in the modes of mobility will mean significant volumes and multidirectional migratory flows. This will exert considerable pressure on India's collective ability, within government and outside, to govern—through progressive policy, transparent regulation, robust institutions, standard operating practices and effective service delivery—and promote human resource capacities across stakeholders in the migration process. It must be noted, though, that with economic growth and India's transformation from a traditional to a modern society, the effects of the migration transition will impact emigration flows. Typically in the 'emigration life cycle' (Hatton and Williamson, 2009) emigration rates will tend to rise with growth in incomes, then slow down till they climb to a peak and after that begin to decline as wage differentials narrow and the incentive to migrate reduces.

India's Migration Future

As India prepares for its migration future it must recognize that international migration is today an important signpost of globalization signifying complex interconnectedness and is in a myriad ways deterritorializing nation states. The future will challenge India as in the past and there will be uncertainty but it is unlikely that closed nation states with homogeneous national communities will continue (Castles, 2002). There are also some trends that signify important departures from earlier patterns and processes and hence pose challenges. First, the numbers of women migrants from India are growing rapidly and a significant proportion today emigrate independently as primary economic migrants. Most of them belong to the low-skilled category as they migrate as domestic workers and low-end service providers; a very low percentage belongs to the semi-skilled or skilled category of workers (Sasikumar and Thimothy, 2012). Gender-based labour market segmentation is pushing them to the margins of the services, health, and hospitality sectors resulting in operational issues relating to their safety, protection, and welfare (Sasikumar and Thimothy, 2012). Second, the diversity of the states of origin is widening. While there is a deceleration in the rate of growth of migration from the traditional states owing to demography and development it is significant that new, populous, and relatively backward states are emerging as important states of origin. These are states with weaker institutional apparatus for migration management and will face considerable challenge to cope with the growing numbers of emigrant workers. Third, the global nature of migration and the changing geography also blur the lines between 'origin' and 'destination' and make India an important pole in the major global migratory circuits. Given the geopolitical security environment, irregular migration is a matter of growing concern with social and security ramifications well beyond mere law enforcement. This has resulted in the growing securitization of migration. Concerns about human smuggling, traf-, ficking, and the presence of unscrupulous transnational intermediary cartels are legitimate and highlight the importance of international cooperation. However, the fact that migrants and their families are often subjected to exploitation, discrimination, and prejudice is sometimes lost sight of. India does not have a clearly articulated migration policy, at least not embedded in its development policy. Policy interventions matter just as much to migrants themselves as they do in addressing the challenges that migration poses to origin and destination societies alike. A key missing element in migration governance in India is both the absence of data and the poor quality of data and analysis, seriously impairing India's ability to plan for the future over longer terms. Fourth, the asymmetry between liberalized regimes for the mobility of goods and capital and restrictive policies on the mobility of people; the deep divide between good economics and populist politics; and the hegemony of the developed world over the international discourse on migration has resulted in the rise of several theoretical constructs—temporary migration, circular migration, seasonal migration, temporary contractual labour, and such like. Bilateral engagements via the free trade agreements or investment protection agreements that India negotiates and sometimes is nudged on to are often devoid of provisions relating to emigration of Indians for work, entrepreneurship, business, or for study.

The Challenge of Temporariness

The vast majority of Indian emigration occurs along the India–Gulf corridor and primarily as 'temporary contractual mobility'. In all of these constructs, the emphasis is on the temporariness of the mobility and the decisive shift to mandatory return. This temporality of the migration process has long-term and life-cycle implications—social exclusion, absence of social security, low access to social and economic opportunity, and denial of family reunifications—and raises operational as well as ethical questions on the instruments of contractual engagement.

Temporary migration in itself is not bad. In fact, in certain market conditions, several kinds of jobs in diverse sectors are necessarily temporary in nature—fruit picking in agriculture, and steel scaffolding in construction are examples—and establish cycles of temporary migratory movements. Temporary contractual labour of the kind prevalent in the Gulf Cooperation Council (GCC) countries, however, is fraught with intrinsic weaknesses. Temporary contractual migration based on sponsorship visas renders migrants more vulnerable and dispossess them of basic rights. Their protection is a serious human rights challenge. Lest we miss the wood for the trees, it must be recognized that restrictive or selective immigration policies, rather than curbing migration, result in unintended effects of catalysing irregular migration and pushing migrants to seek permanent settlement.

Fifth, historically and up until the last quarter of the twentieth century, the direction and pace of migratory flows were largely a function of geographic proximity with intra-regional migrants being more numerous than the inter-region migrants. This was true of India as well. The concerted efforts at regional integration processes and the proliferation of regional free trade agreements combined with inward-looking policy prescriptions only served to reinforce this trend. In recent decades, however, with the emergence of global production and supply chains, rapid progress in transport and communications, structural problems of labour supply and skills shortages due to demographics, and changes being wrought in the global financial architecture as a result of the rise of the emerging economies, emigration from India too has become increasingly complex and the destination of Indian migrants diverse and farther than before.

There is now a global race for talent and skills. Portability of skills, recognition of qualifications and certification of skills are becoming increasingly sector- and job-specific. Developing standardized curricula, pedagogical methods, and independent testing and third-party certification to ensure universal recognition between and across geographies pose serious challenges. India has embarked on a national programme on skills. Yet, there is no specific focus on the skills necessary for emigrant workers seeking overseas employment or to position India as a preferred source for skilled workers. Finally, another visible change is the increasing transnational character of migration with overseas Indians maintaining socio-economic and political ties with India. Giving mainstream attention to the overseas Indian community, extending parity in social, cultural, educational, and economic matters with Indian nationals through the overseas citizenship card and providing for 'voting rights' to non-resident Indians also have implications for governance as also international relations. It is no longer possible for countries of origin or of destination—under the current modes of production it is difficult to be just one or the other—to restrict access to social and economic opportunities on the basis of nationality or indeed to work in isolation with populations that are transnational in character. As people become more mobile, many of them will have political, economic, social, or cultural relationships in two or more societies at once. This tends to be seen as undermining the undivided loyalty to sovereign nation states (Castles and Miller 2009).

The recent economic crisis has raised questions about the welfare and future prospects of expatriate populations. There have been reports in recent months of firms or projects shutting down and laying off workers in many countries. There is a visible rise in unemployment rates across the world. The dominant view emerging across the world is that there will be a significant slowing down of migratory movements, a visible decline in worldwide remittances from overseas communities and large numbers of migrant workers losing their jobs and returning home. In times of global economic crisis it is the migrant workers and their families who are most vulnerable and bear the brunt of the downturn. Typically, migrant workers are the first to lose jobs or face sharp wage-cuts. They are often forced to return home and with no social security cover. India has weathered this storm rather well. Despite the global slowdown there has been a secular growth in remittances. While there has been a deceleration in the rate of growth of emigration, there has not been an exodus of returning workers. One unfortunate result of the downturn, however, is the specious argument that migrant workers cause job losses or conversely that the effect of the downturn would be less severe if there were no migrants. Indeed, the downturn has resulted in populist politics that immigration is bad or, worse still, that immigrants are the cause of rising domestic unemployment. Nothing can be further from the truth. Migrant workers fill labour supply gaps that often cannot or do not want to be met by local workers.

History also points to the fact that in times of economic downturn, governments often adopt protectionist policies thereby exacerbating the negative impact of the crisis on the economy. This only makes worse the condition of the migrant worker. Raising protectionist barriers to the movement of natural persons as a policy response, as some countries are doing, is both short-sighted and counter-intuitive and will only delay the recovery from the economic crisis. However, migration policy is often more influenced by the political economy of migration than it is by informed debate. Apprehensions in destination countries on giving labour market access are fuelled by fears of loss of jobs for locals. The 'cultural capital' argument raises fears of the consequences of permanent settlement of migrants. Saudi Arabia, the destination for the largest number of temporary contractual workers from South Asia, recently announced the Nitaqat law for greater Saudization of the job market and to enforce the prerogative of the 'sons of the soil' to employment by prescribing between 5 and 30 per cent mandatory employment of locals by firms depending on their size. Similar restrictions have been imposed in several other destination geographies especially after the global slowdown since 2008. Yet, the large labour supply gaps emerging in many countries owing to ageing and the considerable shortage of skills sets across key sectors are structural and not cyclical in nature. They are realities that the global economy has to come to terms with and find solutions to.

The migration of women is transforming traditional gender roles. The number of women emigrating from India has been rising steadily across all skills levels. What is even more encouraging is that women from newer states of origin are considering emigration as an opportunity. The growing presence of women migrants signifies the positive long-term benefits to them, giving them autonomous identity and economic independence. Women migrants constitute nearly half the world's migrant population. They often face the hardship of separation from their families and are vulnerable to various forms of exploitation at the workplace. They are more susceptible to forced labour, violence and sexual abuse than are men. They are more likely to accept poorer work conditions, lower salaries, often below the market wage and experience unhealthy living conditions. Although it is evident that international migration has a significant gender dimension, most country policies—of both origin and destination—do not mainstream gender-specific problems of women migrant workers. In theory and in practice, the women emigrant is invisible and her contribution unseen. There is need for a 'rule-based' framework for the protection and welfare of women emigrants that will govern working and living conditions, as well as inter-state measures and mechanisms, to provide an institutional and legal basis to protect the dignity of women migrant workers. In the Indian context this assumes urgency since a large number of women migrate to the Gulf for work primarily in the household sector and the risk of being lesser-skilled and of being rendered irregular is compounded by ethnicity and gender. This influences access to the entitlement of family reunification, access to the labour market and social services (Piper, 2005).

Migration matters to India and Indians and it will matter even more in the future. India has a long history of migration but there is much that it needs to unlearn if she is to articulate a policy and strategy that will position her as a responsible leader in migration. Over the last five centuries, mass migrations have played a major role in human history yet international migration has never been as pervasive, or as socio-economically and politically significant, as it is today (Castles and Miller, 2009). In present-day India, the defining principle is that her states are as diverse and as different as countries can be. They are also at different stages of development and demography. For some states, migration has contributed and continues to contribute, to important goals such as economic development, social dynamism, and cultural diversity. For others, the sense of urgency comes from questions on how to adjust to new migratory situations and develop effective policy responses to emerging challenges. Much of migration policy and interventions have been in the exclusive preserve of the federal government, often to the near-complete exclusion of the provinces. It is time that labour mobility and migration become legitimate areas of governance in the domain of the states in India. Policy and practice in migration matters must be embedded in the development policy of the country. It must also be more proximate to the ground for, after all, the states are the theatres of migration engagement.

Making Migration Work

A good starting point to imagine the future of migration is to glean its history, even if briefly. In the not-so-distant past, emigration was more difficult than immigration is today. Countries used exit controls to prevent their citizens from leaving the country. Ironically, as recently as in the middle of the last century, and even up to the late 1960s, people from South Asia and the Caribbean could move without restriction to the United Kingdom and within the Commonwealth. Until the formation of nation states, missionaries, traders and workers travelled far and wide freely. For much of the twentieth century, free movement of people took place without restrictions. Ironically, in a rapidly globalizing world, legal migration is being rendered increasingly difficult. While there is growing consensus on lifting border controls for the flow of capital and goods and, more broadly, to further globalization, when it comes to immigrants the nation states assert their sovereign right to control their borders (Sassen, 1996). In the Indian context, though, for a large part migration is the story of colonialism and the coercive mobilization of workers through the system of indentured labour. Several million people were recruited as indentured labourers to work on plantations in far-flung territories of the European empires. It is also the inspiring story of an independent India that has over the last sixty-five years come to be seen as the homeland of a knowledge diaspora of over twenty-five million comprising doctors, engineers, scientists, teachers, entrepreneurs, and workers with a presence in every part of the globe.

To understand our future, we must pause to understand our past. Though emigration is structurally embedded in India's economy and society, in varying degrees across states and over a long period of its modern history, the future of emigration is difficult to predict. Despite the considerable diversity of the modes, pathways, and the destinations in the emerging patterns of emigration from India, much of the immigration focus in most countries today is on high-skilled workers, often to the exclusion of low-skilled workers. Such selective and segmented migration management represents a dichotomy between political compulsions and economy-wide needs. Future brain drain is likely to be multidirectional (Li, 2008) and there is already a perceptible contraction in low-skilled workers in developed countries as a result of demographics as well as upward mobility of the native population. In particular, sectors like health care, hospitality, construction, and agriculture are facing chronic shortages that will continue into the foreseeable future. Demographic imperatives will influence the pace and the direction of migration and determine who moves where in the twenty-first century.

The convergence of a coherent and progressive national policy and the administrative capacity to enforce the policy, combined with sagacious diplomatic initiatives, are necessary conditions to foster safe, orderly, and efficient migration that will maximize the benefits to the emigrants and their families, to India and to the world. Striking a balance between the need to protect overseas Indian workers, professionals, students, service providers, entrepreneurs and business while not creating conditions that would decrease their competitiveness in the global marketplace is a challenging task. India's ability to balance global competitiveness, protection and welfare of its citizens, and the perceived infringements upon sovereignty of the countries of destination weighs heavily in designing and implementing a migration praxis framework. Migration will not be in one direction alone. India's economic transition is already providing incentives for its overseas migrants to return. As opportunities increase, it will attract foreigners too. India will be a major player in international migration and will need a migration praxis framework that will best enable it to face the challenges of a rapidly globalizing world. The first principle to enhance India's capacity for migration governance is to engineer a paradigm shift in the roles and responsibilities of the principal actors engaged in the process. India must rethink the role of the state and implement a migration praxis framework that marshals the capacities of local governments, the private sector, and civil society to position it as an important migration hub for the southern hemisphere. To do so, it will need a medium- to long-term strategic vision, effective institutional architecture, innovative instruments of engagement and significant capacities. Migration has shaped her past and will, doubtless, influence her future. The time is at hand for India to demonstrate leadership in international migration. The time is now.

11

Looking Back in Anguish

We have never been as aware as we are now of how oddly hybrid historical and cultural experiences are, of how they partake of many often contradictory experiences and domains, cross national boundaries, defy the police action of simple dogma and loud patriotism. Far from being unitary or monolithic or autonomous things, cultures actually assume more 'foreign' elements, alterities, differences, than they consciously exclude.

—Sake Dean Mahomet (1793)

Migration and Empire

The Indian migration story is inextricably intertwined with its colonial history. The development of modern colonial capitalism between the nineteenth and the twentieth centuries generated in South Asia— creative disruption—the fundamental impulse that comes from the new consumers, goods, the new methods of production or transportation, the new markets, the new forms of industrial organization that capitalist enterprise creates (Schumpeter, 1975). It transformed the old modes of economy and society and brought in its wake new forces that compelled the migration of people, set in motion new avenues of coercive mobilization and catalysed the mobility of labour across vast distances. In some ways the migration experience of the present parallels that of the past. Yet, in significant ways there is divergence that points to the future. Not too long ago, in the early twentieth century, migration was frowned upon, the widely held view was that only the desperate left home for strange places, and that under compulsion or false advertising by those who enlisted them for various jobs. In the present age of migration, crossing the 'Kalapani' has become a coveted and much-sought-after symbol of success (Lal, 2007). The roots of migration from India can be traced to various forms of slavery in the eighteenth century, typically the result of wars and famines and often of the distress sale of children under the British East India Company. Sheikh Din Mohammed, the first Indian writer in English, was reportedly sold as a 10-year-old boy following the great Bengal Famine of 1769. He later went on to become an accomplished and well-respected Indian immigrant in the United Kingdom, the author of the 'Travels of Dean Mahomet' and the founder of the first Indian curry house restaurant in Britain (Mahomet, 1793). In fact, famines, slavery, and migration were so widespread that Lord Cornwallis appeared helpless in his efforts to prosecute those indulging in slavery and famously said of Calcutta that hardly a man or woman exists in town who does not own a slave child either stolen from its parents or bought in exchange for rice in times of scarcity (Lord Cornwallis, 1789). Besides the export of starving migrants as slaves, this period of merchant capital also saw involuntary labour migration as kidnapping and deception were resorted to by many unscrupulous intermediaries for financial gain. The slave market circuits operated primarily around the European merchant settlements—French, Portuguese, and Dutch.

Slavery was abolished on 1 August 1834 but only children under the age of six were freed immediately under the terms of the 1833 Emancipation Act though 'The Abolition of the Slave Trade Act' was passed as early as in 1807 (the National Archives, Government of the United Kingdom). This signalled the beginning of a harsh exploitative system of coercive mobilization to supply cheap labour to the colonies under the British Empire across Africa, Southeast Asia, the Indian Ocean, and the Pacific Ocean. The early Indenture System, a form of legalized slavery that mimicked many of the features of slave traffic, was doubtless one of the most shoddy and shocking episodes in the whole violent history of the British Empire. The mushrooming of recruiting agents, the ubiquitous presence of intermediaries preying on the poor and the starving populations, and deception in the terms and conditions of work and inducements were stark reminders of the past and are ironically similar, even if to a lesser degree, to the present. The wage differential for Indian labour working in the colonies was five times and hence incentive enough to suffer considerable privation and penal sanctions. Improvements in transportation across the high seas, new technology in mining and sugar production and rapidly growing population made it economically viable for cheap colonial labour to be recruited from India and transported to distant lands. The vast majority of the indentured labourers from India were agricultural labourers with little or no education (Madhaven, 1987). Cheap labour then, as now, was invaluable and prompted Sir George Grey, the then Governor of Cape Colony, to observe that introduction of coolie labourers from India would greatly tend to promote the wealth and security of Natal, and render it of value and importance to Great Britain (Magubane, 1975). An important aspect of India's colonial migration history was 'convict migration'—the transportation of Indian convicts to penal settlements across the East India Company territories. Convict migration occurred from the major presidency sea ports of Calcutta, Madras, and Bombay and this workforce was instrumental in the development of roads, railways, canals, and bridges in the European settlements. Testimony to the remarkable contributions of the convict migrants from India stand in the form of the St Andrews Cathedral and the Isthana in Singapore built in 1862 and 1869 respectively (Anderson, 2005). Since accurate records are unavailable, we can only estimate that over a hundred thousand convicts were transported between 1825 and the end of the Second World War (see Table 11.1).

Under the indentured labour system between 1834 and 1937, it is estimated that over six million emigrants travelled to distant lands and formed the basis for what is now called the 'old diaspora'. Of these, 1.5 million travelled to Ceylon, 2 million to Malaya and 2.5 million to Burma (UN, 2014). From 1834 up until after the Sepoy Mutiny of 1857 when the British Monarchy took over the East India Company, the terms and conditions of indenture varied vastly between the settlements. The process was characterized by exploitation and coercion. The Colonial Emigration Act of 1837 recognized for the first time that the indentured labourers being recruited did not fully understand the terms of the contract that they were being bound to or even that they would have to go away for long periods

Table 11.1 Emigration of Indentured Labour from India, 1834–1916

Destination	Period of Emigration	Number of Emigrants
Mauritius	1834–1900	453,063
British Guyana	1838–1916	238,909
Malaya	1844–1910	250,000
Trinidad	1845–1916	143,939
Jamaica	1845–1913	36,412
Natal	1860–1911	152,184
Réunion	1861–1883	26,507
Surinam	1873–1916	34,304
Fiji	1879–1916	60,965
East Africa	1896–1921	39,282

Source: Lal (2007).

to places so far from their native county. They were required to appear before an authority appointed by the provincial government. Recruiters sending migrant workers by fraudulent means were to be fined or imprisoned. A sample contract setting down the wages, period, and conditions of work was also introduced (Lal, 1980). Despite the regulation, in 1940 a committee of the Government of India reported that there was no doubt that the coolies exported to Mauritius and elsewhere were mostly induced to come to Calcutta by gross misrepresentation and deceit practised upon them by middlemen, contractors, and shippers who were aware of these frauds, and who received a very considerable sum per head for each coolie exported (House of Common Papers, 1840). Based on the reforms recommended by this committee, the Government of India Act of 1842 provided for regulation and supervision by appointing an emigration agent, a protector of emigrants and licensing of ships.

The Protector of Emigrants

A key lacuna, however, was that there were no provisions for enforcement. Despite the regulations in force, malpractice in recruitment continued unabated and minors continued to be abducted, kidnapped, and enticed (Sarup, 2006), prompting the Mauritius

Reformatory Enquiry Commission Chairman H.D.N. Beyts to report that recruits unwilling to go to one colony were forcibly sent to another in open defiance of the local laws while the Protector of Emigrants was powerless to prevent the abuses in at least 90 per cent of the cases (Report of the Commissioners, Mauritius, 1848). Based on these investigations further reforms were introduced in the Emigration Act of 1864. The protector of emigrants was now required to interview each emigrant at the port of embarkation, recruiters were licensed on a yearly basis and the emigration depots were inspected by the police regularly. Emigration then faced widespread corruption just as is the case today and was likened by some to sending wolves and vultures to look after and take care of lambs (Lal, 2007). This was an obvious reference to the heavy hand of regulators. In 1880, Natal began to requisition, for the first time, specifically for agricultural labourers, railway workers, domestic servants, cooks, washermen, blacksmiths, and drivers. The terms included free return passage after ten years of service. Mauritius refused free return passage, in violation of the Colonial Emigration Acts that specified five years as the period after which free passage was an entitlement (Sarup, 2006). Colonial emigration under the indenture system was driven primarily by the demand for cheap labour in the colonies and by famine and starvation in the provinces in India. The report of the Protector of Emigrants, Calcutta, for the year 1868 noted that emigration to Mauritius had reduced considerably in the two years past as a consequence of the poor agricultural prospects caused by successive droughts (Annual Report on emigration from the port of Calcutta, 1868). Indian emigrants were willing to face considerable exploitation in the hope of a better life overseas. It must be recognized that coercive mobilization was not the only mode of migration. Indian masons, carpenters, and other craftsmen were the preferred workers in the Indian Ocean island settlements. Significant numbers of these voluntary migrants followed by tailors, shopkeepers, priests, and doctors formed the early overseas Indian communities in the European colonies. The demand for Indian workers came from all the colonies because of their hard work and discipline. This is best illustrated by the observation in 1870 of the medical inspector of emigrants on the excellent sanitary condition of the Georgetown, Demerara depot, and the zeal, ability and energy displayed by Dr Ramsahay Persaud who worked to prevent any outbreak of disease when the depot was unavoidably overcrowded (Report of the Government Medical Inspector of Emigrants, 1870). In 1882, the government passed a comprehensive Emigration Act that remained in force till 1922.

While the indenture system was predominantly prevalent in north India, the 'Kangani' and 'Maistry' systems of recruitment of cheap labour on a significant scale developed in south India (Lal, 2007). Both systems were based on 'labour gangs' with an overseer or supervisor and relied on an extensive network of intermediaries. Central to both systems of recruitment was the debt relationship created with the migrant worker. Every worker under these systems began his journey with indebtedness. Money would be loaned to the family for labour services of the potential migrant, costs would be debited to the worker for his passage and the cost of food and this debt would be deducted from the wages payable to the worker. The wide network of *kangani*s who would mobilize the gangs of 25–30 workers ensured that they could reach remote parts of the country and recruit from multifarious locations. By and large the system of debt bondage recruitment remained unchanged from 1837 till 1921. That this was a form of bonded labour was beyond doubt and the official view was that the coolies under a kangani were little better than slaves bound hand to foot because of their debt to him. The view was that this unjust system ought to be abolished and the workers encouraged to enter into contracts directly with the employer. The widespread abuse of Indian emigrant workers, both under indenture as well as the Kangani and its variant, Tundu, systems in the colonies and the findings of the Marjoriebanks—Marakkayar Commission on the indebtedness of Indian labour drew the attention of Mahatma Gandhi and other nationalists. They had denounced the conditions under which indentured labourers emigrated in the British Empire leading to its abolition in 1917, and campaigned vigorously against discrimination against economic migrants (Pebbles, 2001). The critique of emigration within the Indian national movement was broader-based: that workers in the colonies had no freedom, they could be prosecuted even for labour offences, they were prevented on risk of imprisonment from quitting the estate on which they were employed, false charges were often trumped up and the recalcitrant coolie sent to jail.

The Wages of Coercion

Colonial recruitment was not all bad though. It provided an avenue for thousands of starving and abjectly poor people to begin a new life. From the long shadow of the indenture system, there emerged the 'jahajis' who were to establish themselves in distant, alien lands and by dint of their hard work become eminently successful. Despite the offer of free passage upon completion of five years of their contracts, several chose to continue and settle in the colonies to which they were taken forcibly. Indeed, many indentured workers returned to India with considerable savings and often went back after a brief sojourn home. Trinidad and British Guyana appeared the better colonies, providing better working and living conditions and greater economic opportunities. The annual report of the Protector of Emigrants for the year 1877 noted that many migrant labourers return home with considerable savings, enlarged ideas, and some education demonstrating the advantages (Annual Report of the Protector of Emigrants, 1877). In fact, several of the labourers were able to embark on return to the colonies paying for their own passages. Bringing back considerable savings in cash, jewellery and other valuables made indentured labour migration appear lucrative. Table 11.2 as part of the report of the protector of Emigrants, Calcutta, for the year 1877 is revealing:

There is, however, no gainsaying that the lives of the indentured workers were essentially one of harsh bondage and for many it was also lives of penury in old age or upon return. Dr J.G. Grant, the legendary Protector of Emigrants at Calcutta, was compelled to make a special mention of the need for appropriate social security cover for

Table 11.2 Statement from the Annual Report of the Protector of Emigrants, 1877

Colonies	No. of Ships	No. of Souls	Average Amount Saved (Rupees)	Aggregate Amount Saved (Rupees)
Mauritius	5	1326	154	205,206
Demerara	2	868	136	118,683
Jamaica	1	247	56	13,875
Trinidad	2	485	379	183,982

Source: Annual Report of the Protector of Emigrants, 1877, contained in Sarup (2006).

the workers returning after completion of their contract periods. All pauper emigrants returned home at the expense of the colony from which they returned; but in some instances these workers were not merely poor, but abjectly so and with no means of earning a livelihood. The need was felt for either the workers themselves or their employers to subscribe to a pension fund for the support of such cases. It is clear that the return to his native village of one such worker, utterly poor, would go far towards neutralizing all the persuasive powers of the most successful recruiters (Annual Report of the Protector of Emigrants, 1877). Though the colonial government was unwilling to discontinue emigration, in 1921 the Viceroy proposed a new bill by which emigration would be prohibited where Indians were denied equal rights and that the government would protect Indian migrant workers. This resulted in the Emigration Act of 1922. But the continuance of coercive emigration was short-lived. Export of labour to Burma was stopped in 1937, to Malaya in 1938 and to Ceylon in 1940. Nevertheless, the legislation of 1922 was a landmark and was to form the basis of future migration praxis from India. It specified that emigrants had to be 18 years of age, regulated the working hours and the wages to be paid, contained welfare provisions for housing, medical, and sanitary facilities, prohibited recovery of advances paid in India and provided for free repatriation within one year of arrival (Government of India Act VII, 1922). It must be said of the colonial administration that they did put in place an effective regulatory framework at both origin and destination to oversee emigration to the colonies. It also legislated from time to time reforms in the process to ensure better protection of workers. That this was done to ensure profits for the East India Company and later to serve the imperial interests of the crown is a different matter altogether. The conquest of India beginning with the defeat of the Nawab of Bengal in 1757 and the ascendancy of the East India Company; and the rule by the British Crown from 1858 following the 'Sepoy Mutiny' till India's independence, coincided with the remarkable European expansion in Southeast Asia. This was also the period of mercantilism and the growth of commercial production of tea, coffee, rubber, sugar, and rice. It was no surprise that in the conflict between the British, the French, the Dutch, and the Portuguese for supremacy in the region, the proletariat as well as the petty bourgeoisie in the colonies would be mobilized. The East India Company first employed Asian seamen known as *lascar*s, in the seventeenth century. The articles for the East Indiaman in 1746 recorded that the lascar crew would be paid a fixed monthly wage for the voyage from India to London. When in London, they were to get bounty money and maintenance while waiting for a return passage to their port of origin. In practice, the East India Company simply abandoned lascars once they were in London, and the Merchant Shipping Act of 1823 made the Company legally responsible for their upkeep in England. In 1855, in an attempt to provide for destitute foreign seamen, the Church Missionary Society founded the Strangers' Home for Asiatics, Africans, and South Sea Islanders in London (Sarup, 2006).

The Europeans also recruited sepoys from the local communities in the Madras and Bombay Presidencies, the emphasis being on recruits having adequate physique and being of 'appropriate caste'. In the Bengal Army, however, recruitment was only amongst high-caste Brahman and Rajput communities, mainly from the eastern Uttar Pradesh and Bihar regions. Recruitment was undertaken locally by battalions or regiments, often from the same community, village, and even family. The Indian sepoys who served overseas were amongst the first migrants to settle in far-off lands. From 1858 through the end of the First World War at least, Sikhs, and the martial regiments of the British army that they manned and led into battle, remained the stout right arm of British Imperial power (Wolpert, 1999).

India, as were the other colonies, was drawn into the colonial capitalist market as an appendage of the metropolitan nations to supply raw materials and exotic commodities to the industrial centre (Robinson, 1979), opening up trading opportunities and the emergence of new trading posts and commercial centres dominated by the British. Even before the advent of the Europeans in Asia and Africa, first as traders and later as rulers, Indian traders and businessmen were active along the mercantile routes of the Indian Ocean to the Gulf and the east coast of Africa as well as via the land routes to West and Central Asia. Though a dominant trading community from as early as the fifteenth century, Indian merchants constituted a small number till the beginning of the nineteenth century. However, there was significant emigration of traders, businessmen and moneylenders between 1880 and 1930 to the European colonies resulting in a dramatic increase in the size of the overseas Indian merchant community estimated at nearly a quarter of a million at the end of the nineteenth century (Carter, 1996). The more pioneering mercantile communities—the Marwaris, the Chettiars, the Sindhis, the Bohras, and the Sikhs—showed admirable entrepreneurial spirit to set up businesses as diverse as textiles, banking, construction, and commodity trading, including rice, timber, edible oils, sugar and household appliances. Their interests took them across Southeast Asia—Singapore, Malaya, Indonesia, Burma, Africa, and the Caribbean. They settled into their new environment and found the prosperity they were seeking; acted as magnets, attracting their kinsmen, nurtured links with the homeland and provided resources that allowed others to migrate (Kudaisya, 2011).

At about the same time, at the turn of the century, Sikh farmers were seeking new lands to work outside British India. Fragmentation of land had reduced farm size while the high water rates and land revenue were imposing considerable stress on the Sikh farmers in Punjab. Sikh troops returning via Canada from the Diamond Jubilee celebration of Queen Victoria reported it was possible to make as much as $2.00 a day in the mills and on railroad construction in Canada and the United States, nearly ten times the average wage in Punjab at the time. It is estimated that 7,348 Asian Indians migrated to the United States and Canada between 1899 and 1920 (Dusenbery, 1989). The Punjab province in India was a great source of Asian Indian immigration to the United States and Canada. The composition of the immigrants from 1900 to 1917 included 85 per cent Sikhs, 13 per cent Muslims and 2 per cent Hindus (Dusenbery, 1989), though almost all who arrived were termed Hindus, even if the label was inappropriately applied. The California State Board of Control (CSBC) submitted a report to Governor Stephens in 1920 titled 'California and the Orientals: Japanese, Chinese and Hindus'. It indicated that since 1910, the number of Asian Indians in the United States had increased by 33.5 per cent. The CSBC perceived these immigrants as an economic threat, or competition for native farmers (California State Board of Control Report, 1920). They were referred to as a group of labourers becoming landowners and threatening the monopoly of the majority group. These Punjabi farmers migrated as far as California and Canada but not without encountering racial discrimination and hostility. The 'Komagata Maru' episode in 1914 in which about four hundred Sikh migrants were not permitted to disembark at Vancouver despite the fact that the Japanese ship carrying them was sailing from a British colony to another British territory and part of the Commonwealth Empire and returning to Calcutta Port after a year at sea remains a stark reminder of the pervasive racist undertones of modern neocolonialism. The early emigrants to North America displayed remarkable tenacity and pioneering spirit. It is no surprise therefore that their descendants—the Indo-Americans and the Indo-Canadians—are today amongst the most successful across the world. This is testimony to the courage and enterprise of these early Indian emigrants. It is only in recent years that countries, including India, have begun to recognize the 'soft power' of their diasporas. Yet, as early as in 1913, overseas Indians had undertaken advocacy by launching the 'Gadar Movement' for India's independence. This represents an exceptional example of how the knowledge and resources of overseas communities can be mobilized for 'home country' causes.

Independence and New Beginnings

The end of the Second World War and India's independence signalled a paradigm shift in Indian emigration. There emerged a new migration pathway from India to the metropolitan centres of the western world. Immediately following India's Independence, migration to England gained momentum as a result of old colonial relations as well as the unique Anglo-Indian community seeking to move to the Empire-Commonwealth. Thereafter, migration to the White Dominions—Australia, New Zealand, and Canada—gained impetus after the cessation of the 'Whites only' policies. The most dramatic transformation in the character of Indian emigration occurred from the 1960s onwards with the emigration of high-skilled professionals—doctors, engineers, scientists, and entrepreneurs—to the United States of America. This was the beginning of a strong wave of knowledge migrants that was to continue unabated till the Great Recession of 2007–8 after which questions began to be raised even in the United States on immigration imperatives. In the golden age of economic growth from 1945 till 1973, the

United States of America was the bellwether for immigration and demonstrated the virtues of fostering the transnational mobility of people and successfully attracted the best and the brightest from across the world. A seminal work on innovation and entrepreneurship carried out in Silicon Valley at the turn of the millennium had indicated that innovation and enterprise was driven primarily by immigrants—Indians and Chinese—with nearly a quarter of all the high tech firms run by them in 1998 (Saxenian, 1999). An interesting update on that study carried out in 2010 showed that several of these innovators were heading home since they perceived conditions at home better for further innovation and that the United States was losing out. It pointed out that in the era of exponential technologies, education and skills matter more than ever. Small teams of people can do what was once possible only for governments and large corporations—solving grand problems.

Diversity in backgrounds, in fields of knowledge, and in thinking is a great asset. The United States needs the world's best and brightest more than ever before. Yet, her visa policies are doing the opposite: chasing away this talent (Wadhwa, 2012). A significant development in the last few decades has been the active 'student migration' corridor. India perhaps is one of the leaders in the number of its overseas students. There are growing numbers of students from the developing world seeking out foreign schools because of excess demand for domestic higher education and the need for internationally recognized qualifications in emerging regional and global markets for highly skilled labour (Bashir, 2007). The bulk of them seek out schools in the United States which boasts a student population of over one hundred thousand from India. But other countries like the United Kingdom, Canada, and Australia also attract a large number of Indian students. This mobility through the education route adds in significant measure to high-skilled Indian migrant stocks across the world. In fact, there is growing evidence that student mobility fosters 'brain circulation' or the back and forth movement resulting in the emergence of strong networks (Kuznetzov, 2006a).

Ironically, even while the 'new world' was applauding freedom of movement of people for education, employment, and entrepreneurship in the United States and to a lesser degree in the other metropolitan centres, there was a less than optimal mobility corridor emerging rapidly in Asia. The 'oil crisis' and the resurgence of the Gulf, West Asia, and North Africa as major oil producers meant the return of 'temporary contractual labour' spurring in a short span of a few decades the most active South–South migration corridor which was to see migration of significant numbers of contract labourers from South Asia moving to the oil-producing countries. Difficult as it might appear to acknowledge for a country aspiring for a place at the high table of the comity of nations, India is known in the Gulf as an ABCD country—a country that sends ayahs (housemaids), butlers, cooks, and drivers. This constitutes the bulk of the emigration from India and is a grim reminder of the fact that India was once a nation of colonial natives. Central to India's migration praxis in the future will be the imperative to diversify her destination base and help move emigrants up the value chain. The most visible 'benefit' of migration is the significant and growing volume of remittances. In India's case not only have they been secular in their growth, they constitute the bedrock of her foreign exchange reserves and are less fickle than foreign institutional investor (FII) flows. Yet, it must be said that remittances have few multiplier effects and in some ways have resulted in 'remittance dependent' development. Speaking of Kerala, a significant state of origin, although remittances have helped improve the welfare of the migrant households and raise levels of economic activity in construction, trade, transport and personal services, their contribution to the state's economic development is not significant. There is a need to interrogate migrant remittances and see how they can foster 'remittance independent' development.

It would be useful at this juncture to take a bird's-eye view of Indian emigration and the nature of the flows and stocks as well as the pathways and destinations (see Figures 11.1, 11.2, and 11.3).

The decision to migrate is a complex one. Migratory flows are influenced and shaped to a great extent by a host of factors—migrant networks, information flows, assistance of friends and relatives, and intermediation between people in the countries of origin and of destination. The process thus becomes self-selecting and self-sustaining, and after a point ensures that movements are not necessarily limited in time, unidirectional, or permanent (Boyd, 1989). It is difficult to answer the question what makes a person migrate while another next door to him chooses not to. Migration decision-making is at the

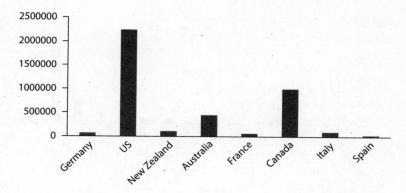

Figure 11.1 Distribution of Indian Diaspora in Some OECD Countries
(as of 2012)
Source: Ministry of Overseas Indian Affairs, Government of India.

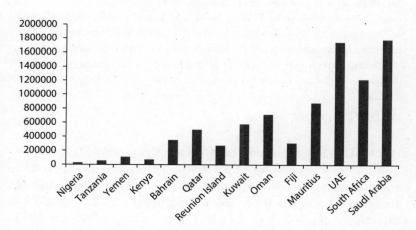

Figure 11.2 Distribution of Indian Diaspora in Selected Middle Eastern and
African Countries (as of 2012)
Source: Ministry of Overseas Indian Affairs, Government of India.

individual level, a matter of choice, and, perhaps ironically, a situation in which one has no choice; at the level of the family or community it is a function of migrant networks and intermediaries and
at the macro level it is the political economy of development or the

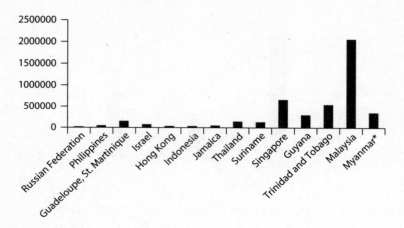

Figure 11.3   Distribution of Indian Diaspora in Selected Countries in Asia, Latin America, and the Caribbean (as of 2012)
Source: Ministry of Overseas Indian Affairs, Government of India.
Note:* The number of Overseas Indians living in Myanmar according to the Ministry of Overseas Indian Affairs (MOIA) as of May 2012 is 356,560. However, there have been different figures quoted by the MOIA. In the past, it was estimated that the size of Indian diaspora was about 2 per cent (945,000) of the total Burmese's population, though the High Level Committee on Indian Diaspora (HLCID) report the size as 2,902,000. The estimates of the Ministry of External Affairs in 2001 were similar (2,800,000).

lack of it. India's emigration history holds significance for its migration future. The regulatory framework, the institutional apparatus, and processes of present-day emigration with all their strengths and weaknesses flow from their colonial origins. The bulk of the policy thinking in the last three decades since the Emigration Act 1983 came into force has focused on rather ad hoc and truncated reform measures to address the inefficiencies and abuses of the system extant rather than on envisioning a modern approach to migration by redefining the paradigm from regulation based on segregation to freer mobility based on information and capacities that will best foster informed choices. Indian emigration must grow out of its colonial shadow and signal childhood's end.

12

Future Tense

The central long-run question facing India is where will good jobs come from? Productive jobs are vital for growth. And a good job is the best form of inclusion. More than half our population depends on agriculture ... while industry is creating jobs, too many such jobs are low productivity non-contractual jobs in the unorganized sector, offering low incomes, little protection, and no benefits. Service jobs are relatively high productivity, but employment growth in services has been slow in recent years.

—*Economic Survey* (GOI, 2013a: 26)

Great Expectations

There are many in India who believe that she is on the threshold of becoming an economic powerhouse. Many others are convinced that she is only a pretender. Arguably, India's economic prospects in the near term hang in the balance and are increasingly seen with circumspection. Striking a cautiously optimistic note the annual economic survey for 2013 observed that while the current environment was difficult, the future held promise provided India could answer the question probably foremost in the minds of India's young population: 'Where will my job come from?' (GOI, 2013a). At the end of 2010, close to 30 per cent of India's population lived below the poverty line—in absolute numbers the figure is a disturbing 300 million plus. A feature of mass poverty in India is that it is largely a rural affliction. It is rural poverty also that is intractable and the condition persists because they live in equilibrium of poverty (Galbraith, 1979). Despite policy prescriptions for inclusive growth, inequality and regional disparity in India have widened considerably. A recent paper analysed data from the 61st and the 66th rounds of the National Sample Survey for the period in which India recorded impressive growth rates—2004–5 to 2009–10—to study the relation between growth and deprivation. It concluded that there was no evidence for pro-poor growth for the lower classes—labourers, marginal and small farmers in rural areas, and casual labourers and the self-employed in urban areas. Essentially, India's growth in recent times has been biased in favour of the middle and richer groups and not in favour of the poor (Motiram and Naraparaju, 2013). While India has made great strides in food production from the time of the famines it would not be out of place to note that the countryside remains stressed with little to cheer about. Little is it recognized that India remains a relentlessly Malthusian country where the pressure of population on land, resources, and incomes is stark. If anything, in recent decades the emphasis on population pressure being at the root of deprivation is muted though the objective conditions of development point to the weight of numbers severely retarding human development—economic opportunity, education, health, and sustainable livelihoods—for an unconscionably large population. That over half of India's population depends on agriculture that produces about 15 per cent of the gross domestic product (GDP) only makes worse the equilibrium of poverty. Not much seems to have changed since independence for those in abject poverty. For the vast majority of India's poor, it is a struggle to escape the equilibrium of poverty—bare existence with no savings, without savings and capital investment there can be no improvement in income (Galbraith, 1979). This is compounded by the fact of risk aversion—the poorer people are, the fewer the assets available to protect them against catastrophe, and hence the more risk averse they are likely to be and with valid reason.

Missing the Manufacture Bus

As a predominantly rural and agrarian economy that, as most analysts recognize, has all but missed the 'industrial' or 'manufacture' stage of economic transition and seems to be trapped at the lower end of the 'services' revolution, India represents many of the characteristics of a poor, post-colonial developing economy—produces in the main raw materials and agricultural products, suffers persistently adverse balance of trade, labour supply far exceeds demand and hence exports labour on a significant scale. The poor state of manufacturing in India is reflected in the fact that the contribution of the sector to India's GDP has stagnated at around 17 per cent during the last decade. India's share of global manufacturing output, which was 1.1 per cent in 1995, increased to only 2.3 per cent by the end of 2010 (OECD, 2013). In contrast, China's share soared from 4.2 per cent to 18.9 per cent during the same period. Innovation can become the force to infuse energy across all levels of the Indian manufacturing sector. Innovations, which will spin off new technologies and require new skills and training, will give rise to disruptive business opportunities creating employment for low-income and geographically remote populations across the value chain. In the absence of a rapidly growing industrial sector, wages are pushed down by labour surplus. The economy-wide problem of unemployment, underemployment, and disguised unemployment has only served to further erode incomes. The most direct and perhaps the largest state intervention to provide employment where there is none is the Mahatma Gandhi National Rural Employment Guarantee Act that provides a legal guarantee of at least one hundred days of employment every financial year to adult members of any rural household willing to do public works-related unskilled manual work at the statutory minimum wage of INR 120 per day at 2009 prices. If they cannot be provided work as envisaged, the government still has to pay the wages at their homes. The outlay for the scheme was INR 33,000 crore (USD 5.5 billion) in the financial year (FY) 2013–14 (GOI, 2013c). While doubtless this programme has given some succour to the poorest amongst the rural poor, it has raised questions on both its economic rationale as well as its effects. Arguably it has resulted in distortions in labour supply to agriculture and allied activities, affected labour market participation rates and adversely impacted wages in the rural economy. In his classic *Inquiry into the Nature and Causes of the Wealth of Nations* (1776), Adam Smith asked why some countries were richer than others. His answer was that it was the division of labour which enabled workers to become more productive by learning specialized skills and performing complex tasks. The employment guarantee programme would appear to run counter to this principle. Besides the issues of corruption, misrepresentation, and fraud, the fact that it assures a wage and some work has had the effect of weaning away labour from agriculture, driven up wages in agriculture and related sectors, and resulted in serious labour supply shortages. It is not uncommon in many states for farmers not to find agricultural workers during peak sowing and harvesting seasons. Besides the fiscal implications of the employment guarantee programme, its long-term effects of shrinking skills in the population and acting as a drag on enhancing productivity are matters for India's leaders to reflect upon in devising their development strategy.

The Missing Jobs

For a country with a burgeoning young working-age population, the most visible manifestation of backwardness, among other things, is the absence of avenues for productive economic engagement for its youth. Despite two decades since the economic reforms, the central question that faces India is the employment rate. Though the Indian economy has been growing at a rapid pace, especially in the years 2004–9, it has been characterized by jobless growth (see Table 12.1).

A disconcerting fact brought out by the 2009–10 Employment–Unemployment National Sample Survey data is the addition of a mere 2.76 million jobs during the period of India's fastest growth (National Sample Survey, 66th Round). The restrictive segmentation between the formal and informal sectors has been at the root of widening income inequality. The pattern of economic growth in recent years has only exacerbated the 'informalization' of the employment market. Besides lower wages, informal workers are susceptible to denial of fair terms and conditions of work. With little job security and limited access to safety nets, most of the workers in the informal

Table 12.1   Employment Generated during the Decade 1999–2000 to 2009–10

Sectors	Employment across Sectors (Millions)		Absolute Change in Employment (Millions)
	1999–2000	2009–10	1999–2000 to 2009–10
Agriculture	237.67	244.85	7.18
Manufacturing	44.05	50.74	6.69
Non-manufacturing	20.84	48.28	27.44
Services	94.20	116.34	22.14
Total	396.76	460.21	63.45

Source: NSSO (2010a).

sector remain vulnerable to loss of income. Not surprisingly, those in the informal sector are more likely to suffer poverty than their counterparts in the organized sector. The data on jobs in the manufacturing sector is somewhat misleading because, in India, the construction sector is classified as 'industry' and more than half of India's 22 per cent share of employment in industry is actually in construction work.

In evaluating India's long-term economic growth prospects it would be useful to understand the growth drivers going forward. For a 'young' country with a demographic surplus, India's growth prospects will be predicated substantially on the growth in labour productivity, proportion of working-age population, labour market participation, and the ability to enhance total factor productivity. In sum, assuming robust savings and investment rates, and reasonable technological innovation, all other things being equal, income growth will be a function simply of how many jobs the economy is able to generate. One problem is that while the services sector is creating jobs, these have been relatively low-productivity jobs. As a result, per capita income in India has not benefited as much from inter-sectoral migration of workers out of agriculture as in other Asian countries. A second problem is that the high-productivity services sector is not able to create employment commensurate with its growth in value added. 'Could the demographic dividend turn into a demographic curse as some have argued?' (GOI, 2013a). Policymakers are reflecting with some trepidation on the missing jobs scenario (see Table 12.2). This raises several concerns, not

Table 12.2 How Many Jobs Will Be Missing? Alternative Scenarios

	2000	2010	2020		
			Baseline	High Labour Force Participation	Low Employment Rate
Share of Employment in Agriculture (%)	60	51	40	40	40
Share of Employment in Industry (%)	16	22			
Share of Employment in Services (%)	24	27			
Labour Force Participation Rates (%)	60	56	56	58	56
Population (15+) (in Millions)	688	850	1010	1010	1010
Labour Force (in Millions)	409	473	561	586	561
Employment (in Millions)	392	456	541	565	552
Employment/Labour Force (in %)	96	96	96	96	98
Employment in Agriculture (in Millions)	234	217	217	226	221
Employment in Industry (in Millions)	63	165	165	165	165
Employment in Services (in Millions)	94	121	154	154	154
Missing Jobs (in Millions)			2.8	16.7	11.8

Source: World Development Indicators, UN Population Division, cited in GOI (2013).
Note: Labor force participation (LFP) rate in WDI defined as labour force/population 15+.

least that emigration may cease to be a choice and may soon be an economic compulsion.

As India's economic survey 2012–13 notes sombrely, there is a major migration of workers out of agriculture and India follows the path of other Asian countries. In addition, the demographic dividend will ensure more workers joining the labour force. How many workers will industry and services have to absorb in the next decade will be a moot question. The population growth rate in India has dropped to 1.4 per cent in 2010 from the peak of 2.3 per cent in the 1970s. Despite this decline in both fertility and the growth rate, India's population is still projected to increase from about 1.2 billion today to an estimated 1.6 billion by 2050. This will be because of the population momentum—the large cohort of women of reproductive age will propel population growth to the next generation even if each woman has fewer children than previous generations did (Bloom, 2011). The 2011 Census points to the sharpest decline in the decadal growth rate of population since Independence from 21.54 per cent in 2001 to 17.64 per cent in 2011. The percentage of population in the age group 15–59, however, will peak at about 65 per cent in 2035 before it begins to decline thereafter (GOI, 2011). The population pressure on land and resources in rural India will continue unabated and so will internal migration from the village to the city. There is mounting evidence that intra-country rural–urban migration in India is of considerable proportions but has received little policy attention. There are, however, significant barriers to mobility even within the country. Migrants remain at the margins of society often constituting an invisible population alternating between origin and destination points. They are a low priority for governments and face multiple constraints—low wages, poor safety and security, inadequate housing, limited access to health and education, lack of social protection—and are often second-class citizens (see Figure 12.1).

That migration improves economic well-being can be seen from the differences in consumption expenditure between migrant and non-migrant households. Migration benefits both the poor and the non-poor. Education and skills constitute the most important factors for poverty-risk mitigation, for migrants and non-migrants alike. Those who are economically better-off and with higher

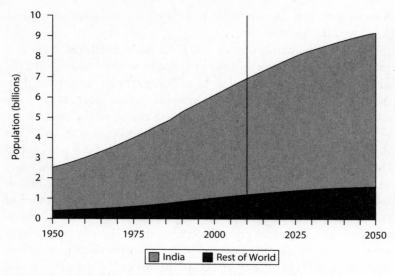

Figure 12.1   India's Share of World Population
Source: UN Population Division, 2009, cited in Bloom (2011).

skills levels benefit more from migration opportunities and the unfortunate poor and unskilled workers less so (Kundu and Varghese, 2010).

The Imminent 'Youth Bulge'

India's demographic changes are also manifest in its age structure. The population pyramids shown later display the share of population in each age group, separately for males and females. In 2010, India had a young population, with many children and few elderly; this gave its age distribution a pyramidal shape. Moving forward in time, the base of the population pyramid shrinks as the number of those of working-age increases relative to children and the elderly.

Figure 12.2 illustrates the changing age structure of India's population: the ratio of the number of working-age persons to the number of non-working-age persons under three UN fertility scenarios. The graph also plots, for comparison, the ratio for East Asia.

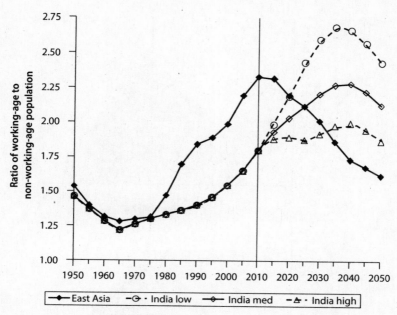

Figure 12.2   Growth of the Working-Age to Non-working-Age Ratio in India, 1950–2050

Source: United Nations, 2009, in Bloom (2011).

Figure 12.3 depicts India's demographic transition from 2010 to 2050.

Intra-country Circular Migration

A celebrated aspect of India's recent development has been the rapid rise of the urban middle class and the growth of its cities and towns. The urban middle class and the 'chattering classes' have come to dominate the development discourse to the near-complete exclusion of the countryside. Images of sprawling cities and a burgeoning middle class have arguably created the mirage of rapid progress. Yet the most important divide that threatens India's development prospects is that between agriculture and industry, between the villages and the cities. Despite the passage of time—after more than a quarter of a century—the ground reality still reflects what Michael Lipton

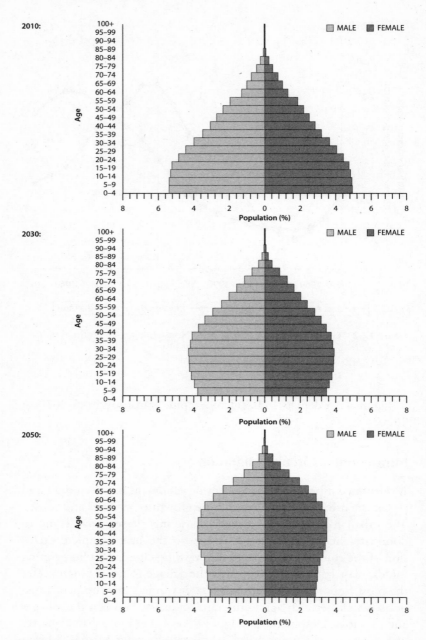

Figure 12.3   India's Demographic Transition, 2010–50
Source: UN, 2009, cited in Bloom (2009).

has famously described. The conflict in poor countries is primarily between rural and urban classes, not between labour and capital or foreign and local. The rural areas hold most of the poor while the cities control power (Lipton, 1977).

India will on average add about fifteen million persons each year to her workforce over the next decade. The Census of India data projects an increase of over 26 per cent in the working-age population over the next decade. Nearly a third of these will be from the states in the north, notably Uttar Pradesh and Bihar, and the vast majority from the rural areas and from amongst the less-educated, economically and socially weaker strata of society. The income gap between farming and non-farming activities has increased dramatically in recent years. India witnesses rural–urban migration of a significant order with poor landless labourers and marginal farmers moving to the city to seek a better livelihood. For many of these people, this represents the first step towards emigrating out of the country. This is a reality that must be recognized. They will need considerable skills education and training. The situation is compounded by the quite remarkable demographic heterogeneity that we see in India. India is heterogeneous, with significant variations on demographic indicators across states. Table 12.3 shows cross-state differences in the main indicator of potential for a demographic dividend, namely, the ratio of the working-age population to the non-working-age population. Here, the comparison of Tamil Nadu and Bihar shows as great a disparity as the current difference between Ireland and

Table 12.3 Percentage of Working-Age to Non-working-Age Population, 2011

Name of the State	% in 15–59 years	Name of the State	% in 15–59 years
Top 5		Bottom 5	
NCT OF DELHI	65.9	BIHAR	52.1
TAMIL NADU	65.9	UTTAR PRADESH	55.8
WEST BENGAL	64.3	JHARKHAND	56.5
KARNATAKA	64.2	RAJASTHAN	57.5
PUNJAB	64.0	MADHYA PRADESH	58.6

Source: GOI (2013b).

Rwanda—giving the economy of Tamil Nadu a much larger potential demographic lift than that of Bihar (Bloom, 2011).

These cross-country differences point to uneven development prospects for the future. Many of the states, particularly in south India such as Kerala and Tamil Nadu, have experienced fertility decline over the past couple of decades, making the Net Reproduction Rate equal to or less than unity. The growth of population in several other states, especially in north and central India has, however, been high in recent years, reporting either no decline or, in some cases, even an increase, which is a cause for concern. However, as a result of general reduction in fertility, the percentage of adults in the age group 20–35 is expected to grow rapidly over the next few decades. This would help these states pick up their growth momentum provided the incremental adult population can be meaningfully absorbed in productive sectors (Kundu and Varghese, 2010). The objective conditions—education, skills levels, health, and infrastructure—in some Indian states are much better than in others to benefit from demographic change. In some of the poorer states, such as Bihar and Uttar Pradesh, the young population would need to ramp up employability and productivity for fruitful engagement in the labour market in ways that would provide them with better entitlements and help propel India forward economically. From a policy perspective this simply means that there cannot be a 'one size fits all' approach that the current programme initiatives of the government appear to follow, especially through what are described as the central sector and centrally sponsored schemes. The states will need to develop condition-specific strategies that best suit their stage of development. India is also at risk of overstating the demographic dividend argument. Demography is no guarantee; an increase in the working-age share of the population does not necessarily translate into higher economic growth. While a large young population will be a decided advantage in terms of its potential, converting that into actual performance will require sustained and consistent policy attention focused on education, skills, and health. In its absence, the youth bulge will likely be a major drag on the economy and pose a challenge to social cohesion.

India presents exemplary evidence on the economic benefits of migration. The scale and spread of internal migration in India holds many lessons for the policy and practice of international migration. Admittedly, it is not without problems but does point to the potential to convert migration into a virtuous cycle benefiting all. Field data on migration generated by the National Census and the National Sample Survey Organisation, even if limited, are invaluable and help us understand the role of migration in livelihood strategies and economic growth in India. Empirical evidence shows that circular migration is the dominant mode of economic mobility in India. Internal migration occurs in significant numbers. The Census of India 2001 had estimated a large population of 309 million as internal migrants. More recent estimates put the number of internal migrants at 326 million or roughly 30 per cent of the population (NSSO, 2010b). Migration is an important route out of poverty. These circular migrants are estimated to contribute close to 10 per cent to India's GDP. Both their importance as also economic contribution go largely under-recognized (Deshingkar and Akter, 2009). For a country of continental proportions, and as diverse and differentiated as India, intra-country migration throws up governance challenges similar in nature and complexity to those in international migration that a discerning scholar, practitioner, or policymaker cannot miss. Just as in the international migration process, a complex network of contractors and agents operates in the internal migration process too; the poor and the uneducated workers face similar problems of the lack of credible information regarding jobs and wages and poor regulation of the intermediation process. Another striking similarity is the policy perspective that migration is a problem and must be stopped. There is, therefore, a need to change the policy view to see migration as an inherent dimension of economic and social change that the development process brings with it.

The Emigration Transition

As a major player in international migration, India's pool of potential international migrants in the age group 18–34 years and which is most likely to migrate will remain high and, in fact, will grow. This large supply pool will be looking for jobs in India and could potentially become international migrants, though this will be determined as much by India's economic performance as by the global economy. As fertility rates and death rates drop in India she will experience the labour bulge when its working-age population peaks. Two demographic features will serve as additional drivers for potentially higher emigration flows. First, the sharp differentials in age structure across the states in India will see significant changes inter se between the states of origin in India. This will alter the composition of the flows and see the emergence of new states as major states of origin and perhaps the gradual deceleration of flows out of the traditional states of origin. The high-growth states (Tamil Nadu, Karnataka, and Gujarat) in the period 1991–2001 had a dependency ratio 8.7 percentage points lower than that of the low-growth states (Bihar, Madhya Pradesh, and Uttar Pradesh) and an average annual growth rate 4.3 percentage points higher. Looking ahead, the low-growth states will benefit more from the demographic dividend, as higher incomes and lower fertility alter demographics (GOI, 2013a). The second is the increase in the share of higher 'age cohort' workers with potentially higher productivity and hence with the opportunities of becoming economically more mobile. Cross-country evidence suggests that productivity is an increasing function of age, with the age group 40–49 being the most productive because of work experience. Nearly half the additions to the Indian labour force over the period 2011–30 will be in the age group 30–49, even while the share of this group in China, Korea, and the United States will be declining. That India will be expanding its most productive cohorts even while most developed countries and some developing countries like China will be contracting theirs in the coming decades can be another source of advantage (GOI, 2013a).

Planning for the Migration Decades Ahead

In India the role of migrant networks has been disproportionately high. These migration networks will also be catalysts for increased mobility. The size and spread of the overseas Indian community will doubtless spread the flow of information and spur higher remittances and will likely reinforce migratory movement. What is less obvious and has received even less attention is the pressure that will be placed on the policy framework, the institutional apparatus on a cross-country basis and the capacities required across stakeholders in the process. Lest she miss the wood for the trees it is necessary that

India's response to migratory pressures must be prescient, recognizing the opportunity to position itself as a supplier of young, skilled, trained, and disciplined workers to the world. India is demonstrating the classic characteristics of demographic transition: a growing labour force, rising investment in physical capital and skills, increasing participation of women in the workforce, and technological and managerial innovation. In this backdrop, emigration will matter in the foreseeable future. Perhaps nowhere and at no time will it matter more than in India in the next two decades. It does seem that the necessary conditions exist to leverage the opportunity of its population age structure. Yet, a caveat will be in order: Demographic transition is a one-way movement. It follows the 'arrow of time'. No country can traverse in the reverse direction. It is also time-bound and does not provide the comfort of procrastination or policy paralysis. So India's opportunity window will be open for the next two decades when its demographic structure can potentially enhance in significant measure its share of young productive workers. It can supply skilled trained workers to the world. After that short window shuts, this period of its demographic history can never be captured again.

Developing capacity for governance, evolving clearly articulated policy goals, building capacity amongst stakeholders, and establishing a strong institutional apparatus can help actualize the demographic dividend. Creating an environment that will catalyse entrepreneurship, innovation, and work opportunities will be central to this effort. A combination of factors present themselves in tandem—India as a young country with a demographic surplus, the rapid rise of education and skills amongst the aspirational generation, the steady ageing of several countries in the developed world causing a demographic deficit and the growing integration of national economies in the march of globalization—to make a compelling case for international migration as a dominant mode of economic engagement over the next few decades. In the medium- to long-term, therefore, it is clear if India has to focus on an agenda to create productive jobs outside of agriculture that will help it reap the 'demographic dividend', overseas employment as a major avenue is not anymore a matter of choice. Indeed, it is a necessary condition that merits serious policy attention. India's position as a major player in migration needs to be built upon. What is striking about the India migration experience is its diversity. The number of women migrants in the last ten years in healthcare, hospitality, and the household sectors has been growing; there is a significant rise in high-skilled migrants going to diverse destinations across a wide gamut of sectors, and a steady increase in the number of student migrants primarily towards North America for tertiary education. On the flip side, there are disconcerting trends of irregular migration and disproportionately high temporary migration flows. In India's economic future, emigration will doubtless emerge as an important driver of income growth for a significant population in India. While as a percentage of the population, emigration will remain small, the absolute numbers of those who can benefit from overseas employment will not be inconsiderable.

With an age dependency ratio of 53 as in 2012, India is a young country. However, between the white-collar minority and the blue-collar majority the combined workforce in the organized sector is minuscule. The number of persons in informal employment in India, as a percentage of non-agricultural employment, is a staggering 83 per cent. Of this, 67 per cent are employed in the informal sector. The share of women with an informal job in the manufacturing sector in India is as high as 94 per cent. Cross-country data suggests that informal employment is paired with low income per capita and high poverty rates (ILO, 2012). The bulk of these are the rural poor with little formal education or vocational training but with the potential to climb the vocational skills ladder. They constitute the current pool of potential migrants. Clearly, the next two decades will be the 'migration decades'. The opportunity that India's migration future must seize upon is its demographic dynamics and the world that juxtaposes a young India with an ageing world for the most part. The result has been structural labour supply shortages and the concomitant skills gaps in many parts of the developed world. The demographic deficit debate cannot continue for much longer without greater liberalization of immigration. In a growing number of countries in the OECD, the population is both shrinking and getting older. As a consequence, there are fewer people working, saving, consuming, and investing. A declining economically active population has to support a much larger number of people who are no longer economically active but depend on welfare support. Over 40 per cent of the world's population now lives in countries that are ageing and in decline. India must gain the first-mover advantage and diversify its destination base. It should also build on sectors in which it has competitive advantages. There is a growing demand across the world for young workers across the skills spectrum. While the demand for highly skilled workers continues, the advent of technology, innovation, and higher capital–output ratios in most sectors are rapidly reducing the low skills space in the international labour market. There is in its place growing demand for 'grey collared' workers who are middle-skilled, trained, and meet global standards. India must seek to position itself as the preferred source country for a vast pool of skilled, trained, and productive workers. The principal challenge is to produce the best and the brightest and on a scale that enables her to significantly enhance her share in the global labour market. This is a formidable challenge.

Moving up the Skills Ladder

The Great Recession as many have termed the global economic slow-down since the financial crisis of 2007 has resulted in job losses to millions across the world. The ILO estimates that over 75 million young people worldwide are jobless—from Europe through North America and from Africa through the Middle East to Asia. The situation in India is no different, compounded by archaic labour laws and governance deficit. While Indian migrant workers are much sought after overseas for their skills, discipline, and hard work, in India it is a different story. To unlock the demographic dividend and catalyse a robust job market India will need to make intelligent choices and wise investments over the next decade to address the twin problems that hold the key to her economic future—the excessively restrictive labour market and the gross mismatch between education and work.

Consider the skills training aspect in India. It does show a relatively dismal picture (see Figure 12.4).

But the more disconcerting aspect is the mismatch between the skills that young people possess and those that the employers need. Data from the National Sample Survey on vocational education in India throws up some startling facts. Surveying over 4.6 lakh people across the country in 2009–10, the results show an astonishing disconnect between formal vocational training and the work done

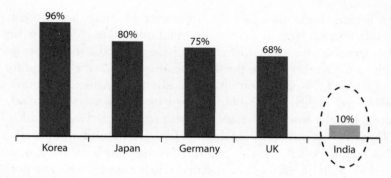

Figure 12.4 Percentage of Workforce Receiving Skill Training (2008)
Source: Planning Commission Report, 2008, cited in FICCI-Ernst & Young (2012).

by those who had received the training. Over 65 per cent of rural labourers working at construction sites or in agricultural fields had training in mechanical or electrical engineering or computer skills. Nearly 58 per cent of clerks had computer-related diplomas (NSSO, 2013). These are serious mismatches that need to be addressed. As a knowledge-based economy with a vast pool of technically qualified and trained people, it must deploy technology and training to re-engineer skills and unleash creative disruption across sectors in which there is a looming crisis. With globalization, India has the opportunity to establish itself as the source country for skilled people. This will require building our global competitiveness. India has significant competitive advantages in skills sets in several sectors in which it can become a world leader. This will require strong linkages between education and industry and a lot of training. The objective must be to create a pool of skilled and trained workers who can meet global standards. This will entail a sustained and sustainable pan-Indian skills programme specifically aimed at overseas employment. On a country-wide basis India will have to focus on developing: capacities, capabilities, and quality standards; institutions that can deliver all of these and a self-sustaining revenue model to ramp up. How well and how soon she can do this will substantially shape India's migration future.

13

The Colonial Compass

We are like travellers navigating an unknown terrain with the help of
old maps, drawn at a different time and in response to different needs.
While the terrain we are travelling on, the world-society of states has
changed, our normative map has not.

—Benhabib (2005: 11)

India's emigration compass is of colonial vintage. Several of the
objective conditions of emigration that overseas Indian workers face
appear as a nuanced reproduction of colonial emigration at least
along the India–Gulf pathway. Till the judgment of the Supreme
Court of India in *Kanga and Others vs the Union of India* in 1979,
laying down guidelines that would govern emigration, the legislative framework that circumscribed Indian emigration was the Indian
Emigration Act 1922. The Emigration Act 1983 was the outcome
of the judgment of the Supreme Court in the Kanga case and today
constitutes the regulatory framework extant. The structure of the Act
is simple and in essence rests on a tripod: first, no citizen of India
shall emigrate without the prior approval of the government; second,
no person shall recruit an Indian citizen for overseas employment
without being registered and third, there shall be a Protector General

of Emigrants (PGE) vested with the authority to grant approval to intending emigrants and to register the prospective recruiting agents. The Act also vests in the Protector General the responsibility of ensuring the protection and welfare of the emigrants and to regulate the recruitment process to prevent malpractice. Ironically the Act, though well-intentioned, mimicked the 1922 Act at least in its objects and institutional architecture. It was similar in form and substance. But it lacks the enforcement apparatus that its precursor had and therefore falls short of expectations in practice. Its representation in practice casts a long colonial shadow over the emigration process. In short, the Emigration Act 1983 suffers from flaws—intrinsic and instrumental. To understand the shadow that falls between the idea and the reality of emigration regulation we need to understand the praxis that emerged from the colonial Acts. Emigration during British Rule in India had already established processes, institutions, and instruments that steered it to serve the interests of colonial empire. With Independence, the policy objectives as also the relationship between India and the other British colonies or dominions were transformed overnight. By the mid-1970s when 'free migration' in large numbers began along the India–Gulf corridor, times had changed and with the passage of time the dynamics of engagement between the country of origin and the country of destination had changed profoundly. The emigration regulation and the institutional arrangements, though, were stuck in a time warp, as it were.

The Emigration Act 1922 and the regulations drawn up by the twelve-member emigration committee comprising both houses of the legislature was a definitive event in shaping the emigration processes in British India. It primarily governed the emigration of unskilled agricultural workers to the British colonies. The regulations specified that all emigrants must be over eighteen years of age and in a progressive leap laid down the norm that two of every three male emigrants must be accompanied by their wives (Lal, 2007). This was intended to maintain the gender balance. Contrast this with the emigration to the Gulf in the modern day where all emigrants are compelled to leave their families behind. The regulations also set normative standards for regulating working and living conditions of the emigrant workers as well as for welfare measures. Following the passage of the 1922 Act the principle of a 'standard wage' was established as opposed to a minimum wage with a committee setting the standard wage after factoring in location and working conditions. But the truly definitive feature that sought to enhance the protection of workers was that an agent of the Government of India was appointed in both the colonies—Ceylon and Malaya—to ensure statutory compliance by employers and recruiting agents alike. The presence of an official at the destination point representing the government of origin enhanced both the reach as well as the enforcement capabilities of the government. The government's agent also petitioned the local government to ensure the enforcement of contract conditions when there were discrepancies or grievances. An emigration commissioner in both Malaya and Ceylon took the responsibility for recruiting workers. The recruiting agents, however, had to take the approval of the local government from where the emigrants were embarking. This gave the provinces some oversight on the recruitment process. Thus the proximate oversight at the point of recruitment as well as at the place of work served as the umbilical cord between origin and destination and unified the emigration process.

The suzerainty of the British Empire over its colonies and dominions gave the then Government of India the strength to intervene in destination countries to ensure some welfare and protection of emigrant workers, such as it was. The terms of the contract and the working and living conditions were, doubtless, abominable. They helped serve the interests of empire and hence were necessarily exploitative. But the process of intermediation was effective and the response was on a real-time basis. Whether it was the Protector General under the indentured labour system or the Government of India agents appointed in destination countries under free migration or the authorities in the provinces, there was a formal administrative apparatus that enabled the government of origin to enforce the law at the destination end. This ensured oversight of the entire migration cycle. It also meant that interventions could be made both in India as well as in the British colony concerned, say, Ceylon. An important feature of colonial emigration was the emphasis on exit controls. Under British rule, emigration of colonial subjects to the metropolis of the empire or indeed to other foreign states was severely restricted. The movement of cheap, unskilled, and mostly agricultural, labour to other colonies and dominions was regulated through the colonial emigration Acts. In the post-colonial world, however, easing of exit controls meant that citizens of the newly independent countries could emigrate relatively easily. This liberalization of exit shifted the burden of regulation to the countries of destination. The destination countries of the developed world represent the metropolises of erstwhile empire and have been focusing all policy energy and attention to entry controls—how to keep people out, or at least restrict entry. This paradigm shift in the migration discourse has shifted focus on border controls at entry. In political economy terms it simply means the continuing hegemony of the erstwhile colonial powers. They were now transforming the discourse: from emigration is good to immigration is bad; and from emigration is a solution to be embraced to immigration is a problem to be tackled. Thus the sphere of influence that the developed world continues to exercise has created a sense of crisis and made the transnational movement of people immigration-centric. A geography comprising colonies and dominions enabling seamless regulatory oversight was transformed but the legislative framework and the administrative apparatus was unable to recognize or anticipate the challenges of a free world.

The Anachronism of Emigration Regulation

The first intrinsic flaw in India's regulatory framework for emigration is that it remains 'exit control' based. It filters who travels overseas and regulates the manner of exit. Arguably it is done in their own interest with their welfare in mind. The idea is noble but in practice the filter only renders the process more difficult for an already burdened emigrant worker. It also drives up rents in the entire cycle of migration. It is anachronistic that in an open society and democratic polity such as India it is mandatory for the vast majority of the citizens to obtain 'emigration clearance' before they can emigrate. The instrument by which this is enforced is that a certain class of citizens (at present all those who have not completed tenth grade of school) are issued a passport that carries an endorsement 'Emigration Clearance Required' (an ECR passport). This makes it mandatory for all ECR passport holders to obtain prior approval from the Protector of Emigrants for travel overseas for employment. What is stark is that this regulation has no statutory basis. It is by administrative instructions that this is being enforced. Neither the Passport Act 1967 nor the Emigration Act 1983 has a provision to make such distinctions or discriminate between citizens while issuing passports stamped as ECR or non-ECR. The criterion for entitlement to a non-ECR passport is relatively arbitrary. Till recently an undergraduate degree was the minimum requirement. This has now been brought down to 10th grade. The underlying assumption in such exit control is that those who are less educated might be less equipped to manage the emigration process and hence more prone to exploitation. So the law requires that such people produce valid documentation—a work visa, an employment contract, and a power of attorney from the foreign employer authorizing the recruiting agent to recruit on his behalf—as proof of legally binding contractual obligations before being cleared for emigration. The situation on the ground points to the fact that this, in itself, does not ensure the protection and welfare of workers. Not only does the PGE have no control over the process after the worker's exit, the documentation meets the letter of the law while violating it in substantive spirit. The work contract produced is only a 'model contract' with the worker being forced to sign a different one on arrival, often with terms and conditions adverse to him; the visa is sponsor based and hence at the will and pleasure of the employer, limiting the mobility of the worker; the recruiting agent washes his hands off the moment the worker is granted the emigration clearance. Notwithstanding the elaborate system of the Protector General set out in the Emigration Act 1983, the first objective condition that defeats the protection and welfare of the worker in the countries of the Persian Gulf is the 'Kafala' system of sponsorship so widely prevalent in the Arab world. It gives the employer immense control over the worker, his legal status, his entry to and exit from the country of destination and prohibits change of employer. The grievances of overseas Indian workers generally relate to non-payment or delayed payment of wages, unilateral changes in the contracts, poor living conditions, and arbitrary changes in the nature of work. In some instances, the workers are denied employment and left in the lurch overseas. In such instances, the PGE steps in and directs the Recruiting Agent concerned to get the workers repatriated at his cost. There is little else that the Protector General can do.

Besides being discriminatory, the result of such exit control has been to create 'second class' citizens of people who happen to be poor, uneducated, low-skilled and predominantly from the country-side. This second-class status of holding an ECR passport results in an economy—society-wide discrimination against these emigrants. They are seen as a market for exploitation and suffer considerable discrimination, privation, and abuse at the hands of government and the private sector alike. The ECR system reinforces an adverse selection process in emigration exacerbated by the asymmetry of market information. The presence of a multitude of intermediaries, many of them unregistered and mostly unscrupulous, creates a moral hazard in the recruitment process. The moral hazard arises essentially from the principal–agent relationship between the foreign employer and the local recruiting agent. For the agent, recruitment is a one-time transaction the conclusion of which absolves him of further responsibility. There are some operational safeguards the regulation envisages to ensure accountability of the agents—security deposits, statutory returns, suspension of registration, and so on—but remain ineffective. They are followed unevenly and seldom enforced. There are no standard operating practices to ensure that the safeguards are followed in letter and spirit failing which penalties would follow. In government it simply emboldens rent-seeking. The proliferation of intermediaries handling ECR emigrants at both the origin and destination ends of the pathway only underscores the negative sum game for the emigrants themselves. In practice, the registered recruit-ing agents rely on a wide network of unregistered sub-agents who serve to mobilize potential migrants from the rural hinterland. Yet, they are not recognized. Typically, when large numbers of workers are duped the complaint is never against a registered agent for he remains anonymous. It is the little-known sub-agent who is named but who is not regulated by the Emigration Act since the law does not recognize sub-agents.

The Conflict of Interests

The second intrinsic flaw is in the system of the PGE. While he is entrusted with the task of the protection and welfare of emigrants he has no control over the emigrant once he leaves the country. Nor does he have more than nominal control over the overseas employer. The contractual relationship between the employer and the emigrant is subject to the national laws of the destination country. Should there be gross violations of contractual obligations and there are aplenty, the Protector General has no jurisdiction and hence can do precious little. The Protector General is an arcane institution that worked well in colonial times but is less than optimal in the modern day. In fact it is ill-equipped to discharge the onerous responsibilities that are expected of it. Not being able to oversee the entire migration cycle and in the absence of jurisdiction to intervene in the event of distress of workers at the hands of the employers renders the Protector General a mere licensing authority in the country of origin. Unlike under colonial rule he remains a titular head of the emigration process and cannot ensure the better protection and welfare of the emigrants. Nor is he able to address the double jeopardy of adverse selection and the moral hazard. In emigration, moral hazard is the direct result of information asymmetry. Adverse selection in emigration occurs as market failure in which undesired results recur when emigrant workers have inadequate information even as the recruiters (both employers and the recruitment agents) have greater access to information. This information asymmetry often means 'bad' products or services in the emigration process often through unregulated intermediaries are more likely to be selected. In particular, moral hazard occurs because the recruiting agents are insulated from risk and have more information about their actions and intentions than the emigrant worker who ends up paying for the negative consequences of the risk. This has resulted in incentives to recruiting agents to behave inappropriately from the perspective of the emigrant worker. The inability of the Protector General to act against the recruiting agent and ensure the protection and welfare of the emigrant worker also arises from the principal–agent problem peculiar to the 'temporary contractual mobility' arrangement that emigrant workers are subjected to. The recruiting agent in the country of origin, in this case India, is in most cases an agent acting on behalf of the overseas employer in the destination country who is his principal. The emigration clearance process itself is based on less than credible documentation—a demand letter from the employer, a model contract, and a power of attorney assigned by the principal to the agent. This is what is required to be produced to obtain emigration clearance. Once the one-time transaction of emigration is completed and the worker exits, neither the agent nor the PGE have the jurisdiction or the means to enforce the terms and conditions of the contract. The fact that there has not been a single conviction for violations under the Emigration Act 1983 is stunning testimony to the obsolescence and the fragmentation of the regulatory regime.

The third intrinsic flaw in the regulatory regime for emigration arises from the conflict of interest in the roles and responsibilities of the PGE. The Protector General combines in his office the role of the policymaker, licensing authority, service provider, and regulator. Each of these roles has a different mandate: the policymaker ought to look at medium- to long-term strategic goals, for instance, making India a preferred country of origin for emigration; the licensing authority must focus on enforcement of the statutory compliance and ensuring that registered recruitment agents maintain high standards of integrity and professionalism; the service provider should focus on dissemination of accurate and authentic information to potential emigrants and facilitate ease of emigration; and the regulator should play the role of a fair and impartial arbiter between the various stakeholders—government, recruiters, employers, and emigrants. The inherent contradiction is between the interests of the emigrants, which is protection and welfare, and the interests of the recruiters, which is profits. In this dialectic the political economy of emigration dictates the outcome. The recruiting agents are a more organized, coherent, and powerful interest group than are the emigrants and hence prevail. A time-and-motion study of the regulatory oversight of the recruitment process and the emigration clearance system leaves no doubt in the minds of observers that it is a case of the tail wagging the dog. Between the multifarious stakeholders in the emigration process, the emigrant is at the centre. The system must work for him or her while all the rest are merely players facilitating the process of migration. The interests of the migrant worker and of the recruiting agent are not necessarily the same. The worker seeks decent working and living conditions while the recruiting agent seeks to maximize his profits. The migrant worker represents a transient group with little ability to mobilize while the registered agents are relatively more permanent and better organized. Finally, the worker is poor and has no ability to lobby while the recruiting agent is wealthier and hence exerts a greater influence over the regulatory process. In the result the interests of the recruiters are better protected at the cost of the interests of the workers. This has meant the emergence of the recruiting agents as an influential lobby that wields considerable power in influencing policy as well as in shaping the discourse. On a workaday basis there is poor enforcement of statutory requirements and service standards. Entry barriers are low and hence there is a proliferation of recruiting agents. But, in reality, only a small percentage of the registered agents, a mere third of them, actually engage in the business of recruiting. Thus in the political economy of emigration the recruiters remain dominant and the worker only a bird of passage. Policy interventions are therefore often far removed from the needs of the emigrant workers. This is compounded by the fact that the Protector General does not have an investigation or prosecution arm and has to rely on the state governments for action against recalcitrant recruiters in India and depend on the Indian missions abroad for action against errant foreign employers. This erodes the authority of the PGE and diminishes his effectiveness as a regulator. Simply put, he has been reduced to a licensing authority. The complaints against registered Recruiting Agents are enquired into with the help of Protectors of Emigrants and the Indian missions concerned. The complaints against foreign employers are taken up with the Indian missions and where there are grounds for punitive action the employer is blacklisted.

The Fragmentation of Praxis

Several other flaws of the regulatory regime extant are instrumental, rendering the system less than optimal and reinforcing practices that often run counter to policy objectives. First among these is the fragmentation in the policy framework and its enforcement. The absence of policy coherence—horizontal and vertical—on a government-wide basis across the various ministries of government at the centre and between the central and state governments has constrained reform so essential to keeping pace with changes over time; hampered real-time response, a necessary condition for effective enforcement; and pre-empted a coordinated effort to govern migration seamlessly. International migration is an integrated process that subsumes several activities that need to be coordinated by the various ministries to enable 'the virtuous migration cycle'. In India, matters relating to passports, visas, and diplomatic initiatives are handled by the Ministry of External Affairs. Labour laws and matters relating to the International Labour Organization are handled by the Ministry of Labour; immigration and registration of foreigners is handled by the Home Ministry; student mobility is the preserve of the Ministry of Human Resource Development; and the welfare of women the mandate of the Ministry of Women and Child Development. In the year 2004, an independent ministry to deal with people of Indian origin and non-resident Indians across the world was established. This ministry was also mandated with the task of dealing with all matters relating to emigration and the return of emigrants. The multiplicity of agencies has only served to compound the problem. There is no institutional mechanism by which policy coherence and an articulation of strategic objectives to achieve national goals can be achieved. There are no formal consultation mechanisms on a workaday basis. As a result, these core ministries seldom talk with each other and can and do take actions that sometimes run counter to national policy objectives. In the last few years since the establish-ment of a new Ministry of Overseas Indian Affairs, this dissonance has only aggravated with the subject of emigration being seen as the job of this one ministry alone, diminishing outcomes that coordi-nated action can otherwise achieve. The diverse facets of migration remain fragmented across government with various ministries laying claim to the legitimacy of their mandates resulting in turf wars and often action that is at cross purposes. Operationally, this has resulted in several practical difficulties: first, India is punching much below its weight in the international discourse on migration with the consequence that its strategic interests are seldom articu-lated. A more recent member of the International Organisation for Migration after long years as an observer, India is seldom heard or seen at this important forum. India's representation at the Global Forum on Migration and Development can best be described as that of a passenger. This is true of other equally important forums as well, for instance the Colombo Process, a regional process of countries of origin in which India ought to have taken a leadership position as a major country of origin. Second, India has not been able to secure its strategic bilateral interests in migration. The growing barriers to the mobility of high-skilled workers to the United Kingdom are a case in point. Less than five years ago the United Kingdom decided unilaterally to discontinue the 'residency' training for Indian students graduating from medical school, which was till then part of the medical school programme. Not only was this discriminatory, it was applied retroactively adversely impacting those who had chosen the course at a time when house surgeon practice was part and parcel of the graduate programme in medicine. It was not Government of India that helped resolve the problem, though feeble attempts were made. The judiciary in the United Kingdom intervened on an application made by the affected students to provide them relief. In a more recent visa policy of the United Kingdom requiring even those applying for tourist visas to deposit a guarantee amount against overstay, India has been clubbed with other countries perceived as high-risk suggesting that Indian tourists are prone to irregular migration. This too is the result of the absence of a coordinated national policy response. It is a different matter that the government of the United Kingdom subsequently realized that this restriction was proving counterproductive and decided to withdraw it. Similar is the case of the mobility of Indian information technology (IT) professionals to the United States. They represent the best and the brightest, yet the IT companies investing in the United States are required to pay higher tariffs for the short-term H1B visas driving up costs and making them less competitive. In the absence of bilateral social security coordination the individual as well as the corporate lose social security contributions made during the period of detachment. This situation is the result of the contradiction between the visa regime and the social security regime that the United States follows. The H1B or the L2 visas that IT professionals going on short-term contracts are issued provide for a maximum stay of six and seven years respectively. It is mandatory for the individual as well as his employer to contribute about 15 per cent of the monthly salary as social security contribution. However, the worker earns a pension entitlement only after contributions are made for at least forty quarters or about a minimum of ten years which means they never get back what they contribute. It is estimated that Indian professionals contribute close to USD 1 billion annually and receive no pension. This again is the result of absence of policy coherence on a government-wide basis at the centre in India.

The scenario is even grimmer when you drill down to the states. It is the states in India that constitute the theatre of action on migration, yet they are peripheral players in the process. The Emigration Act creates a centralized regulatory architecture that concentrates all powers in the Protector of Emigrants with little role for the states. Except for the general penal provisions of the Indian Penal Code and the Code of Criminal Procedure that empower the state police to act on complaints relating to migration, there is no statutory role assigned to the states in the Emigration Act 1983. This is a serious lacuna. The states have no role whatever in the process of registration of recruiting agents, recruitment of workers, or the grant of emigration clearance. They appear on the margins only when things go wrong. The complaints against intermediaries not registered with the Protector General do not come within the ambit of the Emigration Act. Such complaints against unregistered agents are referred to the state governments for investigation and appropriate action as per provisions of the law of the land. The state governments and union territory administrations are also issued a general advisory that all police stations must keep a strict vigil on unscrupulous middlemen. The states play an important role in India's governance. The Constitution of India devolves upon them important responsibilities and in the context of migration 'police', 'labour', and 'women and child development' being subjects in the realm of the states makes them crucial stakeholders in the emigration process. When the states are not actively engaged in policy formulation, operations or enforcement there are both short-term and long-term consequences that manifest themselves. In fact many of the weaknesses are now structural and will require significant institutional and process reforms. First, even major states of origin lack a world view or a policy framework on migration. In practice this simply means that there is no institutional apparatus equipped to design and execute policy or make interventions on a real-time basis. There is little interaction, if at all, and even that rather perfunctory, with the agencies of the Government of India. As a result it is often the case that the state administration is reactive rather than proactive. Some states like Kerala have a semblance of a policy and institutional framework borne more out of long experience than the governance architecture of vertical coherence. But even this remains the exception to the rule.

Second, in the absence of regular engagement with the emigration process and interacting with the Government of India, the states have been unable to develop capacities in key areas so important in migration management—intelligence gathering, information dissemination, outreach and training, mobilizing civil society, and enforcement of the law. This is a pity because close to half a million people emigrate from about ten major states and the vast majority of them are desperately in need of handholding. The facts on ground point to the significant role that the states can play in preventing exploitation and at the very least make the emigration process more humane and orderly. Third, by excluding the states, by design, from playing an active role in the emigration process, we have forsaken the opportunity of mobilizing non-state actors who are important stakeholders in migration—civil society, migrant networks and non-government organizations that are more proximate to the community. Finally, the key missing actors at the sub-national level who ought to be the centre of gravity are the local self-governments in India—the rural and urban local governments. This third tier of governance in India in the form of village panchayats or village governments is closest to a true democracy that is within reach, democracy that is more than rhetoric and within the meaningful grasp of the citizen. The local self-government remains the first post that the rural folk turn to for credible information, relevant assistance, and problem-solving. Excluding the two tiers of governance from migration management has only worsened the generic 'Pareto inefficiency' in migration. Structurally therefore the regulatory architecture and the policy framework have not been constructed bottom-up. The entire migration practice centres on the binary construct of the nine protectors of emigrants and the disparate group of six hundred-odd recruiters who between them determine the emigration future of close to a million people. The result of the top-down excessively centralized regulatory framework has also meant policy interventions that are divorced from ground realities hence proving counterproductive. Because the legislative framework applies only to the ECR passport holders and does not bring within its ambit the 'Emigration Clearance Not Required' (ECNR) emigrants the data is incomplete. Even within the ECR category tracked by the Protectors of Emigrants the data is fragmented since the contracting terms are not captured in the model contract nor do the recruiting agents file the statutory returns as mandated by law. Where data is available there is no management information system to provide for exception analysis and real-time interventions where necessary. A good example of a policy being counterproductive and in fact producing results quite contrary to what the policy had aimed to achieve relates to migration of women. The problem as observed was the exploitation and sometimes the sexual abuse of women emigrants by their employers. The solution considered was to prohibit the emigration of women who were less than thirty years old, the assumption being that those under thirty are more prone to exploitation and those over thirty are better-equipped to handle the problem. In reality however the policy restriction simply drove the women under thirty underground spurring an irregular migration cycle, raised rent-seeking, increased the cost of migration and rendered the women even more vulnerable to exploitation by several interlocutors since they were now part of a process that was unlawful. This is but one example of ill-informed policy. The true scarcity in India's migration praxis is not of resources, nor even of virtue, but of understanding. Keynes famously said, "Soon or late, it is ideas, not vested interests, which are dangerous for good or evil" (Keynes, 1936: 383–4). The real and only structural obstacles to efficient migration governance in India are the obsolete doctrines that clutter migration praxis in India. There is too much of the past in the present and too little of imaginative planning for the future. India needs to catch up with tomorrow.

14

Taking India to the World

> The dust of discord in the Gulf region ... had somewhat subsided. After a brief lull, there was again an upsurge in job opportunities in the oil kingdoms. When a friend ... casually mentioned there was a visa for sale, I felt a yearning I had never experienced before ... How about going abroad for once? Not for long. I am not that greedy. Only long enough to settle a few debts.
>
> —Benyamin (2012: 35)

A Leap of Faith and the Virtual World

Towards the end of the twentieth century India took a leap of faith. Under an unlikely prime minister, P.V. Narasimha Rao, the first from south India, who demonstrated sagacity and courage, India began to emerge from its Third World shadow and into the sunlight of a globalizing world. It made people sit up and take notice as a chain of seemingly unlikely events unfolded. The Balance of Payments Crisis of 1991 compelled fundamental economic reforms that broke from the past, the Indian information technology (IT) industry began to show spectacular success where manufacturing had floundered, and the economy started to grow at an impressive pace defying the 'Hindu rate of growth'. India's economy grew at an annual average rate of 6.86 per cent during the two decades of economic reforms

(1991–2 to 2009–10) as against 4.07 per cent during the four decades prior to the economic reforms (1950–1 to 1990–1) (Saikia, 2012). Less visible but as important was the steady rise in the emigration of high-skilled workers from India primarily to the United States but more generally to other countries in the West. The last decade of the twentieth century thus represents a watershed in India's history. The year 1991 signalled a sharp right-turn in India's political economy and brought in its wake a host of remarkable changes, not least in the pattern of emigration and its impacts. Indian immigrants were primarily and continue to be recruited as labour, but the form has changed from unskilled to highly specialized with a shift from a nation-centred economy to a global economy (Varma, 2007). The structural reforms were significant not just for the fundamental economic changes that they wrought but as much for the fact that they brought the idea of free market economics into the mainstream of political economy discourse dominated till then by the state sector. From being an avowed socialist republic as set out in the 42nd Amendment to the Preamble to the Indian Constitution, India was now courting a new and capricious mistress—the free market. Besides a remarkable turnaround in its economic development prospects, the transition in the 1990s marked the arrival of India as a 'knowledge-based' economy, led by the information technology revolution. It is arguable though whether the structural changes that mimicked the neoliberal doctrine of liberalization, privatization, and deregulation, propagated by the World Bank and the International Monetary Fund (IMF) in the guise of structural adjustment conditionalities, in any way touched the lives of the vast mass of the poor in the country and the 70 per cent of the rural population still dependent on agriculture. If anything, since 1992 income inequality has worsened in India. The challenges have resurfaced and prosperity by exclusion—despite a growing middle class—does appear tenuous and unsustainable. Amartya Sen had observed over twenty years ago that the overall success in the task identified by Nehru, of ending poverty, ignorance, disease, and inequality of opportunity, has been limited (Dreze and Sen, 1995). This holds substantially true even in present-day India.

State capitalism till the 1980s created a humungous apparatus for growth, even if inefficient, and it now seemed that with the sharp shift to the free market economy, the benefits that would flow as a result might be usurped by a small elite. In higher education this proved to be true. The IT industry grew, as many have argued, despite and not because of the government since it did not face the infrastructural and regulatory bottlenecks that the manufacturing sector did. What is less recognized, though, is the importance of science education imparted in India in the decades of the 1960s and the 1970s that served as the foundation for the rapid rise of information technology. India first unveiled its Scientific Policy Resolution in 1958 which resolved to "foster, promote and sustain" the cultivation of science and scientific research in all its aspects. In the early decades of India's Independence, science played an important role in constructing its state-led market economy. The state created a highly skewed public-funded higher education system that subsidized tertiary education at the cost of universal school education (Chakravartty, 2000). The vast majority of the Third World elites, educated at the Indian Institutes of Technology, led the upsurge in the emigration of high-skilled workers. This, combined with the growing demand for scientific and technological skills in the high-wage economies and changes in immigration policies, notably in the United States, accelerated the emigration flows of both high-skilled workers as also students from India to North America, Australia, and, to a lesser degree, the United Kingdom and continental Europe. Unsurprisingly, with the rise of India's economic fortunes, the emigration flows and concomitantly information technology exports grew in tandem. Powerful network effects came into play and in turn spurred migratory movements of skilled workers. As opposed to conventional wisdom, it was not the unskilled poor workers but rather the better-off sections of the workforce that had not just the propensity but also the ability and the resources to migrate that actually did. Indians soon came to be counted among the best-qualified, highest-earning, and most professional ethnic groups, with the United States and Canada as the most-favoured destinations (Khadria, 1999).

In practice, despite beginning at the high-end of computer software development—the design and implementation of complex information systems—by the late 1970s, the Indian IT industry expanded internationally at the lower end of providing software services, routine code writing. Most of the export revenue generated by the IT sector in India was from services performed by information workers and not from product development (Chakravartty, 2000).

In hindsight, this trend was to grow with the bulk of the Indian IT industry revenues being predicated upon wage and time arbitrage exposing it to the charge of body shopping. This continues to be the case. The longer-term consequences were twofold: the IT industry risked being locked in a low-level equilibrium trap that would constrain it from staying ahead, driving innovation, and fostering entrepreneurship on the one hand and second, it would act as a disincentive for students from pursuing higher degrees in science and technology. The Indian Institute of Science, a prestigious school of scientific research, on the occasion of its centenary year 2008–9 published a commemorative volume titled *Pursuit and Promotion of Science*. It sombrely noted the decline in students opting for science after their secondary examination from 32 per cent in the early 1950s to barely 19.7 per cent in recent years. More worrisome was the fact that the 32 per cent in the early 1950s were from the topmost rung, in contrast to the present-day 19.7 per cent from the lower-middle level. Clearly, young students, particularly the brighter ones, are drifting away from science and this was a matter of grave concern (Indian Institute of Science, 2008–9).

Going Beyond the 'Push' and 'Pull' Factors

The economic reforms triggered in 1991 in India and its emergence as an information technology power coincided with the Immigration Act 1990 in the United States which introduced temporary migration under the H-1B non-immigrant visa programme for 'specialty occupations'. This gave impetus to short-term emigration for specific purposes of specialized knowledge workers. The H visa programme was to become the primary vehicle for Indian migration to the United States with Indian workers taking half of the H-1B visas. Indians have doubled their population in the United States (see Figure 14.1). Between 1990 and 2000, the Indian population in the United States increased from 815,447 to 1.9 million. Almost 70 per cent of these Indians are foreign-born (Varma, 2007). The period from 1991–2008 saw a steady tide of high-skilled emigration from India to the United States and, as a matter of fact, 70 per cent of all Indian immigrants in the United States counted at 2.9 million today arrived after 1990 (Li and Lo, 2010).

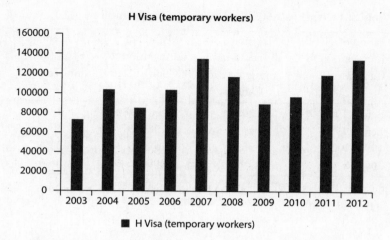

H Visa (temporary workers)

■ H Visa (temporary workers)

Figure 14.1   Non-immigrant H Visas Issued to Indians during the Period 2003–12

Source: US State Department; Annual Reports of Non-immigrant Visas Issued by Classification and Nationality, 2003 to 2012.

After reaching a peak in the year 2007, there was a dip in the two years that followed as a result of the financial crisis and higher rates of unemployment in the United States. It is only since 2012 that we are beginning to see a recovery to the pre-crisis levels.

In Canada, the Immigration and Refugee Protection Act of 2002 (IRPA) spurred increasing inflows of skilled workers from India. The IRPA broadened the category of economic migrants to include not just skilled workers and business immigrants but also those who were not subject to the skilled worker selection regime in order to meet local economic needs such as live-in caregivers who were earlier classified as temporary foreign workers. The new criteria also emphasized language skills and gave easier access to those with English language abilities, thus giving Indians an advantage and making them the preferred source country. In Canada too, 65 per cent of the Indian immigrants came after 1990 (Li and Lo, 2010).

In brief the pattern of migration from India to North America can be discerned from Table 14.1.

The story is similar for the United Kingdom as well, with the emigration flows of high-skilled migrants to the United Kingdom

Table 14.1   Pattern of Migration from India to North America

Period of Immigration to Canada	Percentage of all Indian-born Immigrants in Canada	Period of Immigration to the United States	Percentage of all Indian Immigrants in the United States
Before 1981	20.4	Before 1980	12.7
Before 1991	14.9	1980–9	17.3
1991–2000	35.6	1990–9	35.6
2001–6	29.1	2000–6	34.4

Source: For Canada, Census 2006, and for the United States, Terrazas, 2008, cited in Li and Lo (2010).

increasing substantially after 1990. The United Kingdom saw a 50 per cent increase in its immigrant population between 1993 and 2011; high-skilled Indians, including students seeking tertiary education in the UK, formed an important source for these flows. For instance, Indian-born immigrants constituted the largest group at 10 per cent of the population of London. A labour force survey in the first quarter of 2008 indicated that India with 284,000 non-immigrant workers represented the third-largest foreign workers group in the United Kingdom after Poland and Ireland. Indian migration to the United Kingdom has risen in the last fifteen years. It has also changed in character, defined now by entry to work and study. This trend is likely to continue (Somerville and Dudhwar, 2010).

In tandem with this rise in migration, the remittances to India from overseas Indians grew from a modest USD 2.1 billion in 1990–1 to an impressive USD 70 billion in 2014. What is noteworthy is the secular rise in remittances to India, which appears unaffected by the financial crisis of 2008 or, indeed, the global economic slowdown that the world has been going through since (see Table 14.2).

What is striking is the compounded annual growth rate of 16 per cent over the period. While the effects of the global financial crisis are visible for the years 2009–11 on remittances, and in a more pronounced manner on emigration, the recovery has been quick with the numbers for 2012 quite impressive. It is this robust and sustained inflow that makes remittances an important element

Table 14.2 Remittances Received during the Period 2002–12: Private
Remittances

Year	US ($ Billion)	Year-on-Year (YoY) increment (in %)	Growth in Numbers Emigrating (YoY) (in %)
2002	15.80		
2003	17.20	9	27
2004	22.20	29	2
2005	21.10	–5	16
2006	25.00	18	23
2007	30.80	23	20
2008	43.50	41	5
2009	46.90	8	–28
2010	53.90	15	5
2011	55.90	4	–2
2012	70.00	25	19
CAGR			16%

Source: Authors' calculations based on the figures reported by the Ministry of
Overseas Indian Affairs and the Protector General of Emigrants year on year.

in India's foreign exchange management. Remittances do serve as a
sustainable foreign exchange avenue that helps in management of
the balance of payments. At between 2.5 and 3 per cent of gross
domestic product (GDP), they serve as the bedrock of India's foreign exchange reserves and remain a small but significant factor for
balance of payments stability. For many major states of origin like
Uttar Pradesh and Bihar that are economically backward and have
a disproportionately large population of the poor, private transfers
made by overseas workers are critical both at the macro and micro
levels. This is true as much of in-country migrants as it is of international migrants. The in-country remittances estimated at over
USD 10 billion (UNESCO, 2013) indicate that Indians are truly
on the move.

In traditional states of origin like Kerala, besides constituting a
significant per cent of the gross state domestic product (GSDP)—
31.20 per cent of the state's GSDP in 2011—remittances from
overseas help improve the quality of life of the poor (Rajan, 2011).

With over 60 per cent of these private transfers spent on maintenance expenditure of the families of the workers, they remain an important source of sustenance at the level of the household. In the forex reserves that India held of USD 280 billion as on October 2013, for example, about 25 per cent or USD 70 billion were accounted for by the private transfers of overseas Indians. In turn, remittances also impact the current account deficit (CAD). The significance can be gauged through an adjusted measure of CAD, where workers' remittances are excluded from the current account as these represent broadly the exogenous component not driven essentially by the current pace of domestic activities and employment (Reddy, 2006). The weight of remittances can be assessed from Table 14.3.

The case for remittances should not, however, be overstated. They are in the final reckoning in the nature of private transfers and have limited multiplier effects. Recently measured remittances have risen much faster than emigration. While these income flows have raised consumption, and perhaps educational investments, among family

Table 14.3   Adjusted Measure of Current Account Balance, 1980–2005

Plan Period	Trade Deficit (Average for the Plan Period)	Actual Current Account Deficit (CAD) (Per cent to GDP)	CAD Adjusted for Private Transfers (Remittances) (Per cent to GDP)
Sixth 1980–5	–3.5	–1.5	–2.8
Seventh 1985–90	–3.0	–2.2	–3.1
Annual 1990–2	–2.0	–1.7	–2.7
Eighth 1992–7	–2.7	–1.2	–3.5
Ninth 1997–2002	–3.2	–0.6	–3.4
Tenth 2002–7*	–3.9	0.5	–2.8
2002–3	–2.1	1.3	–2.1
2003–4	–2.3	2.3	–1.4
2004–5	–4.9	–0.4	–3.4
2005–6	–6.5	–1.3	–4.4

Source: Reddy (2006).
Note: * Pertains to the first four years of the Tenth Plan.

members at home, there is a tendency in migration discourse to exaggerate the role of remittances in development. Excessive dependence on remittances can have an adverse impact on labour market participation, savings rates, and investments at the recipient household level.

Another important dimension of emigration from India is student mobility. The shift in emphasis in Indian emigration towards higher skill levels was also reflected in the quest of Indian students for tertiary education overseas. There has been a visible rise in the number of Indian students seeking higher education outside the country. This has been the result as much of the weight of a young aspiring generation as it is of the supply-side constraints in India. The best and the brightest continue to seek out the best schools overseas, especially in America, in search of better opportunities. As a result, Indian students rank amongst the biggest groups in the major destination countries. Student mobility has seen a steady rise in the last few years. The growth in the number of students in the major destinations during the period 2006–10 is depicted in Table 14.4.

In 2009, the United Kingdom overtook Australia as the preferred destination after the United States. In large part this was the result of two important developments: First, the spate of attacks against Indian students in Australia, especially in Melbourne, and second, and perhaps more important, the changes in the Skills Occupation List in 2009 which was perceived by students to adversely impact job opportunities (Figure 14.2). The United States remains the most popular

Table 14.4   Stock of Students in Major Destinations, 2006–10

	2010	2009	2008	2007	2006
United States	103,968	101,563	94,644	85,687	79,219
United Kingdom	38,205	34,065	25,901	23,833	19,204
Australia	20,429	26,573	26,520	24,523	22,039
New Zealand	6,650	5,710	4,094	2,452	1,563
Canada	4,617	4,314	3,257	–	2,826
		(Russia)	(Germany)		
Total	173,869	172,225	154,416	136,495	124,851

Source: UNESCO Institute for Statistics (2013).

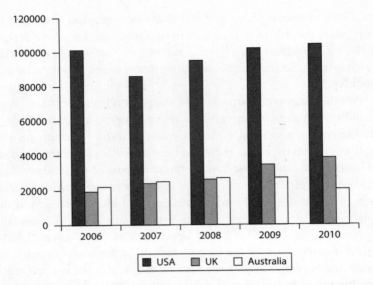

Figure 14.2   The Growth in Numbers in the Three Top Destinations, 2006–10
Source: UNESCO Institute for Statistics, 2013.

destination with more than half of all Indian students abroad choosing schools there. The United States enjoys high academic credibility as well as expectations of better employment opportunities notwithstanding the global economic downturn. The majority of Indian students going abroad join the STEM streams—science, technology, engineering, and maths.

Student mobility thus represents an important migration pathway for high-skilled workers from India and one that needs greater policy support. Student mobility is sensitive to the international labour market conditions. At a macro level, students aspiring for tertiary education overseas do make a cost–benefit analysis that determines their decision on whether, where, and when to go. The Global Recession of 2008 has had its impact on overseas study too.

To illustrate, it is useful to look at the number of student visas issued to Indians for study in the United States in the last few years (see Figure 14.3). The bell curve shows clearly the extent to which the global financial crisis has affected student mobility primarily owing to the difficult employment market in the United States.

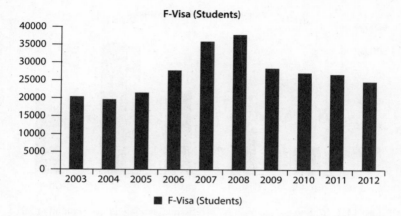

Figure 14.3   Student Visas Issued to Indians for Study in the United States, 2003–12
Source: US State Department, Annual Reports of Non-immigrant Visas Issued by Classification and Nationality, 2003 to 2012.

Despite the decline in numbers in the last few years, student mobility remains one of the more efficient pathways of migration. It attracts talent, gives them an opportunity to integrate, and is in the interests of both countries.

The Dilemmas of Dual Nationality

On 9 January each year India celebrates the 'Pravasi Bharatiya Divas' (PBD), an impressive congregation of overseas Indians comprising foreign nationals who are People of Indian Origin (PIO) and Indian nationals who are not resident in India (NRI). They come from across the world and engage with India and its leadership on economic, social, and cultural matters. This impressive gathering of migrants epitomizes the symbiosis of transnationalism and development in all its dimensions. Less known is the significance of the date. It was on 9th January 1915 that Mahatma Gandhi, the greatest overseas Indian of them all, returned to India to lead a non-violent struggle for independence that not just signalled the end of the British Empire but inspired similar struggles that were to end colonialism everywhere. On 9 January 2006, at the PBD in

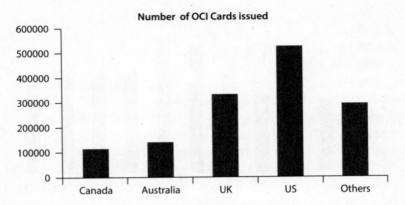

Figure 14.4   Overseas Citizenship Cards Issued, January 2006–September 2012
Source: Ministry of Overseas Indian Affairs, 2013.

Hyderabad, in a small but symbolic act that all but went unnoticed, the prime minister of India presented 'Overseas Citizen of India' (OCI) cards to two foreign nationals of Indian origin. The OCI scheme was thus launched. Ironically, the scheme initially received a rather tepid response (see Figure 14.4). The overseas Indian community and its representative organizations, especially in the United States and the United Kingdom, had been demanding dual citizenship. The OCI scheme fell far short of their expectations. The Government of India had in any event received the demand for dual citizenship with circumspection. India does not recognize dual citizenship so the OCI card does not confer citizenship in the conventional sense of the word. Yet, the OCI card represents an example of an innovative instrument that best meets the needs of mobility in the modern day—one that is characterized not just by circular migration of people between their home and host countries but also by 'step migration' where the person emigrates to more than one country—and the compelling demands of transnationalism shaped by the convergence of the state, the market, and technology. Simply put, the overseas citizenship programme meets a basic minimum set of needs: it enables visa-free travel by a foreign national to his/her country of origin, enables him/her to stay for as long as he/she wants without limitation; it gives national treatment in matters social and economic; and it enables the overseas Indian to work and invest in, as well as benefit from, the opportunities in India. The limitations imposed because of which it falls short of citizenship are that s/he is not allowed to vote and cannot invest in agricultural land.

As time has passed, the benefits of the OCI have resonated with an increasing number of overseas Indians. In the eight years since the scheme was launched, over 1.4 million OCI cards have been issued to overseas Indians residing in over 100 countries across the world. It is indeed an instrument that serves the economic migrant well and has added depth to the overseas Indian engagement with India. The programme has also served to strengthen the migrant networks that function as a bridge between the home and the host countries. The OCI as an instrument of engagement catalyses the three elements that make for successful diaspora networks—bringing together people with strong intrinsic motivation; enabling them to choose to play direct as well as indirect roles in development; and to move from project ideas to tangible outcomes. Thus they help transform diaspora networks into search networks triggering guided serendipity (Kuznetsov, 2006b). This the OCI programme does by forging an identity that enables them to straddle two worlds and belong in both. Despite the small numbers, the high-skilled migrants and Indian students overseas have helped shape perceptions on India as a knowledge economy. They have had an impact far greater than their numbers and have set in motion powerful network effects that are, in turn, beginning to establish a virtuous cycle of circular- and step-migration. Amongst the networks that have shaped the process of taking India to the world are The Indus Entrepreneurs (TiE), the American Association of Physicians of Indian Origin (AAPI) and their counterparts in the United Kingdom as well as Canada, and the Global Organization of People of Indian Origin (GOPIO).

The Deserted Road to the Gulf

We must now turn to the less fashionable, dust-and-grime story of Indian emigration to the Gulf, which accounts for 90 per cent of India's out-migration. Indian migrant workers in the Gulf are unique in that they are 'temporary contractual workers', typically migrating for contract periods of between two and three years, with some luckier than the others perhaps getting an extension of one additional term. This also means that the return flow is rather high. They can never hope to become permanent residents, let alone citizens, in the countries in which they live and work; and almost all are compelled to leave their families behind in India. If there is one feature that defines the Gulf migrant despite the droves, it is loneliness. Overseas Indian workers in the Gulf are estimated at over five million and a substantial number of them are women. Besides facing years of privation in an alien culture, they often face difficult living and working conditions in the host country.

The economic and social significance of these important constituents of overseas Indians can be judged by the spectacular growth in remittances by migrant Indian workers from the Gulf. About 40 per cent of India's remittances—close to USD 28 billion—comes from the overseas Indians in the six Gulf Cooperation Council (GCC) countries. The temporary migration of unskilled, semi-skilled, or skilled workers—mostly to the Middle East is also unique in that the social cost of education or vocational training is modest while the economic and social benefits derived from remittances or skill formation are significant. There is evidence to suggest that remittances in the aggregate as well as per capita from overseas Indian workers in the Gulf are significantly higher than remittances from others. Though overseas Indian workers are at the lower end of the income scale their remittances not only support household consumption back home but also provide resources for investment in the rural sector, particularly agriculture. Return migration, however, increases the incidence of unemployment by exerting pressure on the scarce job opportunities in the rural areas.

Migration to the Gulf is also unique in another important way. The data on emigration of low-skilled workers, defined as those who have not passed the tenth grade of school is captured through the exit control system under the Emigration Act 1983. The migrants are required to obtain 'emigration clearance' or prior approval from the Protectors of Emigrants.

This data captured electronically is accurate and is available up to date. Since the Gulf accounts for the bulk of India's migration, we decided to analyse the complete primary data set for the period

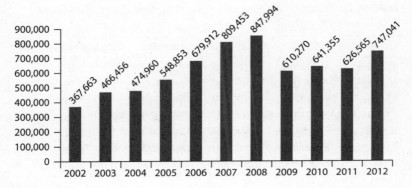

Figure 14.5   Emigration Clearances Given by the Protectors of Emigrants from 2002 to 2012

Source: Authors' construction based on the data from the Protector of Emigrants, Government of India, 2013.

2002–12 (see Figure 14.5). During this period the gross flows of emigrants out of India were a phenomenal 6.82 million. Of this number, 6 million Indians went to the six GCC countries alone. The total emigrating population grew at 7 per cent over the last decade on average, with a peak in 2008 of 847,000 workers. The financial crisis impacted numbers in 2009 but the numbers have since bounced back, particularly in 2012. Despite these large numbers over the last decade, the population of overseas Indians in the Gulf grew by much less. As against the gross flows of a little over 6 million people to the six GCC countries over the period 2002–12, the overseas Indian population in these countries grew by only 2.37 million. The increase in each of the six GCC countries is depicted in Table 14.5 and Figure 14.6.

This implies that about two-thirds of the emigrants, over 4 million, either returned to India on completion of their contracts or migrated to other countries in the Gulf or elsewhere.

The India–Gulf pathway thus represents an example, though in our view a bad one, of circular migration. Typically, the migrant is young, in good health, poor but full of aspirations at the time of leaving and s/he is older, in worse health, often with no old-age security, and with fewer economic opportunities on return. Since the bulk of these workers are unskilled or low-skilled workers recruited by agents

Table 14.5 Population of Overseas Indians in the Gulf Cooperation Council (GCC) Countries, 2002 and 2012

Country	2012	2002	Increase	Percentage Growth
Bahrain	350,000	130,000	220,000	169
Kuwait	579,390	295,000	284,390	96
Oman	718,642	312,000	406,642	130
Qatar	500,000	131,000	369,000	281
S.Arabia	1,789,000	1,500,000	289,000	2
UAE	1,750,000	950,000	800,000	84
Total	5,687,032	3,318,000	2,369,032	71

Source: Authors' calculations on the basis of data from the Ministry of Overseas Indian Affairs (2012).

on behalf of employers overseas they are far more prone to exploitation in the contract terms and abuse by the employers during the period of the contract. This is one of the pitfalls of 'third party' recruitment where regulatory oversight by government is less than optimal. The employer in the destination country is sometimes also a 'victim' of dubious recruitment practices. He is taken by surprise when he receives workers who are less qualified than his expectations and fall woefully short of the job requirements. Yet the cycle goes on as younger cohorts

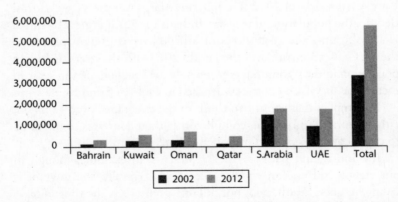

Figure 14.6 Population of Overseas Indians in GCC Countries, 2002 and 2012
Source: Authors' construction based on the data from the Ministry of Overseas Indian Affairs, Government of India, 2013.

emigrate to replace the returnees. The population of overseas Indians in the two biggest destination countries grew significantly both in Saudi Arabia, from 1.5 million to 1.78 million (2 per cent), and in the UAE from 0.95 million to 1.75 million (84 per cent).

The Changing Dynamics of Origin and Destination

During the first decade of the twenty-first century quite remarkable demographic and development transition effects were altering the patterns of migration from India to the Middle East in unprecedented ways. During the period 2002–12 that we analysed the data for, the highlight was that the share of Uttar Pradesh (UP), the largest and arguably the poorest state in India, in the total migrant population increased dramatically from 5 per cent to 26 per cent. International migration from UP has grown at an annual rate of 26 per cent against the national average of 7 per cent (see Figure 14.7).

Tamil Nadu's (TN) share of the total has shrunk from 22 per cent to 10 per cent in the last ten years, with the total number of migrants

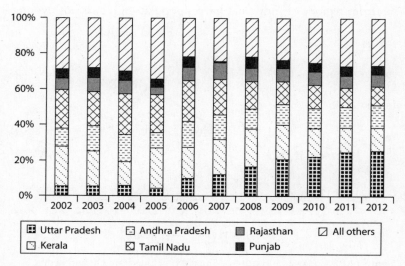

Figure 14.7   Emigration from the Major States of India, 2002–12
Source: Authors' construction based on the data from the Protector General of Emigrants, Government of India, 2013.

in 2012 at roughly the same level as in 2002. The other states to grow faster than the national average were Andhra Pradesh and Rajasthan. The contrasting fortunes of two states is striking—UP has emerged as the biggest contributor to migrant population, growing at 26 per cent annually in the last decade, while Kerala, the traditional bastion of migration to the Gulf, has seen significant deceleration in the emigration numbers and has dropped to second place on the back of 2 per cent annual growth in migrant labour to the Gulf (see Figure 14.8).

The tipping point is clearly 2008 for both states after which there has been a sharp decline in the emigration flows from Kerala while UP shows a sharp rise from 2009. This has a lot to do with the fact that south Indian states in general and Kerala in particular are ageing faster than the states in north India. The new major states of origin in the north are also the traditionally poorer states—notably UP, Bihar, and Rajasthan. The changing patterns of emigration and the emergence of new states as leading states of origin while we witness the waning of traditional states of origin are signs of the demography–development dynamic unfolding in India.

The surge in numbers in the second decade of this century is coming from regions of India that have a population that is both young

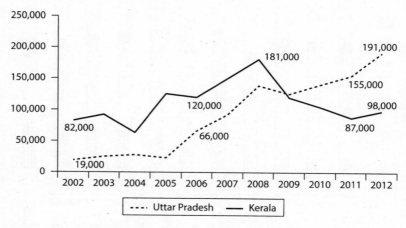

Figure 14.8   Contrasting Fortunes—Emigration Flows from UP and Kerala, 2002–12

Source: Authors' construction based on data from the Protector General of Emigrants, Government of India, 2013.

and aspiring. They have the propensity and the ability to migrate having come out of the throes of dire poverty. Equally, other regions that are decelerating have populations that are ageing and have access to growing economic opportunities and hence are less mobile than in the past. While north and east India show acceleration in the emigration numbers, there is a visible decline in the numbers from the south as also from the west—both these regions are 'older' and more prosperous, just as the former two are younger but poorer.

We looked at the emigration numbers region-wise and the trends are shown in Figure 14.9.

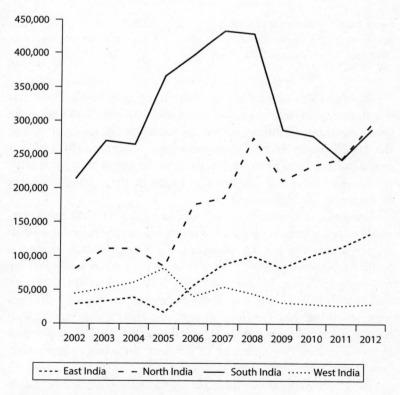

Figure 14.9   Region-wise Trends in Emigration, 2002–12
Source: Authors' construction based on the data from the Protector General of Emigrants, Government of India, 2013.

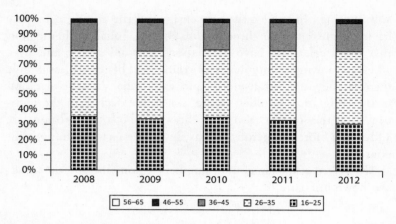

Figure 14.10   Age Mix of Emigrants from India, 2008–12
Source: Authors' construction based on the data from the Protector General of
Emigrants, Government of India, 2013.

The Age Mix: The age distribution of migrant workers has
remained fairly stable in the last five years, with the 26–35 years age
group contributing almost half of the total migrant population, and
the 16–25 group being the second-biggest category. Thus, 80 per
cent of all migrants from India are under the age of thirty-five. This
is reflective of the fact that India will soon be the youngest country
in the world (see Figure 14.10).

Amongst the destination countries, Saudi Arabia is the most popular for Indian migrant workers. Emigration numbers have grown at
14 per cent in the last decade against 7 per cent overall, increasing
Saudi Arabia's share from 27 per cent to 48 per cent or nearly half the
migrant population. Within the GCC, Saudi Arabia, Oman, Qatar,
and Kuwait have grown at or above the overall average of 7 per cent
while the UAE has grown at only 4 per cent. Qatar and Kuwait
have steadily increased their share of overall migrant population
by growing at 17 per cent and 28 per cent, on average, respectively
(see Figure 14.11).

The graph below gives a dramatic representation of the emigration
flows to the major destination countries during the period 2002–12.
Clearly, the year 2008 was one of crisis. In the GCC states, the UAE
in general and Dubai in particular were hit the hardest. Emigration

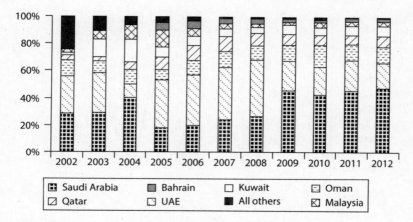

Figure 14.11 Emigration to Major Destination Countries, 2002–12
Source: Authors' construction based on the data from the Protector General of Emigrants, Government of India, 2013.

to the UAE, which had peaked at about 350,000 in 2008, dropped precipitously to a little over 130,000 in 2009 and is yet to recover. In contrast, Saudi Arabia, after a pause in growth in 2010, has recovered to the earlier trend rate (see Figure 14.12).

The migrant workers from South Asia have played a substantive role in building the GCC countries and helping their economies grow. Without them much of the economic activity in these countries will likely come to a grinding halt for, quite simply, they cannot live on petrodollars alone. Thus far, the Gulf has been a magnet drawing a large number of migrant workers. But a combination of diverse factors—stagnating wages, rising costs of living, a growing trend of imposing restrictions on foreign workers, and to a degree the declining fortunes of the Gulf—have somewhat dimmed the sheen of the Gulf as a destination. The Nitaqat Law in Saudi Arabia and increasing Emiratization in the UAE, as also the absence of justiciable workers' rights, including the freedom of assembly, raise serious questions on the human rights record of the Gulf countries. The Kafala system of 'free visas' ironically imposes restrictions on workers that often border on abuse and exploitation. The GCC countries need to urgently reform their immigration praxis. They need to rationalize the visa regime by disbanding the sponsorship system, improve their

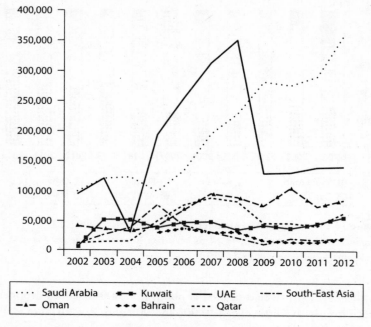

Figure 14.12 Trends in Emigration to Major Destination Countries
Source: Authors' construction based on the data from the Protector General of Emigrants, Government of India, 2013.

human rights record, and modernize their laws if they want to catch up with the rest of the world. Without these steps the oil kingdoms will likely lose young, productive, and skilled migrant workers to other, more progressive, parts of the world. They will also likely face an uncertain economic future.

15

Interrogating Irregular Migration

The image of 'living in the shadows' has been invoked by all sides. For immigrant advocates, 'the shadows' are where the undocumented are harassed by overzealous law-enforcement officers and exploited by unscrupulous landlords and employers. For many ... 'living in the shadows' conjures vaguely sinister intruders using public services to which they are not entitled .... Yet regardless of one's views on the issue, this imagery is profoundly misleading. It helps to perpetuate the myths and exaggerations that have made our immigration debate so fruitless.

—Skerry (2013)

Irregular Migration as a Metaphor

The international discourse on migration has been dominated by the debate on irregular migration as have most national migration polemics. In recent years, irregular migration has in almost solitary splendour, gained visibility at migration forums, captured the public imagination, received sustained policy attention, inspired considerable empirical work and has driven national and supranational institutions to commit significant resources—men, material and money—to 'combat' irregular migration. In this process there is the real danger of missing the wood for the trees. Besides, the outcomes have been far short of expectations and the benefits less than commensurate with the costs. This has raised serious questions on the ability of states to prevent irregular migration by policing alone. It has also raised questions on whether fragmented policy prescriptions that seek to address only part of the puzzle and attempt piecemeal solutions are only compounding an already complex process. Irregular migration remains a hyperbole in the migration lexicon and is increasingly present in its vocabulary. Countries of destination have become selective on whom to admit. Even as the selection criteria has become more restrictive and the policing of the borders more stringent, anti-immigrant sentiments and right wing politics have gained ground. This approach has been buoyed along by the widespread economic gloom following the prolonged economic slowdown triggered by the Great Recession. Irregular migration as metaphor has more than its stylistic use. It is pervasive in everyday life not just in language but also in the policy and practice of international migration at both ends of the pathway—origin and destination—often blurring the thin ethical line that separates right from wrong. The focus on preventing irregular migration at all costs has also struck a blow to the ethical basis for global governance. Nothing brings to the world the enormity of this tragic bind more than the unconscionable Lampedusa boat tragedy. On 3 October 2013 a vessel carrying over 500 emigrants caught fire, capsized and sank in Italian waters off Lampedusa. Over 366 of the migrants died. Writing in the *Financial Times* Bernard Kouchner, the founder of Médecins Sans Frontières and France's former minister of foreign affairs, saw Lampedusa as a metaphor for the European Union (EU): There were once high hopes but there are no longer any expectations. At the bottom of the Mediterranean lie the bodies of fugitives from nearby poverty. They embarked for Europe believing they would find salvation and a new life for their families on a continent that is not even capable of agreeing to throw them a lifebelt (Kouchner, 2013). This is but one, albeit the worst, of a series of boat tragedies carrying migrants seeking entry into Europe. The principal failure in Europe as in many other parts of the world has been its inability to carry member states with it as a result of the absence of political will to forge a harmonized migration policy. The consequence has been little effort by governments to make interventions other than building fences and intensifying policing. Even less has been done to engage with the irregular migrants and help them make rational and safe choices. In a sense the state has ceded ground, now occupied by organized networks of private players who run an irregular migration industry with a seamless presence in the countries of origin, transit, and destination. This includes travel agents, recruiting agents, and brokers who constitute powerful networks. Especially in the Asian migration circuit, movements have been shaped by a host of intermediaries including employers, agents, and brokers who are important players (Castles and Miller, 2009). This begs the question why governance is absent though government is present every step of the way. It also begs the question why governments cannot partner in facilitating safe and regular migration. A part of this failure has been the result of the stereotypes that have been built of irregular migrants and the simplistic solutions that follow. Another part of this failure has been the rise of anti-immigrant sentiments and xenophobia. Instead of dismantling barriers right-wing populism has forced countries to focus on patrolling their borders. Governments have failed to nurture avenues for freer legal transnational movement of people. Transnational networks of intermediaries have seized upon this failure. They seem closer to the socio-economic realities of a changing world and the importance of migration in it.

The Wretched of the Earth

Irregular migrants are not unlike other poor people in search of a better life. Like regular migrants they choose to leave their countries for the same reasons. Their journeys are predicated upon hope and sustained by nothing more than the dreams of economic opportunity. In countries with low average wages and high wage inequality, as appears to be the case in much of the developing world, there is negative selection of emigrants. Those with the greatest incentive to relocate to rich countries with higher average wages and lower wage differentials are often workers who have below-average skill levels in their home countries. The costs of irregular migration are perceived as smaller than the expected gains in wages thus providing the migrant with an incentive at the margin to choose the irregular pathway. Irregular migration is particularly difficult for the poor because the costs are sensitive to border restrictions and enforcement measures. The greater the rigour of restrictions on exit and entry the higher is the fee that an irregular migrant pays to the smuggler. In an exit-control regime, restrictions only serve to drive up rents. Even after incurring these high costs there are no guarantees of jobs awaiting the irregular migrants. All costs, even at the destination end, are higher while wages paid are lower than the market simply because the irregularity makes them much more vulnerable. Despite the exploitative pricing, they are compelled by their circumstances to make risky choices simply because they do not meet the selection criteria that countries apply to restrict immigration. Ironically, many of those migrants, who do not meet the ex-ante selection criteria but still manage to evade border enforcement and gain entry, end up staying by meeting the criteria for regularization, ex-post. Since countries restrict legal migration through quotas and criteria thus raising insurmountable barriers to entry, irregular migration remains the only pathway available for poor low-skilled workers to migrate to high-wage economies. Irregular migration is a complex phenomenon not least because of its aetiology. It is important to understand that there are a lot of ways by which a migrant can become irregular; there are regional differences in the manner in which irregularity is determined; and the status of migrants can often change with time and circumstance (Koser, 2007). In practice, the term irregular migrant covers a broad range of situations. A migrant might become irregular because she has overstayed a visa or residence permit, or a migrant worker can be rendered irregular by an arbitrary withdrawal of sponsorship by the employer. Many are hapless victims of unscrupulous recruiting agents or other middlemen and have been deceived into believing that they are entering or working in a regular manner. It is important to remember that many, if not most, irregular migrants will not have entered the country of destination clandestinely, and that the status of many migrants becomes irregular because of an arbitrary or unlawful act by a state or non-state actor (ICHRP, 2010).

The absence of accurate data makes it even more difficult to analyse and hence much that is written about irregular migration is based on anecdotal evidence. The total migrant population as of 2010 is estimated at about 214 million or 3 per cent of the world's population. At the global level the number of irregular migrants estimated at between 15 to 20 per cent of the total migrant population (UN-DESA Population Division, 2003) is certainly not alarming.

In the EU, overall, statistics suggest that irregular migration is in decline in many EU (member) states; although in some it has risen or stayed the same. The reasons for this are multiple and include indirect factors, such as EU enlargement and the economic crisis in the EU (European Migration Network, 2012; EU, 2013). There were an estimated 11.6 million unauthorized immigrants living in the United States as of January 2006. Nearly 4.2 million had entered in 2000 or later and an estimated 6.6 million of the 11.6 million unauthorized residents were from Mexico (Hoeffer et al., 2007). The Department of Immigration and Border Protection (DIBP) of the Australian Government estimates were that "as of June 2012 there were 60900 people unlawfully in Australia" (DIBP, 2013). A report commissioned by the Greater London Authority and researched by a team from the London School of Economics estimated that the United Kingdom has a population of some 618,000 irregular residents, within a range between 417,000 and 863,000 (Greater London Authority, 2009). All of these numbers while significant do not justify the brouhaha about irregular migration in some quarters. They do lend credence to the view that irregular migration is not just exaggerated but serves as a convenient stick to beat regular migration with. In absolute terms, though, these numbers ought to be a matter of concern for all—governments, policy makers, industry, employers, and migrants alike—since the irregular migration circuits exact unconscionably high human costs. This, we dare say, is entirely avoidable if the immigration countries acknowledged that they need low-skilled labour as much as they do high-skilled workers. The extent of the flows of irregular workers is a strong indication that the demand for regular migrant workers is not being matched by the supply, with migrants serving as the buffers between political demands and economic realities (ILO, 2004).

While it is difficult to put exact numbers to the irregular migrants from India, evidence supports the assertion that they count amongst the lowest in the world both as a percentage of the emigrating population as well as in absolute numbers. The United Nations Office on Drug and Crime (UNODC) report of 2009 on irregular migration from Punjab and Haryana, two major states of India, to the EU made an unsubstantiated and grossly exaggerated claim that over 20,000 Indians attempt to emigrate irregularly each year. Yet the report finally gives all-India deportation numbers that are far more modest. In 2007, according to the report, the all-India deportation numbers were just 7,261. Not all of these were irregular migrants and included those denied asylum or refugee status and others who were fugitives. Of these 4,540 were deportees from Asia and the Gulf. Thus the number of deportees from outside Asia and the Gulf region was a mere 2721. The data from official sources from around the world demonstrates the fact that India is not a major country of origin of irregular migrants. In the United States, there were an estimated 270,000 unauthorized Indians as of 2006. In Europe the numbers are not just small but are declining (see Table 15.1).

In recent years, though, there have been disconcerting reports from some parts of India of attempts at irregular migration, often with unscrupulous intermediaries in the lead. A pattern emerges from several of these high-profile cases of irregular migration that failed: the Malta Boat Tragedy in which 88 Indians were among 389 people on board a sailing vessel *Yohan* who drowned off the coast of Sicily on Christmas Day 1996; the Mauritania desert cases in which 37 Indians went missing in 2004 and 22 Indians were found stranded in 2006 attempting to reach the northern shores of the Mediterranean via the Maghreb; and the Vilvoorde Sikh Gurudwara case in Brussels in 2008 in which several irregular migrants were found sheltered. Most of these attempts have been thwarted and in some instances where they did manage to exit they were denied entry and deported. In terms of flows therefore we would hazard a guess and say there are some high-risk areas from where small streams of people do attempt taking the irregular migration route. The pattern

Table 15.1   Estimates of Irregular Migrants in the EU, 2008–11

Category	2008	2009	2010	2011
Refused Entry at the EU's External Borders	3,140	2,260	2,205	1,720
Found to be Irregularly Present	20,285	16,675	14,945	15,130
Ordered to Leave	18,795	17,025	15,490	15,325
Returned to India	5,125	6,660	7,790	7,165

Source: European Migration Network, 2012; EU, 2013.

discernible from these cases is that there are transnational cartels of human smugglers who handle the irregular migrants. Without their widespread presence at the points of origin, transit, and destination the migrants would likely not have attempted the journeys. Local-level travel agents formed the cutting-edge. It is these agents, who lured the victims or their families to go abroad rather than the families contacting them and persuaded them to go abroad with the promise of better opportunities for work overseas (Bhawra, 2013). The vast majority chooses to travel on visit visas and then overstay to join the grey market workforce in the developed world. Travel agents, recruiting agents, education enrolment agents, and other intermediaries are the prime movers of these attempts. The role of the intermediary networks of agents and brokers cannot be overstated. The intermediary networks explore different country options for irregular migration both to maintain flexibility in their operations as well as to evade action by law-enforcing agencies. This enables them to operate in different countries with intervals as well as to include newer geographies at both the points of origin as well as destination (Saha, 2012). They constitute the driving force of the irregular migration circuits, an invisible, extensive, and transnational network that thrives on an equally wide grey market that, in turn, thrives on supply of cheap labour.

Irregular Migration to the Gulf

The bulk of Indian migration is to the Gulf and it is axiomatic that it is also along the India–Gulf migration pathway that the risks of irregular migration are higher. In the context of emigration to the GCC countries it is important to understand who is an irregular migrant. Besides illegal entry and overstay, a migrant worker can become irregular if he switches employers from the one who sponsored him/her. Such cases result from the practice of trading in visas as a consequence of which though a national may sell a visa he may not be an employer and the worker may not get a job. Though illegal, this is common in the Gulf (Shah, 2008). The GCC countries, however, regularly flush out irregular migrants through amnesty programmes aimed at regularization or return. Under the circumstances we decided to look at some sample survey data of irregular migrants in the UAE. In December 2012, the UAE government announced an amnesty for irregular migrants. They could try and find a sponsor and regularise their stay or choose to return to their home country after paying a small penalty. Amongst the irregular migrants some were from India. While a third of them were able to find sponsors and hence gain regular status, others had to leave the country. A number of these Indian migrants approached the Indian mission in Abu Dhabi for financial assistance and issuance of emergency certificates to help them to return home. The embassy administered a questionnaire to about 2,500 of the irregular Indian migrants who had to either be regularized or issued emergency certificates to enable them to travel back to India. We obtained the data from the Ministry of Overseas Indian Affairs of the Government of India and the findings that we present below are based on our analysis of this survey data.

As expected, the vast majority of the irregular migrants, 83 per cent, did not even have tenth grade qualifications. Only 14 per cent had finished high school. This is not surprising because it does fit the typical profile of those who have in the past attempted irregular migration from India to other parts of the world, including Europe or North America. The typical profile is of a school dropout with no skills, from rather modest backgrounds and predominantly from rural areas. Typically, because of the exit controls and the barriers to entry, irregular migration throws up several business opportunities along the entire migration process that are seized upon by the intermediary and the migrant alike. Along the India–Gulf corridors it is also common to see relatives, community leaders, and other members of the migrant network like shopkeepers and provincial politicians as active middlemen. The high incidence of unskilled school dropouts amongst irregular migrants is one visible network effect where unscrupulous intermediaries entice potential migrants with allurements. The potential migrants are sourced through a network of subagents whose job it is to scout for those who are gullible and desperate enough to risk being fugitives from the law. This engagement is possible because there is no credible avenue for the potential migrant to access information or seek counselling. She is left entirely to the devices of the agent. This informal contract between the dubious recruiting agent and the gullible potential migrant represents in a sense the 'prisoner's dilemma'. In the event of failure they have the choice either to cooperate or to renege. The outcomes are always better for them when they cooperate than when either or both renege on the unwritten agreement between them. It is this 'omerta' that enables the network of middlemen to thrive, mostly at the cost of the migrant, and undermine the sovereignty of both the countries—of origin and destination.

The survey data throws up several interesting facts. The general perception supported by anecdotal evidence of irregular migration from some of the high-risk areas of India—Punjab and Haryana—to Europe would suggest that the typical irregular migrant is young, between eighteen and thirty years in the majority of the cases. This perception is reinforced by the fact that nearly 80 per cent of all migrants to the Gulf in the last decade have been below thirty-five. From those surveyed, however, the profile of irregular migrants to the Gulf seems counterfactual with nearly 65 per cent being over 30 and the largest chunk of 40 per cent of the irregular migrants surveyed being in the age group 36–49 years. Only about 24 per cent were in the 18–29 age group. This would suggest that the irregular migrants to the Gulf are typically more experienced, older, and have perhaps worked in the Gulf before. It is possible that many are second-time offenders who returned to the Gulf after the expiry of the ban period from the time of their prior deportation date. Nearly 90 per cent of the irregular migrants were male. This does not necessarily mean that the number of irregular women migrants is lower. On the contrary, the reason why the legal emigration data shows a smaller share of women emigrants is because significant numbers emigrate to the Gulf on visit visas and then take up work. This is because of the principal regulatory hurdle that they face—of a ban on women under thirty from emigrating. The direct consequence of this policy decision is that it drives potential women migrants underground and makes them willing participants in the irregular migration network. The fact that the survey suggests a much smaller share of only 10 per cent amongst irregular migrants, we believe is because of two reasons: first, the largest number of women are in the household sector which is not covered under the labour laws in the Gulf and hence do not come under the purview of the labour ministry which administers the amnesty. Second, because women who have travelled on visit

visas and work as housemaids do not come forward seeking government assistance, remain under the radar of the enforcement agencies
during the amnesty, and hence seldom get detected. Suffice it to say
that 10 per cent share amongst irregular migrants is significant when
measured against just 2.6 per cent share of women amongst legal
migrants to the Gulf. The conclusion that we draw from this data
and the years of policing and other regulatory interventions that were
attempted by the Government of India is to us self-evident: irregular
migration of women is the single-biggest area for policy intervention
by the government.

Another striking feature that emerges is the parlous economic
condition that these irregular migrants were in back home in India,
which likely was the trigger that compelled them to opt for the irregular migration route. Over three-quarters of the irregular migrants
(an astounding 75 per cent) earned less than INR 5,000—a little
over USD 80—a month, in India. In fact about 16 per cent had
no source of income at all. Only 5 per cent of them earned more
than INR 10,000 a month. In contrast, over 80 per cent earned
more than INR 8,000 in the UAE representing at the minimum an
increase of 65 per cent, and in many cases a much higher increase
in income.

Four major states of India—Andhra Pradesh, Tamil Nadu, Kerala,
and Punjab—contribute almost 80 per cent of the irregular migrants.
This finding on the basis of primary data, in fact, corroborates the
widely held view arising from anecdotal evidence that these states
are indeed the high-risk areas that need concerted action. These are
also the geographies with extensive networks of travel agents, recruiting agents, educational consultants and other active intermediaries
who play the role of catalysts in the irregular migration process. It
is also from these states that the middlemen have proliferated in the
countries of destination. These networks of intermediaries include
earlier migrants who now make a living from supplying cheap labour,
community leaders, teachers, priests, and relatives who are now
well settled in the Gulf. They often visit India to recruit labour on
behalf of other agents and employers. They scout the villages for
people who can be lured with the promise of a pot of gold at the
end of the migration rainbow. They provide the information
and contacts and also facilitate the process. For an overwhelming

majority—57 per cent—of the irregular migrants surveyed, friends and relatives abroad were the primary source of information for emigrating and also the avenue for finding a job. It is perhaps not unique to India's migration experience that the unscrupulous intermediary is often a relative, a member of the local community or congregation, a former migrant, or simply a member of the family. The power of the unscrupulous intermediaries engaged in irregular migration or people smuggling to weave dreams and sell them to unsuspecting, poor, uneducated, and unskilled rural folk in India is profound. It is not surprising therefore that nearly 30 per cent of the irregular migrants surveyed were people who willingly embarked on the journey without an offer of employment or the promise of a job. They were willing to risk emigration in search of a job.

One of the questions in the survey was on how much the migrants had paid to the agent who facilitated their migration. More than 70 per cent of the migrants had paid over INR 50,000. Of these about 30 per cent had paid more than INR 75,000 and about 10 per cent had paid more than INR 100,000. The results from an analysis of their replies are startling to say the least. What stands out is that potential migrants are willing to pay anywhere between 40 and 100 per cent of their future annual incomes to agents to arrange for their new jobs abroad (see Figure 15.1).

Another significant finding from the survey was that almost 75 per cent of the migrants surveyed had emigrated on a work visa.

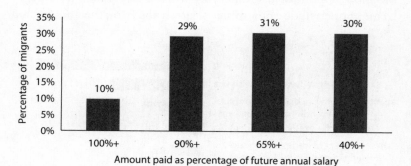

Figure 15.1 Amounts Paid by Irregular Migrants to Agents
Source: Authors' construction based on the analysis of the survey data obtained from the Ministry of Overseas Indian Affairs, 2013.

This runs counter to the conventional view emerging from some of the case studies of irregular migration to Europe which pointed to a trend that the largest number of irregular migrants to the western world proceed on visit visas and then overstay their welcome. In the case of the respondents of this survey, only 27 per cent went on a visit visa and then took up employment. This simply means that most of the workers migrate through a legal process and are rendered irregular during the tenure of their work contract. This throws up a lot of concern on how a person who has entered legally can be reduced to irregular status quite so easily in the Gulf and, worse still, that there does not seem to be any oversight or regulation on the cavalier manner in which sponsors can adversely affect the lives of these workers. This should engage the attention of governments of both origin and destination. The data shows that the reasons for migrants with a legal status becoming irregular almost overnight are myriad. An analysis of the replies of the respondents produced interesting results (see Figure 15.2).

This demonstrates in ample measure that the sponsorship-based visa regime combined with poor worker contract regulation and enforcement have resulted in oppressive living and working conditions for the temporary contractual workers in most of the Gulf. At the root of the widespread exploitation and abuse of temporary contractual foreign workers is the Kafala system. Today it represents the most oppressive instrument of what is not unlike indentured labour or servitude. But this is a gross abuse of the sponsorship

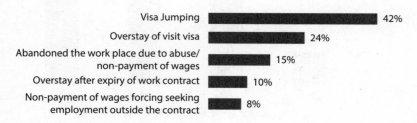

Figure 15.2   Reasons for Becoming Illegal
Source: Authors' construction based on the analysis of the survey data from the Ministry of Overseas Indian Affairs, 2013.

system and occurs for a large part because the governments of the GCC states have turned a blind eye. This was not always so.

The *kafala* system has cultural and historical roots in the Arab world. It comes from the Bedouin custom of temporarily granting strangers protection and even affiliation into the tribe for specific purposes. For instance, if a stranger were travelling across the desert and happened to wander onto a family's camp, it would be customary to take him in, feed him and his animals, and allow him to stay as long as he wishes. (Russeau, 2013)

In the context of emigration to the Gulf all workers are bound by temporary contracts after the completion of which they are expected to leave. They are therefore issued a resident visa for the number of years stipulated in the work contract. Each of these visas has a sponsor who generally is the employer. The system binds the worker to one employer, who is the original sponsor. Without the prior permission of the sponsor, the worker cannot leave or change the employer (Shah, 2008). In a cruel twist, the Kafala system has been made to stand on its head. Under the modern-day sponsorship-based visa regime in most cases the employer confiscates the passports of the worker rendering her immobile. The Kafala system today places the worker under the sole and complete control of her sponsor. Literally it is at his will and pleasure that she lives and works in that country. This, combined with the exclusion from labour law protection, ties the migrant workers to their employers, placing near-absolute power in the hands of the employer to dictate the relationship. This one-sided and exploitative relationship often compels migrants to desperate action. As the results show, 63 per cent of the migrants were rendered irregular either for visa-jumping, abandoning the workplace or seeking employment outside the contract.

Even after the migrant workers became irregular, the majority of them—66 per cent—continued to live and work in the country of destination for between two and five years regardless of the reason why they became irregular. The most dramatic result of the survey is the impact that becoming irregular had on wages. The survey sought information on wages earned per month before and after becoming irregular. Becoming irregular has minimal impact on wages.

As high as 83 per cent of the workers who were earning United Arab Emirates Dirham (AED) 1,000 continued to earn higher than AED 1,000 even after becoming irregular. The effect was more pronounced for lower-income workers. For those earning between AED 300 and 500, the vast majority—96 per cent—were able to earn a higher income after becoming irregular. Similarly, 66 per cent of the migrants who were earning in the range AED 500–1,000 were able to earn more than AED 1,000. This leads to two conclusions: first, that there is a thriving grey market and a sustained demand for workers. Hence even irregular migrants are able to find jobs and earn a reasonable wage. Second, that contract terms drawn up by recruiting agents under the 'third party' recruitment process are loaded in favour of the employer in most cases and the wages are not market related. It appears to be the case that the workers surveyed were locked into contracts where the wages were below the market level. That is why workers who jump visas and change employers are in fact better off and the vast majority of them earned more after they became irregular.

It was no surprise that the survey data points to the fact that over 45 per cent of the workers were in the construction sector after they were rendered irregular. The barriers to entry are low, the skill levels expected are rudimentary and work becomes available on a daily wagebasis even without a formal contract. The fact that 65 per cent of the irregular workers stayed with their relatives or friends during the period of their irregular status demonstrates how strong migration networks are and the wide range of services they provide even to irregular migrants. They search for cheap labour, recruit workers, disseminate information, provide services along the entire migration cycle, have a presence in both the countries of origin and of destination, and operate it as a closed circuit. They also extend assistance and support to irregular migrants in times of need. It is our considered view that this has occurred because of the absence of a coherent policy frame at both ends of the corridor, in India and in the GCC countries. Thus networks of middlemen who man the migration industry have occupied the space that ought to be the legitimate realm of bilateralism. In the context of the GCC countries the excessive emphasis on temporary contractual employment of foreigners through third-party recruitment combined with their unwillingness to conclude bilateral mobility partnership agreements that could govern the emigration and return cycle is at the heart of the problem.

Almost all the irregular migrants surveyed were able to send remittances to their families regularly—monthly or quarterly—and 55 per cent of them were able to send home at least INR 5,000 per month, a significant number of them sending home even more. The data on remittances also blows away many myths about the informal remittance channels referred to as 'hawala'. Contrary to the common perception that irregular migrants do not have access to—or for reasons of wanting to stay beyond the reach of the long arm of the law do not use—formal money transfer channels, the data shows that over 92 per cent of the irregular workers sent remittances through formal channels. A significant 72 per cent used exchange houses while 20 per cent used banking channels. The predominance of exchange houses is to be expected since the GCC countries restrict banking licences to foreign banks allowing a limited number of bank branches of different countries. There has thus been a proliferation of exchange houses.

When asked what help or intervention they wanted from the government, more effective regulation of recruitment practices and institutional support were the most frequently cited areas for improvement. An overwhelming majority of 66 per cent felt that government should act to regulate recruitment of migrant workers and recruiting agents more stringently. About 34 per wanted that the institutional support, particularly in the country of destination, should be strengthened and made more responsive. Despite the grave hardships and the fact that they were being deported, on their future plans nearly half of them said that they would try and go back to the UAE. Left to themselves they will in all probability turn to the migration middlemen once again and embark on yet another journey that will expose them to the risks and vulnerability that irregular migrants are constantly subject to. This can only change when the governments in the countries of origin and of destination show the political will and the commitment to make migration orderly and humane. This will need both the countries of origin and of destination to work together to foster more ethical recruitment practices, beginning with reducing the excessive reliance on third-party recruitment and encouraging direct contracting between employers and workers. It is also time that both governments devote greater attention to institutional mechanisms to guarantee the basic human rights that migrant workers are entitled to. A good starting point and one that is long overdue is for them to sign and ratify the 'International Convention on the Rights of All Migrant Workers and Members of their Families'. Failure to do so will continue to place millions of migrant workers at risk of exploitation and abuse. This will be our collective failure.

16

The Empire of the Mind

Let us go forward in malice to none and good will to all. Such plans offer far better prizes than taking away other people's provinces or lands or grinding them down in exploitation. The empires of the future are the empires of the mind.

—Winston Churchill (1943)

Mobility and the Democratization of Knowledge

The democratization of knowledge has been the prime driver of human progress and the mobility of knowledge providers has been central to the spread of knowledge. Actors in developing economies must have the capacity to acquire new knowledge—to learn new ways of doing things—if they are to compete in the world economy. Learning, in turn, supposes and contributes to the ability to search out and usefully recombine scattered information about production methods, markets, and resources (Kuznetsov, 2006b). The transnational mobility of students, academics, scientists and technologists has been the result of a variety of historical causes. Learning, innovation and entrepreneurship have long been the principal drivers of this mobility. Up until the end of the Cold War, such movement occurred along the axes of political and scientific hegemony. The colonial empires, before, had expanded these corridors to a world scale with scientific talent from a variety of disciplines from geographically distant and diverse colonies moving to the metropolis to learn and train. In the post-colonial world the absence of national education and scientific infrastructure in several of the newly independent countries only served to further catalyse such mobility. Historically, transnationalism has its roots in the movement of people, primarily migrant populations who then founded their own ethnic communities in the countries of destination. In this backdrop, network diasporas are but the latest bridge institutions connecting developing economy insiders, with their risk-mitigating knowledge and connections, to outsiders in command of technical know-how and investment capital (Kuznetsov, 2006b). It was in the second half of the twentieth century, though, that the phenomenon of 'brain drain' entered the lexicon of international migration when the countries of the 'north', notably the United States, became decisive magnets drawing the best and the brightest in search of tertiary education and those with high skills. The mobility of 'knowledge workers' in the modern day in some ways is the reproduction of the mobilization patterns of the past. The pathways, though, have diversified as has the depth which is now centred on the frontiers of scientific research and development. The aetiology of 'the flight of the intellectuals' remains largely the same: inadequate conditions for excellence, particularly, in higher education; the absence of certain branches of study for students in the pursuit of new knowledge; the quest for better infrastructure for scientific research; the scarcity of suitable jobs for the highly qualified; the lack of professional recognition, which alone perhaps accounts for considerable migratory movement and the predominance of the public sector in the scientific establishment. Government has expanded to occupy every nook and corner of research and development very nearly shutting out private enterprise or initiative. The dominant presence of government in and the excessive bureaucratization of the scientific establishment in many countries like India has often been a trigger for some of the best talent graduating from schools and colleges to migrate. Not unexpectedly, the steady streams of outmigration of brainpower has received little policy attention in the countries of origin while the countries of destination in the developed world have demonstrated considerable success in policy design to attract the best talent from wherever it might reside across the world. Whether scientists and high-skilled workers choose to stay in the home country with the hope of making it better or leave in pursuit of better prospects appears to be a function of peer group dynamics and the decision of the critical mass number to stay or leave. The direction in which such critical mass moves is a function of expectations. Suppose each scientist in a home country reference group were to make plans to stay or leave depending on his or her expectation about how many others will stay or leave. These expectations are summarized in a reaction function in Figure 16.1 (Ellerman, 2004).

Given the information that X per cent of the scientists in a group is staying, Y per cent will consider that sufficient for them to stay. If given that 40 per cent are staying, only 35 per cent consider that sufficient for them to stay, then 40 per cent would not be equilibrium (where expectations match reality). The numbers would spiral downward to some low-level equilibrium. If given that 75 per cent would stay, at least 80 per cent consider that sufficient to stay, the dynamics would work the other way (Ellerman, 2004). This pattern seems true even today for India as it does for the rest of the developing world for both emigration from as well as return to the home country. In effect this has only reinforced the sphere of influence of the developed world. In a delicious irony, the biggest Research and Development Centre of General Electric (GE) outside of the

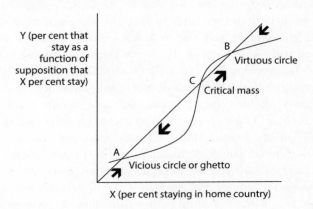

Figure 16.1 Critical Mass Dynamics of Emigration
Source: Ellerman (2004).

United States is located in Bengaluru, India. It is doing some pioneering work for GE globally and employs over 3,500 PhDs, many of whom are American nationals of Indian origin while others are Indian nationals who have relocated from the United States. Providentially, just when a critical number of Indian expatriates who had emigrated to the United States in the 1970s and 1980s were beginning to take leadership positions as chief executives and senior management at American technology companies, these companies were beginning to expand their operations in new geographies. These executives played a critical role in giving their companies the confidence to outsource work to India. They were also patient sponsors as Indian firms gradually learned how to meet American quality and delivery requirements (Kuznetsov, 2006). Thus, the emergence of a mobility pathway for the two-way movement of high-skilled workers was less because of national policy and had more to do with externalities of globalization. In essence, the migration and, more recently the return, though yet a trickle, of the best and the brightest has been occurring in a policy vacuum.

The Emergence of the Knowledge Diaspora

India's occupying a small but significant part of the global mindspace is of rather recent origin, in fact, led by its information technology revolution in only the last two decades. Colonial emigration took Indian workers to distant lands to keep the wheels of Empire turning and in doing so gave rise to a vast overseas community often described as the 'old diaspora'. Yet, it was the new economy that took India to the world in the new millennium. Towards the end of the twentieth century the character of Indian migration began to change significantly, showing greater confidence and rapidly climbing up the value chain. Led by progressive policies for high-skilled migrants especially in the United States, Canada, Australia, and to a lesser degree the United Kingdom, Indian migration to these countries was dominated by students, academics, scientists, engineers, doctors, and information technology professionals—many of whom showed considerable entrepreneurial ability. They thrived in the entrepreneurial environment that these countries provided; established themselves as leaders in their respective disciplines and led cutting-edge innovation with many of them emerging as pioneers of global big business. The mobility of high-skilled professionals of the knowledge economy from India to the Global North has been significant even if in relatively small numbers. A distinguishing feature of this recent phase in India's migration history has been the remarkable role of student mobility with Indian students having a significant presence in most western countries, not least, the United States. Student mobility today represents perhaps the best migration pathway, an exemplar of the best elements of migration. The students are young, they are amongst the best and the brightest, they adapt well to the cultural milieu of the host country and should the market need their skills, they integrate well into the economy and contribute significantly to the destination country. It is also the perfect supply chain to fill the significant labour shortages and the skills supply gaps in countries with declining fertility and ageing populations. It is surprising therefore that student mobility has received little attention, except perhaps in the United States and, to some degree, Canada. This is a pity since there is surplus capacity in several universities across Europe for instance. As for the countries of origin, with possibly the exception of China, there has been no coherent and coordinated effort at enabling student mobility. This is myopic simply because there is empirical evidence to suggest that these students continue to maintain active economic, social, and cultural ties with their home countries and constitute a robust bridge for transfer of knowledge as well as economic engagement.

During this period, the perception of professionals leaving India also underwent a dramatic change—transformed from 'brain drain' to 'brain gain'. The globalization of economic activity at the dawn of this century witnessed the emergence of overseas Indians as key players in transnational networks. Rapid developments in transportation, communication, information technology and the emergence of global supply chains spurred innovation and entrepreneurship in a 'virtual world'. In addition to being a valuable source of capital, technology, and innovation, the Indian Diaspora was also increasingly seen as building bridges for a two-way flow of science and technology between India and the host countries. The emergence of transnational networks of Indo-Americans, for instance, such as The Indus Entrepreneurs (TiE), a global network of entrepreneurs and professionals founded in Silicon Valley in 1992; the American Association of Physicians of Indian Origin (AAPI), an apex organization of doctors and the Pan IIT Alumni Association, to name a few, led to robust Indo-American Diaspora networks acting as bridges, enabling better understanding, leading investment and building transnational businesses. The widespread recognition of Indians as 'nerds' who not merely win at Spelling Bees or Math Olympiads but also make their presence felt in high-end scientific research has even entered the popular lexicon in the United States—comic books, television shows, and books—as well as made legends of several Indians outside India. Over the last decade, we are beginning to discern a pattern of movement of overseas Indian scientists, technologists, and entrepreneurs from various countries to India—reverse migration, in a sense—drawn by the opportunities in India. This has led to the emergence of the phenomenon of 'circular migration', representing a virtuous cycle of mobility of professionals enriching both the country of origin as well as the country of destination, strengthening business and entrepreneurial ties and drawing upon the best of both worlds to spur innovation and development.

The Virtuous Cycle of Migration

While there are already some active networks and mobility corridors, the challenge is to catalyse 'circular migration' in select sectors through policy interventions that create conditions to foster scientific research and drive innovation. The 'mobility of knowledge' has typically over time and geographies been characterized by three key ingredients:

- the pace and direction of migration is predicated upon the economywide demand for technology and innovation;
- this demand manifests itself through specific policies aimed at attracting talent in learning, research, and innovation and;
- economic expansion in the countries of origin combined with policies that open new opportunities for scientific work, and incentivize return.

India is on the threshold of becoming a formidable global economic power and the time is at hand to bring a strategic dimension to its engagement with the Indian knowledge community. It is important to take a medium- to long-term view and forge a partnership that will best serve India as a knowledge economy—to drive innovation and entrepreneurship. Equally, it must meet the aspirations of the overseas Indian community of academics, scientists, and technologists. The opportunity that India must now seize is to enable a mutually beneficial and symbiotic relationship—of bringing 'Indian S&T to the world' and 'the S&T world to India'. In the last two decades, several countries with significant overseas scientific communities have consciously adopted policies to attract the return of their expatriate 'knowledge workers'. These policies have met with considerable success in South Korea, China, and Taiwan. They centred on the notion of incentivizing return. A string of incentives were offered to attract academics, scientists, and engineers. Fostering transnational mobility is not really a matter of compensation or perquisites. It has everything to do with creating conditions for learning, discovering, and innovating; allowing independence of the scientific temper; building institutions that encourage innovation and promoting a market-friendly environment that rewards scientific discovery and innovation. In the countries that have consciously attempted to benefit from 'brain circulation', it is clear in hindsight, that more than the individual incentives, four factors contributed to significant return migration of high-skilled professionals:

- Conditions were ripe for entrepreneurship and innovative business models in response to consumer demand.
- Institutional partnerships enabled centres of higher education and excellence in destination countries to establish a campus presence in the country of origin.
- Funding by industry and angel investors catalysed programmes to link the expatriate scientific community with the scientific establishment in the home country on an institutional basis.
- Enhanced frequency and quality of the exchanges in potentially high-performance verticals within the national research system that reflected grand societal challenges.

It must also be recognized that for the return process to materialize and succeed over the long term, more than mere voluntary policies are required. The structural problems are many and any policy to attract return must be mainstreamed into the 'National Development' policy. This will require a policy framework that can reinforce the idea whose time has come—of making such mobility strategic, sustainable, and symbiotic.

The Virtues of Strategic Engagement

Taken together, the size and spread of the overseas Indian community is impressive—25 million across 189 countries—and widely recognized as the 'Knowledge Diaspora'. As migrants they have distinguished themselves as innovators, entrepreneurs, and thought leaders. Their 'virtual presence' across sectors and in most parts of the globe thus makes them a strategic resource. India would do well to bring a strategic dimension to engaging its overseas community. As an important country of origin and an emerging country of destination, India can and should by example influence the global discourse on migration. The focus must be on establishing a framework for sustainable engagement to lead the knowledge, expertise, skills, and resources of the vast and diverse overseas Indian scientific community into home country development efforts. Such a framework must pull in the Diaspora as 'knowledge' partners, the institutions in India as 'stakeholder' partners, and the governments at the Centre and in the states as 'facilitators'. The key objective of this exchange must be to catalyse overseas Indian entrepreneurship and innovation across sectors and geographies in India. Equally, it must enable overseas Indians to benefit from the growing research and development opportunities in India. In articulating this medium- to long-term strategy, the various stakeholders who will impact the sustainability of this partnership and who potentially can influence policy choices as well as the outcomes need to be recognized and incorporated in the endeavour.

From a strategy perspective the stakeholder analysis and their ability and willingness to influence outcomes is set out below. When the potential stakeholders are assessed on an ability–willingness engagement matrix, they would get distributed in four quartiles. An ABC analysis would suggest that we engage first with those in the first quartile A, who are high on ability and high on willingness (professional groups such as, for instance, AAPI and TiE, academics, scientists, and technologists). We must establish a robust partner institution programme that will constitute the platform for engagement. The second target group would be those in quartile B, who are high on ability but low on willingness. This group (including potential investors in S&T, philanthropists) needs to be incentivized to engage with India. This incentivization must be by creating transparent institutional support and demonstrated good practices. Those in the third quartile C are high on willingness but low on ability. There is need to facilitate their engagement. This will require developing creative programmes and products that can be offered to them, including through the principle of mutualization. There are many challenges, however, that face such an effort to build strong partnerships in science and technology between the home country scientific community and its diaspora counterparts. Globalization is changing the way science is pursued and in the systems by which scientific knowledge is produced. Scientific professions are increasingly coming out of the academic sphere to enter the field of business. Consequently, scientific creation (and the capacity for scientific creation) comes more and more out of the public sector and is considered a commercial weapon that should not be shared (Gaillard & Gaillard, 1997). The development of a strong national scientific community will be a precondition for creating an enabling environment. It will also be necessary to build a broad convergence of priorities between the national scientific community and the expatriates if the partnerships are to produce results that match the potential that these future partnerships might hold. After all there can be no compromise on the strategy to deal with the grand societal challenges (see Figure 16.2).

There is, however, no great Indian Diaspora. In fact there are communities within communities, each differentiated by time and distance and with distinct expectations from both the home and host countries. India's need, therefore, is to develop an inclusive agenda that will draw on this eclecticism, provide for the wide range of roles and expectations, and maximize the impact that these economic migrants can have on development. The opportunity that must be seized is to demonstrate a mutually beneficial and symbiotic relationship between migrants and their home and host societies. Consider just one but important aspect of the impact

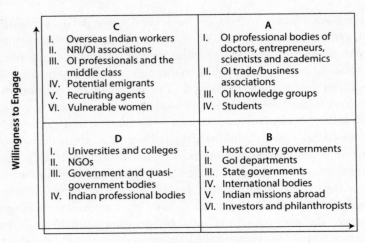

Figure 16.2   Stakeholder Engagement Grid
Source: Authors.

of migration—economic engagement—as a reasonable measure of the success or the lack of it, in the state's efforts. The measure of success would be the extent of overseas Indian investments that have flowed into India. Overseas Indians worldwide who are India's brand ambassadors are estimated to produce an economic output of about USD 400 billion and to generate an annual income equal to about 30 per cent of India's gross domestic product. From an economic perspective, though, it is clear that so far overseas Indians have been looking at India from a short-term horizon of three to five years. That is why while India is the highest recipient of remittances in the world—USD 70 billion in 2014—the share of overseas Indians in foreign direct investment has been far short of its potential. The bulk of the overseas Indians' resources are in bank deposits. The challenge therefore is to transform migrants from being mere savers to investors, and on a longer-term basis. This will be a function of several factors, not least the governance standards and the investment policy regime but, perhaps from a strategy perspective, the degree of convergence that the government's efforts have at an economy-wide level.

We asked the question what can be strategic about India's engagement with its Diaspora. To our mind, the strategic dimensions of engagement that need to be recognized include: the size, spread, and the growing influence of the overseas Indian community; the steady emergence of India as growing power seeking its legitimate place at the global high table; the fact that for the youngest country that she will be, the economy will not be able to generate enough jobs and hence overseas employment should constitute a real option; global demographics and ageing societies in several parts of the world resulting in structural shortages in the international labour market; and the humungous need for energy, natural resources and food security that India will have to ensure. The strategic role that the Indian Diaspora can play in all of these dimensions cannot be overstated.

A moot question is whether the current policy framework has enabled India through its institutional structure, its programme content, its outreach capabilities and intra-government consultation processes to establish its engagement in international migration on a robust path of convergence on a government–communitywide basis? Figure 16.3 sets out the operational environment that needs to be considered to achieve its mandate from a strategic perspective.

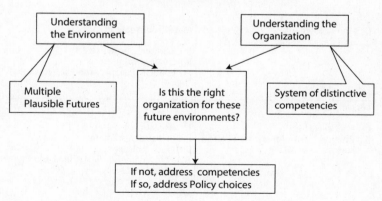

Figure 16.3 Purpose of Strategy
Source: Authors.

In the sections that follow, we will deal with the key elements of strategy.

The Need for Policy Coherence

The mainstreaming of migration policy across government will be central to achieving strategic outcomes in an increasingly globalizing world. The interests of diverse stakeholders and those of countries of origin as also countries of destination, hitherto seen as adversarial, centre on the question 'How can we maximize the development impact of migration for all?' India was one the early pioneers to attempt devoting mainstream attention to its overseas community. In 2004, it was among the first countries to establish a separate ministry of overseas Indian affairs and remains one of only about a dozen countries in the world to do so. However, while this has helped strengthen the economic, social, and cultural bonds between India and its overseas community, it is yet to reap its full benefits. Equally, while the problems and concerns of overseas Indians are now beginning to be addressed, considerable work remains to be done. Simply put, engaging the Global Indian is yet a work in progress and there are a slew of challenges that need to be addressed. The changing dynamics influenced by external factors as well as by structural and political economy factors 'in-country' are depicted in Figure 16.4 on a predictability–importance scale. India will

I. Unemployment II. Skill development	***More Predictable*** I. Economic growth (GDP) II. Demography III. Political (Europe, America & Australia)	
Less Important	***More Important***	
I. Political (Africa) II. Political (South America & Ex-USSR states)	I. Recession II. Investment climate III. Trade policies IV. Political (Middle East, China and South-East Asia) ***Less Predictable***	

Figure 16.4   Scenario Structuring Matrix
Source: Authors.

Four Likely Scenarios (five-year time frame)

Scenario 1 (Indian Eagle)	Highly Globalized, Non-recessionary, and Non-protectionist
Scenario 2 (Pigeon)	Highly Globalized, Non-recessionary but Protectionist
Scenario 3 (Peacock)	Globalized, Recessionary but Non-protectionist
Scenario 4 (Woodpecker)	Globalized, Recessionary, and Protectionist

Figure 16.5 Four Likely Scenarios
Source: Authors.

have to build on those elements of the operational environment as are reasonably predictable and seek to mitigate those that are uncertain. This will significantly enhance the capacity to prioritize from amongst competing demands, ensure optimal allocation of resources, and work a positive sum game where the outcomes achieved would be significantly higher than the sum of the parts.

It can also ensure optimal results in the design quality of the policy regime as well as the programmatic interventions that the country can provide. We have postulated four possible scenarios that could emerge over the next five years. This provides an analytical framework for India to fine-tune the elements of its strategy as well as its operational priorities suitably. We suggest four broad scenarios as given in Figure 16.5. The government in pursuit of its strategic objectives can develop many more.

The Four Fundamentals

I. Fostering Circular Migration

It is inconceivable and, indeed, counter-intuitive to want or to expect overseas Indians to relocate to India to engage in her development process. While the overseas Indian community can serve as an important 'bridge' to access knowledge, expertise, resources, and markets to give impetus to India's socio-economic development effort, the success of this bridge is predicated upon the capacity of the home country to establish conditions and identify institutions for application of this knowledge in spheres germane to development imperatives. Institutions in the public, private, and non-government sectors at the national and subnational levels must drive the demand for, and provide opportunities to, professionals—individuals and organizations—amongst overseas Indians to engage as partners in development projects in chosen sectors/fields. Professionals with the desire, ability and willingness to dedicate time, knowledge and effort to partner in the development of, or assist in, projects in India must be invited to register as members of a 'social entrepreneurs network'. The focus of the mobility strategy and the knowledge transfer programme must be on generating applications, products, and services to address 'Grand Societal Challenges', with the objective of catalysing social sector development and innovation (ideas to market), thus enabling India's rural/urban middle class youth to become science entrepreneurs as opposed to job-seekers. Sectors that need innovation and technological interventions to improve service delivery, can benefit from community capacity-building through training and visits, and attain critical mass in measurable outcomes, should be the priority. These could include:

- higher/technical/vocational education
- energy, including non-conventional sources
- information, communication and transportation, including rural roads
- youth development, including skills upgrading
- community health, including rural health care delivery
- school education, including standardized testing

II. Nurturing Soft Power: Overseas Indians as a Strategic Resource

In a rapidly globalizing world the diasporic community is both the result as well as the driver of globalization. The Indian diaspora is characterized by distinct communities across the globe whose uniqueness has been determined by the circumstances of their migration. Thus we have the 'old diaspora' represented by people of Indian origin who are the descendants of those who migrated in the nineteenth century as part of the indentured/Kangani system of labour. This community has overcome considerable adversity and today represents the triumph over tribulation. Several of the representatives of this community now occupy a leadership position in many walks of life and exercise considerable influence on the 'political economy' as also the development of their host countries. We count among them several heads of state as well as of government. This old diaspora therefore constitutes a significant strategic resource. Equally, we have a large 'new diaspora' that is essentially a twentieth-century phenomenon wherein workers—blue, grey, and white—as well as professionals went in search of opportunities to the western world. Today, the Indo-American, Indo-Canadian, Indo-British, and Indo-Australian communities represent remarkable and pioneering success in the knowledge-based sectors as scientists, technologists, academics, and entrepreneurs. They have begun exercising in recent years visible political influence and shaping policies that might impact India. The role of the Indo-American community in the conclusion of the Indo-US civil nuclear deal is an important example of diaspora advocacy. There are many of Indian origin who are serving in the higher echelons of government in these countries and can, if engaged sagaciously, provide India a relative competitive advantage. India must, therefore, position the overseas Indian community and support it as a strategic reserve to be leveraged over the medium- to long-term primarily for advocacy of India's interest on the global stage. Whether it is India's position on climate change, economic development, the new and emerging global financial architecture or, indeed political issues such as its bid for a permanent seat at the United Nation Security Council (UNSC), India would be well advised to engage eminent overseas Indians who represent civil society. As India takes its place at the global high table, overseas Indians, individually and collectively must be mobilized on issues that are of global significance to India and in forums where her voice needs to be heard.

III. Positioning India as a Preferred Country of Origin

India is a major player in international migration. As a major country of origin, transit, and destination, India has a strategic interest in how international migration policy is articulated. While from a policy perspective to migrate or not to migrate is an individual choice exercised by a free citizen, India certainly can benefit from a robust, transparent, and orderly migration management framework. To transform the migration of Indians for overseas employment as a demand-driven process and to position India over the next few decades as a reliable country of origin to source skilled and trained workers and professionals, it is imperative that it puts in place a modern legislative framework for migration. Modernizing the migration regulatory regime should really mean re-engineering the role of the state. The state must focus on strategic interventions—bilateral and multilateral engagement—and policy formulation, leaving regulation in the responsible hands of an independent market regulator and providing services to the private sector. Central to the robustness of such a migration law will be substantive provisions to counter irregular migrations and people-smuggling for these can, if unchecked, become the scourge of mobility in the future. To support the operational requirements of a modern migration management framework, India as a major information technology power must implement electronic governance of emigration that will help build an electronic database on the flow as well as stock of Indian migrants abroad and enable all stakeholders in the migratory process to manage their roles and responsibilities in an efficient and transparent manner.

The key challenge that India needs to address is to see how the much-talked-about demographic dividend potential can be transformed into real job opportunities for Indians abroad. The mismatch in the demand for and supply of workers in most countries with serious demographic deficits, will be structural and not cyclical. Most ageing economies will, therefore, have to source foreign workers. If India is to benefit from this opportunity it must focus on building a large workforce that can meet international skills standards. This will require significant domestic, bilateral, and multilateral interventions over the short to medium term. Central, however, to position India as a preferred country of origin to source human resources will be her ability to build a strong cadre of skilled, trained human resources. In achieving this objective India's focus should be threefold:

- developing standard curricula on a par with international standards;
- introducing standardized testing of skill levels; and
- independent third-party certification of skills.

India must pursue an action plan that will entail identification of select sectors and select skill sets in which she has competitive advantages and implement a 'skills for employment abroad' programme over the next five to ten years. The second element of the strategy should be to identify the select destination countries where, on a demand-driven basis, India can then match the skill sets required over the medium to long term. To illustrate, focus should be on the health care sector to produce the best paramedics and nurses, the hospitality sector to produce the best chefs and front-office staff, the automotive sector to produce the best mechanics and tool and dye makers and the construction sector to produce the best carpenters, electricians, masons, and steel scaffolding workers.

IV. Establishing Strategic Economic Depth in New Destination Countries

India is an emerging economic power and will also in the foreseeable future be the youngest country in the world. This will potentially give it great appetite for savings and investments. But it will also mean that, as a nation, it will have a humungous appetite and demand for energy (oil, gas, and nuclear power), food, natural resources, and jobs. Opening up its economy to the world, integrating with the global economy, and facilitating greater mobility of the best talent from and to the country will best serve its long-term interests. Greater mobility of skilled and trained people across a wide gamut of sectors and geographies will also enable it to build strategic economic partnerships with countries that are resource rich and relatively underdeveloped. The African continent beckons in this regard. India's economic migration priorities must subsume the need to diversify her destination base—going beyond the traditional countries in the

Middle East, Southeast Asia and the western world—and include select countries in Africa, the Caribbean, and Latin America. Gaining strategic economic depth will also imply that there has to be a change in the patterns of 'out-migration'—going beyond blue-collar, grey-collar and white-collar workers—to include the migration of farmers, small and medium entrepreneurs, and service providers. Gaining the early mover advantage in focusing on agriculture, horticulture, mining, commodity trading, providing utility services and engaging in infrastructure sectors in these newer destinations will give India the strategic economic depth that it will need to develop its sphere of influence in the emerging global financial architecture. It will also be able to play a role in shaping the future economic progress of those countries too.

A strategic intervention capability to reach out to those in need, intervene with the host government or extend emergency relief as well as travel advisories on a real-time basis will be critical if India is to extend its sphere of influence and shape the course of the international migration discourse and praxis. This will presuppose the development of an extensive, country-specific data base of Indians abroad through a registration process; designing outreach capabilities through the migrant networks; and developing policy customized to specific regions, countries, and categories of overseas Indians as might be appropriate. Developing user groups and common resource centres managed by the community but overseen by the government through its missions overseas would help build capacity for self-help, dissemination of information, and building the modus vivendi of intra-diaspora engagement. The focus should be on fostering institutions, support infrastructure and knowledge transfer mechanisms owned and managed by the community. Deploying technology platforms and enlisting the support of the local government will need to be factored in. The migration futures that are possible are myriad but all of them envisage a borderless world. While nation states will remain for some time yet and borders will be more difficult to cross, there is a certain inevitability to the process of free movement of people. It is not just an economic imperative, it is a historical process of movement towards a shared future. If India is to play its rightful role in the migration futures of the world it will do well to recall the perspicacious words of Jawaharlal Nehru, its first prime minister who at the stroke of midnight when India gained independence, speaking of India's tryst with destiny said and we quote:

> And so we have to labour and to work and work hard to give reality to our dreams. Those dreams are for India, but they are also for the world, for all the nations and peoples are too closely knit together today for anyone of them to imagine that it can live apart. Peace has been said to be indivisible; so is freedom, so is prosperity now and so also is disaster in this one world that can no longer be split in isolated fragments.

These words have greater resonance today than ever before.

17

The Way of the Future

Every day, I try to live by that cautious optimism. I hold on to a
degree of faith—faith that the nation's great self-confidence will prove
prophetic rather than merely boastful, that the tremendous wealth of
a few presages a prosperity of many, and that the great churning that
is modern India will eventually settle into some kind of equilibrium.

—Kapur (2012: 259)

Migration as More Than a Binary Function

India's migration praxis, it would appear, drifts between a present
that cannot continue and a future that is hard to achieve. Despite
its impressive strides as an important country of origin and destination, an astute observer would find it hard to shake off the feeling
of sliding back. It does seem like one step forward and two steps
back. The vast majority who emigrate are mostly poor and largely
unskilled, the numbers only greater; an assortment of intermediaries, not least the recruitment agents, still dominate the emigration
process and occupy much of the regulatory time and space; women
emigrant workers receive little policy or operational attention,
perhaps even less so in recent years; irregular migrants continue
to be deported with regularity, if anything in bigger numbers; bilateral engagement with countries of destination is undertaken with

hesitation and the multilateral, grudgingly at best; the problems of exploitation and abuse revisit migrants with regularity causing a never-ending sense of déjà vu. There is an elaborate regulatory apparatus that is engaged actively but what seems to be missing is a migration praxis framework that mobilizes all the relevant stakeholders in a coherent and coordinated manner that makes the effort efficient and purposeful. There is a sense of fatigue with the same old rituals of engagement—the restrictions on direct recruitment by foreign employers, licensing of recruiting agents, imposing a ceiling on the fee charged by recruiting agents, the ban on deployment to certain countries, prescribing minimum-age restrictions for women workers, the customary blacklisting of erring recruitment agents, the annual consultations with the Indian missions and the states, and the occasional policy pronouncement of yet another new initiative. There is only anecdotal evidence on the impact or the effectiveness of these regulatory measures. There is a widely shared yearning for something new though, relative to the immense opportunities, little seems to move. International migration is not a binary function between the government and the migrant, as it often tends to be viewed. It is a complex process in which several other stakeholders play important roles and need to be engaged. Migrant workers are especially susceptible to oppression arising from the intersection of various forms of subordination including class, ethnicity, low income, gender, non-citizen and undocumented (Lee and Piper, 2013). The main features of labour migration—temporary, intra-regional, predominantly low-skilled and low-wage, significant women migration and, the widespread presence of middlemen (Asis, 2006)—in Asia are relevant to the multiple identities of migrants and how their intersection exacerbates discrimination and inequality. The seamless dynamic between the countries of origin and destination arising from the temporary contractual nature of the mobility, the sponsorship-based visa regime, and the high incidence of mandatory return essentially means that in the Asian migration theatre subordination, discrimination, and exploitation overlap between the origin and destination countries and are intrinsically interlinked. For instance, in the case of women migrant workers, it is not the conditions in destination countries alone that influence the vulnerabilities of migrant domestic workers;

the lack of consciousness and knowledge of rights and entitlements developed in countries of origin also affect the way in which migrant women view their status (Mora and Piper, 2011). The one-dimensional view of migration in narrow economic terms—countries of origin counting the benefits from remittances and the countries of destination measuring the benefits of cheap temporary labour supply—has resulted in the other important dimensions of migration such as the demographic, social, and societal being overlooked and there is little effort to address the migration process on a medium- to long-term basis. The quest for state control of the migrants and the process of migration, even if the avowed objectives are the protection and welfare of migrant workers, has meant severe limitations on the rights of migrants thus undermining their access to opportunity and choice. The tunnel vision has also limited India's global view of migration and of the role that it can play on the world stage.

From Paternalism to Empowerment

It is clear as day that India, though important in the global governance of migration, is currently operating far short of its potential. It is also our assessment that India's global engagement on migration is sub-optimal and hence falls well short of meeting its strategic goals in the global political economy of migration. Several bottlenecks—a policy vacuum that does not articulate clear goals despite the ubiquitous presence of government; fragmentation of the migration function into silos for immigration, emigration, and consular services, making strategic interventions difficult; absence of coherence, both vertical and horizontal, precluding coordinated planning; inadequate institutional infrastructure limiting the ability to reach and mobilize other stakeholders; an obdurate and entrenched network of intermediaries pre-empting much-needed reforms; little imaginative commitment rendering it a low political priority; and bureaucratic inertia—taken together have severely constrained new directions for policy and practice. The principal challenge is to recognize that paternalist approaches to the protection and welfare of migrant workers, in essence, creates in them a path of dependency that straddles both ends of the migration pathway; disentitles them from taking responsibility for their own rights, and deprives them of the freedom to exercise choice. In essence, paternalism deprives them of autonomy thus making them more vulnerable to being controlled by a host of intermediaries. The consequences of depriving migrants of autonomy typically includes low self-esteem, loss of motivation, lack of effort and, adverse effects on work, health, and social interaction. Paternalist approaches to the protection of migrants often neglects the costs of reducing them to helpless victims as a result (Lee and Piper, 2013). There is an urgent need to place the migrant at the heart of the migration process and bring together the different strands of international migration policies and practices extant, weaving them into a progressive, inclusive, and seamless narrative through which the whole can be more than the sum of its parts. The sheer weight of numbers, the complexity of the composition and the multidirectional patterns of the flows has meant that the regulatory apparatus in the countries of origin and destination alike have been overwhelmed. Its place has been usurped by the migration industry, regulated yet unregulated, that has taken over the intermediation process by which the migrant is disempowered.

What might be the basis of a new framework? The experience of the past has shown that the state must take a pragmatic turn and move away from exit controls as the basis for improving the protection and welfare of migrants. In their place the basis must be: empowerment of the migrant. Such empowerment must achieve fuller and informed mobilization of the migrants themselves in the process to enable them to understand the migration process better, engage in the free market equitably, and mitigate the risks encountered along the way. This turn towards empowerment of migrants as the organizing principle for migration praxis is premised on the idea that a migrant must have the information and knowledge, the required skill sets and the freedom to make her own choices rather than being patronized, either by government(s) or by the recruitment industry. The practical case for the gains from empowerment is a compelling one. It entails three significant shifts: first, adopting a 'life-cycle' approach to risk-mitigation covering the four phases of pre-recruitment, recruitment and exit, living and working abroad, and return and resettlement; second, enhancing the returns to the migrants in their living and working conditions and; third, enhancing their access to education, health, safety, social security, and to a life of dignity. This will entail mobilizing the principal non-state actors including the civil society organizations, non-government organizations, advocacy groups and the private sector, as well as restructuring the institutional apparatus of the state.

Migration Praxis: Bridging the Distance between Policy and Action

International migration is essentially a self-selection process. Generally, who migrates and who does not is determined by the income, skill, and education levels of the population. It is ability more than willingness that is the differentiator between those who migrate and those who do not. The emigration pattern from India to the Gulf is not necessarily a self-selection process. In fact, the vast majority of those who migrate are poorer, less-educated, and largely unskilled. This adverse selection process is given impetus to by intermediaries who scout for possible recruits. The process is increasingly influenced by migrant networks that span the countries of origin and destination. Policy emphasis, therefore, has been primarily on the protection of migrants from exploitation. The consequence in the Asian migration context has been the excessive focus, often to the complete exclusion of other approaches, on the legal framework and the regulatory regime. Even a lay but intelligent observer would not miss the obvious. The first gaping hole, ex ante, is really in matching the normative postulates enshrined in the laws and the policy with action on ground. Observing the migration process as it occurs, listening to grievances and demands from the ground and understanding the presence or absence of different actors in the migration theatre do provide valuable insights for empowerment of migrant workers. It also enables state and non-state actors to situate the injustices that surround migrant workers in the context of the multiple axes of the economic, social, geographic, and cultural inequality that typifies the migrant. This would also serve to assess on a real-time basis, how far removed from reality the policy frame is from the felt needs of the migrants.

But the compelling imperative is to achieve the actual from the potential, translate policy into action; and convert potential energy into kinetic energy by mobilizing the government, civil society, the non-government sector and the private stakeholders towards the same goal. An important pre-requisite is to understand the gaps that exist between current migration praxis and the objective conditions that the migrants face on ground. To get a sense of these gaps we carried out a pan-Indian survey of 1,000 intending migrants who prior to their exit were on the verge of applying for and obtaining emigration clearance from eight offices of the protectors of emigrants located at cities in eight major states of origin in India. The intending migrants were administered a simple questionnaire on the emigration process. The survey was carried out at eight offices— Delhi, Mumbai, Chennai, Thiruvananthapuram, Kochi, Hyderabad, Chandigarh, and Kolkota—of the Protectors of Emigrants during May–June 2013. The data throws up interesting information on the migration process at the point of origin.

Profile of the Migrants Seeking Emigration Clearance

Let us begin with who these potential migrants were and where they came from. About 75 per cent of those surveyed at the pre-departure stage came from six states—Punjab, Kerala, Tamil Nadu, Uttar Pradesh, Andhra Pradesh, and Maharashtra. This broadly corresponds with the macro-level data for the ten-year period 2003–12 in which except Maharashtra which is at the eighth position and Punjab at the seventh position the other states are the top four states of origin. Interestingly, the states of Andhra Pradesh, Tamil Nadu, Kerala, and Punjab also figured as the top four states for irregular migrants surveyed in the UAE during the amnesty and analysed in an earlier chapter (see Figure 17.1).

The social groups that the migrants surveyed belonged to are depicted in Figure 17.2.

Contrary to popular perception that the vast majority of migrants are socially underprivileged, nearly two-thirds of the sample of intending migrants surveyed belonged to the general category of castes, though nearly half of them were Muslims and hence would be counted as minorities.

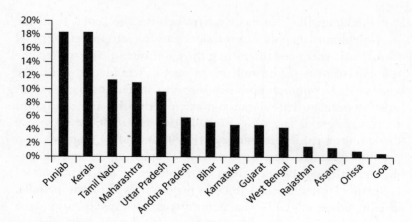

Figure 17.1   States of Origin of the Migrants Surveyed at the Time of
Emigration Clearance
Source: Authors' construction of the data from the survey: Protector General of
Emigrants, 2013.

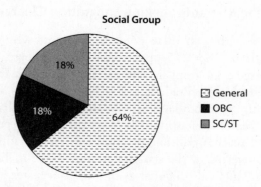

Figure 17.2   Social Grouping of the Intending Migrants
Source: Authors' construction of the data from the survey: Protector General of
Emigrants, 2013.

In terms of skill levels, the respondents, as expected, were predominantly unskilled (see Figure 17.3).

Nearly 60 per cent of the potential migrants were unskilled and
a mere 25 per cent were skilled workers or professionals, slightly

Category of Workers

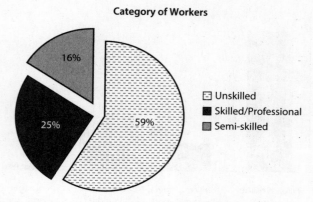

- ⊡ Unskilled
- ■ Skilled/Professional
- ▨ Semi-skilled

Figure 17.3   Workers Surveyed Categorized on the Basis of Skills
Source: Authors' construction of the data from the survey: Protector General of
Emigrants, 2013.

higher than the 14 per cent with more than higher secondary education found amongst irregular migrants surveyed in the destination
country and analysed in the previous chapter. The high proportion of
unskilled workers at about 60 per cent matches the macro-level data
of emigration for the ten-year period 2003–12.

On the question of what the motivation was for migration, an
overwhelming majority—70 per cent—of the intending migrants
chose to migrate because of the expectation of higher wages. This
points to the fact that amongst the poor, uneducated, and unskilled
youth in rural India, the hinterland for large scale migration—
internal and international—there is a widely held perception of the
destination countries in the GCC region as high-wage economies
for foreign workers. This perception has gained ground from the
dreams that middlemen sell about the Gulf, on the one hand, and
the outward symbols of prosperity that the 'Gulf returnees' publicly
display, though the hard life they encounter and the privations that
they suffer are hidden and seldom spoken about. This perception
of the Gulf as the 'El Dorado' is at once a reflection of the fact that
the defining feature of the Indian emigrant to the Gulf is that she
is very poor, often with no work and hence no wage at all. This
latter fact fuels much of the migration circuit driven by unscrupulous intermediaries who offer attractive terms and conditions to

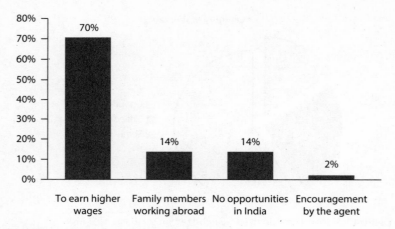

Figure 17.4   Reasons Why They Choose to Migrate
Source: Authors' construction of the data from the survey: Protector General of Emigrants, 2013.

entice workers. The wages offered by the recruiting agents are not necessarily honoured by the employers, who often renege on the contract terms after the migrant workers arrive. Contract substitution is common. The facts on ground in the destination countries are far from flattering. The average wages for different occupations indicated in the model contracts filed by recruiting agents with the protectors of emigrants are modest (see Figure 17.4).

In fact, in most occupations the wages are similar to what obtains in India. The only silver lining is perhaps that the employer provides for food and housing and thus a substantial part of the wage of the migrant worker constitutes savings that can be remitted back home (see Table 17.1).

The moderate wages in two of the biggest and rather prosperous state in the GCC across occupation types however points to a deeper malaise borne out of the political economy of migration in Asia—poor contract enforcement. In a migration industry in which recruiting agents dominate the process, and third-party recruitment is the norm, they also emerge as the most powerful lobby. They exercise undue influence on the decision-making process ensuring that regulation and enforcement remains light-handed and uneven. Over time they have manipulated the system to ensure that this becomes

Table 17.1 Average Wage for Different Occupations in the UAE and Saudi Arabia, 2010 and 2011

Occupation	The UAE		Kingdom of Saudi Arabia	
	Average Wage (INR)	Average Wage (INR)	Average Wage (INR)	Average Wage (INR)
	2010	2011	2010	2011
Electrician	9,900	9,600	7,000	6,400
Mason	6,200	5,500	6,100	5,000
Plumber	9,000	8,700	7,100	5,500
Seaman	12,000	13,000	14,000	9,000
Tailor	5,400	5,000	5,500	5,300
Painter	7,200	6,800	5,300	4,300
Carpenter	5,100	5,000	5,700	5,200
Labour	4,200	4,100	3,800	3,700
Cleaner	4,200	4,000	3,800	3,900
Housemaid	6,200	7,000	6,800	7,000
Domestic Driver	4,800	4,400	6,300	6,500
Other Unskilled	5,600	5,500	4,400	5,200

Source: Authors' calculations based on data from the Protector General of Emigrants, Government of India, 2013.

the inbuilt bias that everybody knows of yet turn a blind eye to. In sum, the regulatory system has abdicated its primary responsibility.

The potential migrants were asked what the principal source of their information on migration was. Again, about 70 per cent of the respondents said that they got the first information about emigration and related matters from friends and relatives or recruiting agents. The fact that less than one per cent of the potential migrants relied on government advertisements was an eye-opener. What is even more disturbing is the fact that a mere 20 per cent of the respondents got their information from the protectors of emigrants or the migrant resource centres (see Figure 17.5).

It seems clear that the agency of government despite its ubiquitous presence, being directly engaged in the emigration process, and positioned as the only service provider for emigration clearance does not enjoy credibility in information dissemination.

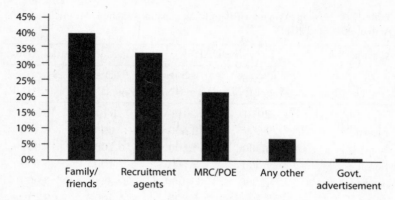

Figure 17.5   Principal Sources of Information to Potential Migrants
Source: Authors' construction of the data from the survey: Protector General of Emigrants, 2013.

That space has been captured by migrant networks and dubious recruiting agents. This creates severe asymmetries in the emigration process since the migrants are exposed to the risk of acting on less than credible information—indeed, more likely than not, on information that is not just wrong but deceitful. It can be the first wrong step for the migrant in a long journey of exploitation and injustice.

When asked what the most difficult aspect of emigration was for an intending migrant, more than half the respondents—54 per cent—identified accessing correct information as the most difficult. Ironically, it is in this area that the absence of the government is most felt. It is a reflection of our policy priorities that considerable resources are spent on the functions that rank much lower in the felt needs of migrants—emigration clearance, passport issues, reviewing model work contracts—but little attention is paid, if at all, to information and awareness. The critical path for an orderly and fair emigration process is the 'first mile connectivity'. It is the first effort of the poor, country-based, unskilled worker to seek information on migration that is crucial to the success of the emigrant as well as of the process as equitable engagement for one who is at the centre and around whom the other service providers revolve. The first Golden Mile, if you will, can make or mar the process. It is along this critical

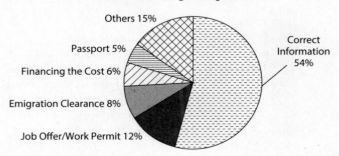

Figure 17.6   What Intending Migrants Find to Be the Most Difficult Aspect of Migration
Source: Authors' construction of the data from the survey: Protector General of Emigrants, 2013.

path that credible government intervention can dramatically change outcomes (see Figure 17.6).

In many ways, the first seemingly authentic and credible voice that an intending migrant listens to also becomes the voice that he turns to for assistance. If this happens to be an intermediary, whether from migrant networks or from amongst the many middlemen in the migration industry, the marginalization of the regulatory process becomes complete. Here on it becomes well-nigh impossible to ascertain whether the normative standards are being met and regulatory compliance ensured.

On the question of whose assistance they sought during the emigration process our survey results throw up startling facts: An overwhelming 89 per cent of the intending migrants sought the assistance of either family/friends (47 per cent) or the help of recruiting agents in India (42 per cent) (see Figure 17.7).

The complete absence of the government or its agencies in this process is testimony to the fact that governments—national, provincial, and local—have ceded ground to an intermediation process, led by an assortment of middlemen. These include a disparate group of ill-informed, poorly trained, unscrupulous travel agents, education enrollers, recruiting agents, immigration consultants, sub-agents, tour guides, and unemployed migrants. It matters little whether they

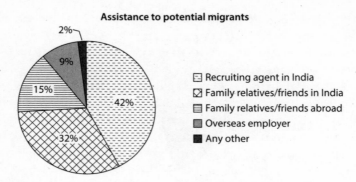

Figure 17.7   Assistance to the Migrant through the Emigration Process
Source: Authors' construction of the data from the survey: Protector General of
Emigrants, 2013.

are registered or not. They all provide much-needed assistance, have
occupied the space vacated by the government service providers and
are able to do so because the regulators have abdicated their responsibilities. Thus regulatory capture is near-complete. In the survey we
did ask the intending migrants what help they needed from the government. The responses in our view struck at the heart of the Asian
migration malaise. Two key areas dominated: contract enforcement
and migration financing (see Figure 17.8).

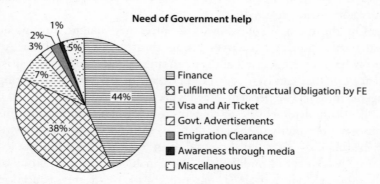

Figure 17.8   Areas Where Government Help Is Needed
Source: Authors' construction of the data from the survey: Protector General of
Emigrants, 2013.

The responses were perspicacious and in our view reflected two of the root causes for the exploitation and abuse of migrant workers that is so widespread in the Asian migration theatre. The importance of these two issues arises from the fact that migrant workers have separated the grain from the chaff and zeroed in on one issue each in the countries of origin and the countries of destination that form the basis for the discrimination and injustice that they face routinely in the emigration process. It also reflects the experiential learning of the migrants that these are two domains in which government and only government can intercede on their behalf effectively. A significant 44 per cent felt that government must help them with the financing of the migration process. Put in perspective, this is a desperate plea of the migrant workers to help them counter the usurious fees charged by a chain of intermediaries which, when added up, works out to a tidy sum. It is commonplace for intending migrants to borrow money or sell property to finance the costs of migration. These costs are far from transparent and are significantly higher than the tariffs for the work permit, passport, visa, and travel services that the migrants need. The high costs of migration as a consequence result in debt bondage of migrant workers. Equally significant is that 38 per cent of the respondents wanted government to help ensure that the foreign employer fulfils his contractual obligations. Again, to put it in perspective, ensuring a fair contract and ensuring the terms and conditions are fulfilled is perhaps one of the most vexatious issues in the emigration process in Asia. These in our view are the central questions that migration praxis must grapple with if migration is to be transformed into an efficient and equitable process for the millions of people on the move in the Asian migration circuit which accounts for nearly half of global migration.

The Sunny Side of the Story so Far

Prior to the oil boom in the Middle Eastern kingdoms most of South Asia, including India, had rudimentary emigration policies and practices. The principal mode of recruitment was direct recruitment by employers. The last quarter of the twentieth century witnessed a surge in demand for foreign workers resulting in the economy-wide commercialization of migration services—recruitment, skills training, logistics, money transfer, and passport and visa services. With the large-scale movement initially of skilled workers in the oil industry and later semi-skilled and unskilled workers in the construction sector and other services, the number of complaints and grievances of exploitation and cheating grew. This compelled governments to enact new laws to regulate emigration and expand their migration management institutions to establish and enforce standards. This migration infrastructure was not just top-heavy but relied almost entirely on state controls. It created an elaborate panoply of rules and regulations based on licensing and protectionism aimed at preventing fraud in recruitment and securing the protection of the worker. Recruitment was sought to be regulated by restricting direct hiring by foreign employers; licensing of recruiting agents, and prior approval of job offers. Similarly, work contracts were sought to be regulated by prescribing standard terms and conditions; screening of foreign employers, and prescribing minimum age, especially for women migrant workers. Despite all these measures, there is little evidence of success and the problems remain ubiquitous in the region. Regulations that establish normative standards remain dead letters unless energized into coming alive through effective enforcement. This should not be understood to mean that there have not been initiatives for better governance that have not been successful. There are, in fact, some programmes that have indeed advanced the welfare of migrant workers. Two of these deserve mention: first, the Indian Community Welfare Fund established in the Indian missions in countries with a significant Indian population. Funded from fees collected from consular services and with some budgetary support, the fund provides, on a means-tested basis, welfare services, including boarding, lodging, medical aid and other support services to Indian migrants in distress overseas. Since the fund operates in the country of destination and provides welfare support 'in situ', it has proved effective and useful. Second, in Abu Dhabi, an electronic work contract attestation process has been implemented with the participation of the governments of both countries. This has been piloted successfully and has established a robust protocol for ensuring authenticity and better enforcement of work contracts. However, these success stories are exceptions. Bringing rule-based standards to bear on the entire migration cycle and empowering the migrants in both the country of origin as well as destination must become the touchstone for India's migration praxis.

Back to the Future: First Principles for Migration Governance

It is axiomatic that protectionism is bad for any economy at any time. This is as true for migration. A good start is to recognize that in a country of origin, whether India or the rest of South Asia, supply far outstrips demand for cheap labour, and migrant workers are willing to pay what the market will bear. Most payments are informal and leave no paper trail. Despite the legal bar, the recruitment system in India relies on a widely dispersed informal network of unregistered subagents who scout for migrant recruits in far-flung rural areas. This makes regulation through licensing controls rather difficult. The policy of not allowing direct hiring by foreign employers without prior approval and the restrictions on the participation of foreign-owned recruiting agencies has resulted in the formation of a cartel by local recruiting agents. There is no evidence to suggest that direct participation by foreign employers or foreign-owned recruiters would in anyway harm the interests of migrant workers aspiring to go overseas for employment. These protectionist measures raise migration costs besides encouraging rent-seeking; expose the migrant worker to enhanced risk of non-compliance by the employer owing to 'third party' recruitment, and leave the migrant workers with no choice. The verification of the contract terms and conditions by the protectors of emigrants is the basis for exit control. This verification is cursory at best. Consider these facts: The annual average of emigration clearances given by the seven protectors of emigrants during the five-year period 2008–12 is 700,000. This means a humungous 100,000 verifications done by each protector in a year comprising approximately 240 workdays. After providing time for other functions, on average the protector would likely spend a miserly five minutes for each clearance in which he ascertains the authenticity of the offer, the credibility of the employer, and whether the terms and conditions adhere to the normative standards prescribed. Clearly, this cannot constitute good-practice regulation of recruitment. The first major policy change, then, should be to allow direct hiring by overseas employers and to remove restrictions on foreign-owned recruitment agencies on operating in India.

Second, India should move away from the narrow objective of 'protection' of emigrants to the broader rationale of liberalizing the mobility of economic migrants. The Emigration Act 1983 which forms the legislative framework for migration is based on the principle of exit control of specified categories of citizens. It provides for protection by exception to only those with poor educational qualifications or to those going to destination countries with relatively weak labour laws and inadequate legal redress for workers. These are also countries whose record on upholding human rights leaves much to be desired. This protection by exception is exercised through a dual system of passports introduced by administrative instructions rather than by legislation and has been in practice for several decades. All passports are classified, at the time of issue, into two categories determining exit control: those in respect of which prior 'Emigration Clearance is Required' (ECR) before travel overseas and those for whom 'Emigration Clearance Not Required' (ECNR). Designed as a means of safeguarding the emigrant workers who are generally issued ECR passports, in reality this distinction has not served the cause of their better protection. Worse still, it has created an underclass—of the poor, uneducated, and largely rural citizens—that in a highly stratified and segregated society like India has been stigmatized. The fact that an Indian is an ECR passport holder immediately places her at a disadvantage in the migration process. It drives up transaction costs and makes her a victim of the protection system in which she ends up paying significantly higher sums that the ECNR passport holder is not subjected to. India must, therefore, move towards a system of a single class of passport for all citizens irrespective of their educational attributes or intended emigration destinations. This will be a far-reaching reform that will, over time, enable citizens to take responsibility for their own decisions on international migration.

The logical third step would be to abolish the ECR system for the migrant worker. No citizen who is in possession of valid travel documents should require prior approval to travel overseas legally (Kumar and Rajan, 2014). The system of placing certain countries that do not conform to international standards in non-discrimination and equal treatment; have poor labour laws; less than credible justice systems; substandard living and working conditions for foreign workers and a poor track record on upholding human rights in a negative list for purposes of more rigorous oversight and enforcement in the emigration process should continue. The regulatory oversight on the emigration of Indian citizens, especially the low-skilled migrants to the countries in such a negative list; the enforcement of the normative standards enshrined in the migration regulation—of ethical recruitment, fair employment, and acceptable working and living conditions—on the foreign employers and foreign recruiters as also local recruiting agents from these countries must be made more rigorous. This will shift the burden of regulatory compliance and meeting the migration process standards to the recruitment industry.

Finally, the regulatory framework extant should be replaced with a governance framework that will be based on three fundamental institutions: First, the time is at hand to establish an independent regulator for international migration in India. The presence of multiple service-providers in the migration process and the conflicts of interest between the various stakeholders suggests that an impartial and independent regulator can be the prime institutional intervention to ensure that normative standards are met by all. The independent regulator can help a nascent 'migration industry' transform into a robust overseas employment services sector. Second, there is a need to establish a standard-setting body of which the foreign employers and foreign and local recruiters will be members. The charter of the body will be to develop and enforce adherence to standards amongst its members. This body will be akin to professional bodies like the Institute of Chartered Accountants or the Institute of Cost Accountants and such like. Third, the offices of the protectors of emigrants must be converted into 'migrant resource centres' tasked with information dissemination, creating awareness on migration matters, providing counselling and advisory services, providing pre-departure orientation and imparting skills training, and undertaking advocacy on behalf of the migrants with the regulator.

These essential reforms will require determination and development of human resource capacities. They will also require redesigning the migration governance architecture and mobilization of a remarkable reservoir of human resources that are today dormant, but if deployed can dramatically enhance outreach and penetration capabilities for both policy as well as real-time interventions on the ground in times of need. Currently, two of the most important stakeholders who are proximate both to the migrants as well as the migration process as it unfolds on the ground, are on the margins. The provincial governments and the local self-governments are mere spectators because they have not been given a formal role in migration management by the government at the centre. The third tier of governance in India comprises the village panchayats or the village councils in which the elders of the village as elected representatives of the community in the local self-government exercise considerable influence. They have the powers of moral suasion and considerable authority and can therefore be a powerful bulwark against many of the ills of the system, including recruitment fraud and duplicity as well as in mitigating the problem of irregular migration. They can also be opinion leaders in shaping the impressionable minds of young first-time migrants. These panchayats with remarkable presence even in remote rural India can play an important role in information dissemination and raising awareness. Besides being the eyes and ears of policymakers and law-enforcement agencies, they can serve as the frontier posts and provide the first mile connectivity. In terms of how this can be brought about there are many options. One institutional network that people in rural India are familiar and comfortable with and has deep penetration is India Post—a trusted national institution. Part of its mandate is to serve as the interface between the citizen and the government. The Indian postal network can be marshalled to provide information, pedagogic tools, and support services to the panchayats and the local communities.

The state governments too have a major role to play. They can undertake the task of capacity building, providing the infrastructure for the migrant resource centres and partnering with the private sector and the non-government sector to undertake pre-departure orientation and skills training programmes. They will also be the bridge between the government of India and the non-government agencies and civil society organizations. Finally, empowerment of the migrant cannot be achieved unless the community that he belongs to is empowered. Hence the importance of mobilizing civil society organizations to strengthen the voice of the migrant and reinforce the imperatives of transparency and fair play in the migration process. They can do this doggedly if they are encouraged to do so and given the space for it. After all, the migrants are an inseparable part of our society. India is today the youngest country in the world and a young aspiring generation wants change. India has reasons to be optimistic about her migration future and the role she will play on the global stage if it can catalyse its people to action towards the future. As humanity traverses the twenty-first century in a globalised world, problems and opportunities hang in a fine balance. While there is no Utopia, the human quest for a good and just world must continue. All great ideas that have advanced human progress—liberty, equality, and fraternity—were hard-fought and won. India has the opportunity to demonstrate leadership as an exemplar of an equitable, progressive, prosperous, and open society. This idea of India needs to be reinforced and fully realized. Equally, the idea of one world in which people can move freely across countries is an idea whose time has come. India must work with the rest of the world with a greater sense of purpose to make that a reality.

Postscript

At the turn of the century, as the world waded its way into the third millennium, it was clear that the two central, and in the medium- to long-term, decisive problems it faced were demographic disequilibria and development deficits. The predictable movement of world population was bound to increase disequilibria in various regions. Surrounded by poor countries with large numbers of young jobseekers looking for a better life, the rich countries with declining numbers—mostly elder citizens and some children—faced a Hobson's choice: of either allowing freer immigration that now seemed inevitable to maintain their economic progress or raise barriers, restrict immigration, and risk significant economic and social decline. No country could remain untouched by these imperatives.

As always, policy has lagged behind real-life events and our ability to respond to the twin challenges remains unclear and uncertain. In fact, the rapid developments in transport and communications and the wide disparity in wages between the rich and the poor countries has meant that policymakers on both sides of the divide are simply overtaken by events. For many, mobility is simply the means to earn a higher income in an alien land without making too many demands of the host country while being rooted in their own home country. Straddling two or more states has emerged as a unique characteristic of mobility in the new century creating new dynamics between foreigners and natives while giving impetus to multiculturalism.

Recent events of large numbers of displaced people seeking to reach European shores through the Mediterranean, and the tragic and avoidable death of thousands of children, women, and the old in the process at sea, have once again captured the mindspace in politics, policy, and populism across the world. The spectre of 'crisis-migration' or 'migration crisis', take your pick, has been reprised yet again, widening the chasm between the lived experience of the asylum seekers, refugees or the migrants as the case may be, on the one hand and the political spin-doctors and the policymakers that serve them on the other. Migration as a symptom or the cause of a crisis, depending on where you stand on the divide, has returned to the center-stage as the favourite tautological argument in international policy discourse. It is mobilized by political actors to whip up public sentiment and thence to greater restrictions that constrain rather than enable migration and mobility as a process that is embedded in a wider social and economic context shaped by the ironies and inequities of history. The Sustainable Development Goal (SDG) number ten (in the 2030 agenda) is but a modest beginning towards a more progressive path that must follow for international migration governance.

Even if looked at in isolation, the prospects for expansion of the world economy are being seen with circumspection, perhaps even a touch of trepidation. Especially for the poor, the prospects for the future appear dim. Technology is deepening capital intensity, squeezing out labour from the production process while transnational capital is shifting production facilities to low-wage countries and, consequently, depressing wage rates. This is the market at work with seemingly no effective mechanism to moderate the devastating effects of social upheavals as a consequence of economic crises. The era of full employment seems a distant past. The development experience of the last four decades runs counter to the belief that unrestricted international trade would help the poor countries bridge the gap with the rich. There is now enough evidence to suggest that strident neo-liberalism has combined with the growing barriers to the mobility of people to produce globally negative outcomes.

It is paradoxical that at a time of unprecedented globalization and an upsurge of interest in international trade and capital, scant attention is paid to mainstreaming international migration praxis within development strategies. The importance of the mobility of people in global development seems fully comprehensible only to a handful of experts. The very realm that can significantly enhance development prospects for all, that perhaps matters to us most, should engage the attention of governments, and be accessible to all by virtue of our humanity, seems not to have captured the serious attention of policymakers or statesmen. Global efforts towards universal development goals hence remain poorly served on the human side of the development story. This is especially regrettable since, largely unnoticed by policymakers, the positive impact of international migration on presentday development concerns can scarcely be exaggerated.

In fact, one of the biggest lacunae of the Millennium Development Goals (MDG) programme was the complete absence of the recognition of the mobility imperative as a necessary condition for achieving the MDGs.

As we went past its sunset, it was clear, disappointingly, that the results are rather modest. Arguably, the MDGs would perhaps still not have been met in full measure but it can be said with some degree of certainty that the achievements would have been enhanced and significantly higher if freer movement of people had been dovetailed into the framework to support the initiative.

The work on the post-2015 development agenda presented another opportunity to the global community to act wisely and decisively. Wisdom would have been to recognize that a growing number of human problems have now become world problems—they cannot be resolved within the confines of a community, country, or region. The demographic dynamic is clearly and visibly one of them. Equally, the precondition to successfully addressing the challenge of global inequity is to embrace radical change—not just in the organizational arrangements for global governance but also in the deep-rooted tendency amongst people and leaders of nations that no great change is called for. The least likely future should be one in which we continue to muddle through as we have done in the past; governments continue to show no more leadership than they have to date and it is business as usual. While the world can no longer anticipate a happy ending, it is important that our collective institutions regain control over the human consequences of our collective actions.

Action Plan

The report of the Special Rapporteur (UN, 2013) on the eve of the High Level Dialogue (HLD) in 2013 was encouraging. He advocated the governance of international migration rather strongly. In his report to the Secretary General, he said, "Any future model for global migration governance should encompass several functions, including standard setting and normative oversight; capacity building and technical assistance; platform for dialogue and collaboration and political facilitation and developing a knowledge base or capacity through data indicators and dissemination" (UN, 2013: 38). We find ourselves in a world in which in the age of migration there is no lead agency to govern it or provide any sense of policy coherence. Since the world we live in has always tried to seek solutions to problems after considerable damage is done, we must move with a sense of urgency on international migration.

We make a modest attempt to suggest how we might make haste wisely and decisively. The action plan set out below envisages three tiers:

Tier 1: A Global Compact on Mobility and Skills (GCMS)

A global compact that would harmonize the commonalities on international migration should constitute a good starting point and serve as the first pillar. Since there is a considerable number of 'convergences' in policy recommendations at the global level pertaining to 'economic migrants' that has found a resonance and recognition either in policy or popular opinion at the national level, this compact can take these convergences forward by forging a multilateral agreement and basing them on principles that work. Demographic futures, technological change, globalization of aspirations, labour shortages and skills gaps, increasing avenues for low-skilled migration, providing access to social security for migrant workers, and universal recognition of skills and qualifications should constitute the common but binding building blocks to be covered in such an agreement. The GCMS should also aim to provide for a structure of reciprocity to enable balancing the economic gains and losses between the countries of destination and the countries of origin. This could be achieved through potential linkages between market access for economic migrants in destination countries with market access/tariff reduction for international trade in countries of origin. Another important element of the global compact can be to encourage the use of an international migration-specific instrument that would enable countries to conclude bilateral Human Resource Mobility Partnerships to transform the mobility of economic migrants into an orderly and well-calibrated process that best serves both countries. This global compact should lead up to multilateral negotiations and the reduction of barriers to mobility and result in welfare gains being distributed equitably. The compact must seek to achieve a market-driven (demand and supply equilibrium) migration and mobility framework with adequate reciprocal arrangements to balance outcomes for all sides.

Tier 2: A Global-Mobility Action Plan (G-MAP)

A G-MAP can address the divergences in policy at the global and national levels. Doubtless there are several points of disagreement or divergence on the specific steps that need to be taken to better govern international migration. These differences are for a large part the result of various perspectives and hence objectives pursued. The G-MAP will serve to set in motion consultations to narrow the differences and iron out the divergence over time. This can perhaps be set as a desired goal through a ten-year Transition Action Plan (TAP) to address the divergences between the global approach and national policy. This will help narrow down the differences through specific actionable steps over the transition period that countries of origin and destination alike can undertake. The transition action plan will, however, require a Compensatory Adjustment Mechanism to mutualize the pains and the gains that arise and thus build a modicum of reciprocity.

Tier 3: The Global Mobility Council (GMC)

The Global Mobility Compact and the G-MAP supported by the Transition Action Plan should ease the path towards building consensus for what might serve the global community as a normative institutional framework for the governance of economic migration. A GMC comprising all members of the United Nations could administer a broad, binding, rule-based, progressive, democratic, and liberal multilateral framework as discussed in an earlier chapter. It can serve as a precursor to a global lead agency for international migration and mobility.

As a corollary to these three tiers, a national institutional structure to meet and comply with international commitments arising therefrom, for building capacities, and for ensuring adherence to standard best practices will be necessary. Such an institutional structure should be uniformly adopted across members of the GMC. Given the myriad benefits of migration, it was inexplicable that it was not included in the post-2015 sustainable development agenda action plan. Migration finds no mention at all and this may prove irreversibly costly an error, the price of which could well be conflict, displacement, and upheaval of unprecedented scale.

In 2000, there was perhaps not enough evidence on the positive impact of migration on development nor was there sufficient political support for its inclusion in the agenda. This is no longer the case. A group of countries, international agencies, and non-governmental organizations (NGOs) had, in fact, made a strong case to the UN Open Working Group on Sustainable Development Goals (the body that was responsible for facilitating deliberations on the post-2015 agenda) that migration would help reduce poverty and generate economic growth (Sutherland and Swing, 2014). The 2030 agenda for sustainable development that was adopted, with the international migration imperative merely at its periphery, will remain a lofty and worthy statement of intent—a statement of intent far removed from the ground reality. There is little in it to suggest that the world has learnt its lessons on recognizing the inevitable and inexorable historical process that international migration is for the future. If the goal of the 2030 agenda for sustainable development of travelling on "the road to dignity by 2030: ending poverty, transforming all lives and protecting the planet" must be achieved the progressive countries in the international community must seize the opportunity and provide leadership to make freer mobility of people a reality. The real challenge is in the praxis. The time is at hand for the progressive countries to act decisively and with sagacity. Else, we will be guilty of wasting yet another fifteen years and countless precious lives, with no excuses to salve our collective conscience.

Bibliography

Abella, Manolo. 2006. 'Policies and Best Practices for Management of Temporary Migration'. UN/POP/MIG/SYMP/2006/03, *UN International Symposium on International Migration and Development*, Turin.

Acemoglu, D., S. Johnson, and J. A. Robinson. 2001. 'The Colonial Origins of Comparative Development: An Empirical Investigation'. *American Economic Review* 91(5): 1369–401.

———. 2002. 'Reversal of Fortune: Geography and Development in the Making of the Modern World Income Distribution'. *Quarterly Journal of Economics* 117(4): 1231–94.

Alba, F. 2013. 'Mexico: The New Migration Narrative'. Country Profiles, MPI. Available at *http://www.migrationinformation.org/Profiles/display.cfm? ID=947* (accessed on 8 November 2013).

Amaral, E. F. and W. Fusco. 2005. 'Shaping Brazil: The Role of International Migration'. Country Profiles, MPI. Available at *http://www.migrationinformation.org/Profiles/display.cfm?ID=311* (accessed on 14 March 2013).

Anderson, C. 2005. 'The Ferringees Are Flying, the Ship Is Ours—The Convict Middle Passage in Southern and Southeast Asia, 1790–1860'. *Indian Economic and Social History Review* 41(3).

'Annual Report on Emigration from the Port of Calcutta, 1868', in L. G. Sarup, *Colonial Emigration 19th–20th Century*, vol. I. Aldrich International, 2006.

Asis, M. M. B. 2006. *Gender Dimensions of Labour Migration in Asia*. New York: Commission on the Status of Women, fifth session.

Attardo, A. C. (2003). *France: Immigration Law and Policy*. Legislation Online.

Balaji, J. 2013. 'India Getting Saudi Exit Visas for Nitaqat-hit Emigrants'. *The Hindu.* Available at *http://www.thehindu.com/news/national/india-getting-saudi-exit-visas-for-nitaqathit-emigrants/article4866440.ece* (accessed on 23 July 2013).

Bashir, S. 2007. 'Trends in International Trade in Higher Education: Implications and Options for Developing Countries'. Education Working Paper Series, Number 6. World Bank Publications.

BBC News. 2013. 'Brazilian State of Acre in Illegal Immigration Alert'. Available at *http://www.bbc.co.uk/news/world-latin-america-22184870* (accessed on 28 May 2013), alternatively *http://www.bbc.co.uk/news/world-latin-america-22106284* (accessed on 28 May 2013).

Benhabib, S. 2005. 'The Right to Have Rights in Contemporary Europe'. Available at *http://ww8.georgetown.edu/centers/cdacs/benhabibpaper.*

Benyamin. 2012. *Goat Days.* New Delhi: Penguin Books.

Berne Initiative Report. 2004. 'Chairman's Summary: The Berne Initiative—Managing International Migration through International Cooperation: The International Agenda for Migration Management'. Berne II Conference, 16–17 December 2004, Berne, Switzerland.

Betts, A. 2010. *Global Migration Governance: The Emergence of a New Debate.* University of Oxford.

———. (ed.). 2011. *Global Migration Governance.* Oxford: Oxford University Press.

Bhagwati, J. 1992. 'A Champion for Migrating Peoples'. *The Christian Science Monitor.* Available at *http://www.csmonitor.com/1992/0228/28181.html* (accessed on 15 June 2013).

———. 2003. 'Borders Beyond Control', *Foreign Affairs*, January–February. Available at http://www.foreignaffairs.com/articles/58622/jagdish-n-bhagwati/borders-beyond-control.

Bhawra, V. K. 2013. *Irregular Migration from India to the EU: Evidence from the Punjab.* CARIM-India Research Report–2013/3.

Biswas, S. 2010. 'Why Are Indian Students Being Attacked in Australia?' *BBC News.* Available at *http://www.bbc.co.uk/blogs/thereporters/soutikbiswas/2010/01/why_are_indian_students_being_attacked_in_australi.html* (accessed on 31 July 2013).

Bloom, D. E. 2011. *Population Dynamics in India and Implications for Economic Growth.* WDA-Forum, University of St Gallen.

Borjas, G. J. 1989. 'Economic Theory and International Migration'. *International Migration Review* 23: 457–85.

Boswell, C., S. Stiller, and T. Straubhaar. 2004. *Forecasting Labour and Skills Shortages: How Can Projections Better Inform Labour Migration Policies?* EC, DG Employment and Social Affairs.

Boyd, M. 1989. 'Family and Personal Networks in International Migration: Recent Developments and New Agendas'. *International Migration Review* 638–70.

Brown, D. 1987. 'A Hungarian Connection: Karl Polanyi's Influence on the Budapest School'. *Journal of Economic Issues* 339–47.

California State Board of Control. 1920. *California and the Oriental: Japanese, Chinese and Hindus.* Report of State Board of Control of

California to Gov. Wm. D. Stephens. Sacramento: California State Printing Office.

Carter, M. 1996. *Voices from Indenture: Experiences of Indian Migrants in the British Empire*. London: Leicester University Press.

Castles, S. 2002. 'Migration and Community Formation under Conditions of Globalization'. *International Migration Review* 36(4): 1143–68.

———. 2010. 'Understanding Global Migration: A Social Transformation Perspective'. *Journal of Ethnic and Migration Studies* 36(10): 1565–86.

Castles, S. and A. Davidson (eds). 2000. *Citizenship and Migration: Globalization and the Politics of Belonging*. Psychology Press.

Castles, S. and R. D. Wise. 2008. *Migration and Development: Perspectives from the South*. IOM International Organization for Migration.

Castles, S., M. A. Cubas, C. Kim, E. Koleth, D. Ozkul, and R. Williamson. 2011. 'Karl Polanyi's Great Transformation as a Framework for Understanding Neo-Liberal Globalisation'. *Consultado a* 9(20): 2.

Castles, S. and M. J. Miller. 2009. *The Age of Migration*. The Guilford Press.

Chaisson, E. J. 2007. *Epic of Evolution: Seven Ages of the Cosmos*. Columbia University Press.

Chakravartty, P. 2000. 'The Emigration of High-Skilled Indian Workers to the United States: Flexible Citizenship and India's Information Economy'. Working Paper 19. The Centre for Comparative Immigration Studies.

Challinor, A. E. 2011. 'Canada's Immigration Policy: A Focus on Human Capital'. *Migration Information Source*.

Chang, H. J. 2003. 'The East Asian Development Experience'. In H. J. Chang (ed.), *Rethinking Development Economics*. Anthem Press.

———. 2006. *The East Asian Development Experience: The Miracle, the Crisis and the Future*. Zed Books.

Charnovitz, S. 2002. 'WTO Norms on International Migration'. Paper Prepared for IOM Workshop on Existing International Migration Law Norms.

Chellaraj, G., K. E. Maskus, and A. Mattoo. 2005. 'The Contribution of Skilled Immigration and International Graduate Students to US Innovation'. World Bank Policy Research Working Paper (3588).

China Law and Practice. 2013. *China's New Immigration Policy*. Available at *http://www.chinalawandpractice.com/Article/3060403/Channel/9931/Chinas-new-Immigration-Law-explained.html* (accessed on 8 November 2013).

Churchill, W. 1943. 'The Price of Greatness'. Speech at Harvard University, 6 September. Published in *Finest Hour 80, Third Quarter*, 1993.

Citizenship and Immigration Canada. 2013. Official website. Government of Canada. Available at *http://www.cic.gc.ca/ENGLISH/department/lawspolicy/index.asp* (accessed on 4 November 2013).

Clemens, M. 2007. *Do Visas Kill? Health Effects of African Health Professional Emigration* (No. 114). Center for Global Development.

Clemens, M. A. and L. Pritchett. 2013. *Temporary Work Visas: A Four-Way Win for the Middle Class, Low-Skill Workers, Border Security and Migrants.* Centre for Global Development Brief.

Collins, J. 2013. 'Multiculturalism and Immigrant Integration in Australia'. *Canadian Ethnic Studies* 45(3): 133–49.

Cousineau, J. M. and F. Vaillancourt. 1987. 'Investment in University Education: Regional Income Disparities and Regional Development'. In William J. Coffey and Mario Polese, *Still Living Together*, 357–79. The Institute for Research on Public Policy.

Crafts, N. 2004. 'Globalisation and Economic Growth'. *The World Economy* 27(1): 45–58.

Curtis, M. 2013. 'Italy's Immigration Debate Turns Racist, Sexist and Personal'. *The Washington Post*. Available at *http://www.washingtonpost.com/blogs/she-the-people/wp/2013/09/06/italys-immigration-debate-turns-racist-sexist-and-personal/* (accessed on 8 September 2013).

Czaika, M., and M. Vothknecht. 2012. 'Migration as Cause and Consequence of Aspirations'. University of Oxford IMI Working Paper, 57.

Dadush, U. 2009. 'WTO Reform: The Time to Start Is Now'. Policy Brief–September. Washington, DC: Carnegie Endowment for International Peace (CEIP).

———. 2010. *The WTO Must Be Reformed in the Interest of the Poorest Countries.* Geneva: Ideas Centre. Available at http://www.ideascentre.ch/wp-content/uploads/2013/10/Governance-Uri-Dadush.pdf.

Dahrendorf, R. 2002. 'Towards the Twenty-First Century'. In M. E. Howard and W. R. Louis (eds), *The Oxford History of the Twentieth Century*. Oxford University Press.

———. 2013. 'The WTO Must Be Reformed in the Interest of the Poorest Countries'. Based on a Carnegie Policy Brief by the author entitled 'WTO Reform: The Time to Start Is Now' prepared in September 2009.

Dalrymple, W. 2008. "The Shabby-Genteel Apheem Chichis'. *Outlook Magazine*, 16 June.

De Haas, H. 2007. 'Turning the Tide? Why Development Will Not Stop Migration'. *Development and Change* 38(5): 819–41.

———. 2010a. *Migration Transitions: A Theoretical and Empirical Inquiry into the Developmental Drivers of International Migration.* International Migration Institute 24.

————. 2010b. 'Migration and Development: A Theoretical Perspective'. *International Migration Review* 44(1): 227–64.

————. 2011. *The Only Way to Reduce Immigration Is to Wreck the Economy*. Available at: *http://heindehaas.blogspot.in/2011/11/only-way-to-reduce-immigration-is-to.html* (accessed on 31 July 2013).

————. 2013. *The Decline in UK Immigration Is Exaggerated and Signals a Broader Crisis in Society and the Economy*. LSE European Politics and Policy. Available at *http://blogs.lse.ac.uk/europpblog/2013/06/29/uk-immigration-decline/* (accessed on 25 July 2013).

Department of Immigration and Border Protection (DIBP). 2013. Fact Sheet 87. Government of Australia. Available at *http://www.immi.gov.au/Pages/Welcome.aspx*.

Desai, M. 2002. *Marx's Revenge: The Resurgence of Capitalism and the Death of Statist Socialism*. Verso.

Deshingkar, P. and S. Akter. 2009. *Migration and Human Development in India*. UNDP, Human Development Research Paper, 2009/13.

Dobbs, R., A. Madgavkar, D. Barton, E. Labaye, J. Manyika, C. Roxburgh, and S. Madhav. 2012. *The World at Work: Jobs, Pay, and Skills for 3.5 Billion People*. McKinsey Global Institute.

Drèze, J. and A. Sen. 1995. *India: Economic Development and Social Opportunity*. Oxford University Press.

Drèze, J. 2010. 'Unique Facility, or Recipe for Trouble'. *The Hindu*, 25 November. Available at *http://www.thehindu.com/opinion/op-ed/unique-facility-or-recipe-for-trouble/article911055.ece*.

Dummett, A. 1992. 'The Transnational Migration of People Seen from Within a Natural Law Tradition'. In B. Barry and R. E. Goodin (eds), *Free Movement: Ethical Issues in the Transnational Migration of People and of Money*, 169–80. New York and London: Harvester Wheatsheaf.

Dusenbery, V. A. 1989. 'Introduction: A Century of Sikhs Beyond Punjab'. In N. Gerald Barrier and Verne A. Dusenbery, *The Sikh Diaspora: Migration and Experience beyond Punjab*, 1–28. Delhi: Chanakya Publications and Columbia, Missouri: South Asia Publications.

Dutta, N. 2012. 'The Myth of the Bangladeshi and Violence in Assam'. *Kafila*. Available at: *http://kafila.org/2012/08/16/the-myth-of-the-bangladeshi-and-violence-in-assam-nilim-dutta/* (accessed on 31 July 2013).

Dyson, T. 2001. 'A Partial Theory of World Development: The Neglected Role of the Demographic Transition in the Shaping of Modern Society'. *International Journal of Population Geography* 7(2): 67–90.

Dyson, T. 2011. *Population and Development: The Demographic Transition*. Zed Books.

Eliot, T. S. 1988. *The Hollow Men*. IC Press.

Ellerman, D. 2004. *The Dynamics of Skilled Labor Migration: What Can Be Done about the Brain Drain?* DIFID-WB Collaboration on Knowledge and Skills in the New Economy.

European Migration Network, EU, 2012; EU, 2013. Practical Measures to Reduce Irregular Migration.

Eurostat, EUROPOP 2008 populations projections.

FICCI–Ernst&Young. 2012. 'Knowledge Paper on Skill Development in India'. September 2012. Available at *http://www.ey.com/Publication/vwLUAssets/FICCI_skill_report_2012_finalversion/$FILE/FICCI_skill_report_2012_finalversion_low_resolution.pdf.*

Florida, R. 2004. *Cities and the Creative Class.* Routledge.

Foucault, M. 1995. *Discipline and Punish: The Birth of the Prison.* New York: Vintage.

Freeman, R. 2005. 'The Great Doubling: Labor in the New Global Economy'. *2005 USERY Lecture in Labor Policy.* University of Atlanta, GA.

Fukuyama, F. 2006. *The End of History and the Last Man.* Simon and Schuster.

Gaillard, J., and A. Gaillard. 1997. 'Introduction: The International Mobility of the Brain: Exodus or Circulation'. *Science, Technology and Society* (2): 195–228.

Galbraith, J. K. 1979. *The Nature of Mass Poverty.* Cambridge, Massachusetts: Harvard University Press.

Gamble, A. 2009. *The Spectre at the Feast.* Basingstoke: Palgrave Macmillan.

GCIM. 2005. *Migration in an Interconnected World: New Directions for Action.* Switzerland. SRO-Kundig.

GFMD. 2007. *Summary Report. Global Forum on Migration and Development, First Meeting.* Brussels, 9–11 July.

GFMD. 2008. *Protecting and Empowering Migrants for Development. Final Conclusions and Recommendations of the Chair.* Manila, 30 October 2008.

———. 2009. *Special Session on the Future of the Forum: Summary of Discussions.* Athens.

———. 2010. *Partnerships for Migration and Human Development: Shared Prosperity; Shared Responsibility—Report of the Proceedings.* Mexico.

———. 2011. *Taking Action on Migration and Development: Coherence, Capacity and Cooperation—Report of the Proceedings.* Geneva, Switzerland, 1–2 December, 2011.

———. 2012. *Enhancing the Human Development of Migrants and their Contribution to the Development of Communities and States—Report of the Proceedings.* Mauritius.

Ghosh, B. (ed.). 2000. *Managing Migration: Time for a New International Regime?* Oxford University Press.

Goldin, I., G. Cameron, and M. Balarajan 2012. *Exceptional People: How Migration Shaped Our World and Will Define Our Future.* Princeton University Press.

Gollerkeri, G. 2007. 'Keynote Address: IOM-IDM Workshop on the Free Movement of Persons in Regional Integration Processes'. Geneva, 18 June.

Government of India. Act VII, 1922.

Government of India. 2011. Census of India: Census Data 2011. New Delhi: Office of the Registrar General and Census Commissioner, Ministry of Home Affairs.

Government of India. 2013a. *Economic Survey (2013).* New Delhi: Ministry of Finance, Government of India.

Government of India. 2013b. Social and Cultural Table Highlights, 2013. New Delhi: Office of the Registrar General and Census Commissioner, Ministry of Home Affairs.

Government of India. 2013c. Union Budget 2013. New Delhi: Ministry of Finance, Government of India.

Graham Jr., Otis L. 1995. 'Tracing Liberal Woes to '65 Immigration Act'. *Christian Science Monitor* 88(23): 19–23.

Grant, J.G. 1877. Note contained in the Annual Report of the Protector of Emigrants, 1877. In L. G. Sarup, *Colonial Emigration, 19th–20th Century,* vol. I. Aldrich International, 2006.

Gray, J. 1998. 'False Dawn: The Delusions of Global Capitalism'. The New Press Excerpted in F. J. Lechner and J. Boli. (eds), *The Globalization Reader* (Oxford: Blackwell, 2004).

Greater London Authority. 2009. *GLAeconomics.* Report of the London School of Economics.

Green, D. 2012. 'Why Is Migration a Cindrella Issue in Development?' *From Poverty to Power,* Oxfam Blogs. Available at *http://www.oxfamblogs. org/fp2p/?p=10831* (accessed on 15 June 2013).

Greenstone, M. and A. Looney. 2012. 'What Immigration Means for U.S. Employment and Wages'. Brookings Institution Blog. Available at *http:// www.brookings.edu/blogs/jobs/posts/2012/05/04-jobs-greenstone-looney* (accessed on 22 July 2013).

Guillén, M. 2010. 'Mauro Guillén's Indicators of Globalization, 1980–2008'. Wharton School, University of Pennsylvania, Philadelphia. Available at *http://wwwmanagement.wharton.upenn.edu/guillen/2010-docs/ Global-Table-1980-2008.pdf.*

Guiraudon, V. 2001. *Immigration Policy in France.* Brookings Institution Center on the United States and France.

Hall, R. E. and C. I. Jones. 1999. 'Why Do Some Countries Produce So Much More Output Per Worker Than Others?' *The Quarterly Journal of Economics* 114(1): 83–116.

Hallward-Driemeier, M. 2003. 'Do Bilateral Investment Treaties Attract Foreign Direct Investment? Only a Bit—And They Could Bite'. Policy Research Working Paper Series 3121, The World Bank.

Hamilton, B. and J. Whalley. 1984. 'Efficiency and Distributional Implications of Global Restrictions on Labour Mobility: Calculations and Policy Implications'. *Journal of Development Economics* 14(1): 61–75.

Harris, John R. and Michael P. Todaro. 1970. 'Migration, Unemployment and Development: A Two-Sector Analysis'. *American Economic Review* 60(1): 126–42, JSTOR 1807860.

Harvey, D. 2011. *The Enigma of Capital and the Crises of Capitalism*. Profile Books.

Hatton, T. J. and J. G. Williamson. 2009. *Vanishing Third World Emigrants?* No. w14785, National Bureau of Economic Research.

Helton, A. 2003. *People Movement: The Need for a World Migration Organisation—Open Democracy.* Available at *http://www.opendemocracy. net/people-migrationeurope/article_1192.jsp* (accessed on 15 June 2013).

Hemme, B. 2006. *Global Migration as a Solution to Worker Shortages in Industrialised Economies.* Forum on Public Policy.

Hipsman, F. and D. Meissner. 2013. 'Immigration in the United States: New Economic, Social, Political Landscapes with Legislative Reform on the Horizon'. MPI Country Profile. Available at *http://www.migrationinforma- tion.org/Feature/display.cfm?id=946* (accessed on 4 November 2013).

Hobsbawm, E. J. 1994. *The Age of Extremes: A History of the World, 1914–1991.* New York: Pantheon Books.

Hobsbawm, E. J., and D. J. Kertzer. 1992. 'Ethnicity and Nationalism in Europe Today'. *Anthropology Today* 8(1): 3–8.

Hoefer, M., N. F. Rytina, and C. Campbell. 2007. *Estimates of the Unauthorized Immigrant Population Residing in the United States: January 2006.* Department of Homeland Security, Office of Immigration Statistics.

House of Commons Papers. 1840. *Great Britain, Parliament, House of Commons Papers*, Volume 12, Google Books.

Huntington, S. P. 1993. 'The Clash of Civilizations?' *Foreign Affairs* 22–49.

ILO. 2004. 'Towards a Fair Deal for Migrant Workers in the Global Economy', International Labour Conference, 92nd session, Report VI. In *The World Economy*, Academic Foundation Indian edition 2007).

ILO. 'ILO International Standards for the Protection of Migrant Workers'. Available at http://www.ilo.org/migrant/areas/international- standards-on-labour-migration-and-protection-of-migrant-workers- rights/lang--en/index.htm.

Indian Institute of Science. 2009. *Pursuit and Promotion of Science, Centenary Publication, 2009.*

Inglis, C. 2004. 'Australia's Continuing Transformation'. Migration Information Source (Washington, DC). Available at: *http://www.migrationinformation.org/Profiles/display.cfm.*

International Conference on Population and Development. 1994. 'Programme of Action'. Available at: http://www.iisd.ca/cairo/program/p10003.html (accessed on 25 October 2013); http://www.iisd.ca/Cairo/program/p10000.html (accessed on 27 October 2013).

International Conference on Population and Development. 1994. 'Synthesis of the Report of the Expert Group, ICPD, Cairo, 1994'.

International Council of Human Rights Policy (ICHRP). 2010. *Irregular Migration, Migrant Smuggling and Human Rights: Towards Coherence.*

International Covenant on Civil and Political Rights (ICCPR). 'Adopted and Opened for Signature, Ratification and Accession by General Assembly Resolution 2200A (XXI) of 16 December 1966'.

IOM. 2001. 'International Dialogue on Migration'. Available at: http://www.iom.int/cms/idm.

⸻. 2005. 'Migration and Citizenship', Section 3.7: 'Essentials of Migration Management'. Volume 3: 'Managing Migration'. Available at *http://www.rcmvs.org/documentos/IOM_EMM/v3/V3S07_CM.pdf* (accessed on 31 July 2013).

⸻. 2007. 'Free movement of Persons in Regional Integration Processes'. Background Paper. Available at *http://www.iom.int/jahia/webdav/site/myjahiasite/shared/shared/mainsite/microsites/IDM/workshops/free_movement_of_persons_18190607/idm2007_backgroundpaper_en.pdf.*

⸻. 2010. 'World Migration Report 2010: The Future of Migration—Building Capacities for Change'.

Johansson, Å., Y. Guillemette, D. Turner, G. Nicoletti, C. de la Maisonneuve, G. Bousquet, and F. Spinelli. 2013. *OECD Looking to 2060 Long-Term Global Growth Prospects.*

Kapur, A. 2012. *India Becoming: A Journey through a Changing Landscape.* Penguin Viking.

Keynes, J. M. 1919. *The Economic Consequences of the Peace,* cited by Angus Maddison in *The World Economy,* Academic Foundation, Indian edition (2007).

⸻. 1933. 'Economic Possibilities for Our Grandchildren' (1930). *Essays in Persuasion,* 358–73.

⸻. 1936. *The General Theory of Employment, Interest and Money.* United Kingdom, Palgrave Macmillan.

Khadria, B. 1999. *The Migration of Knowledge Workers.*

Khan, M. 2007. 'Governance, Economic Growth and Development Since the 1960s'. UN DESA Working Paper No. 54 (ST/ESA/2007/ DWP/54).

King, A. and B. Schneider. 1991. *The First Global Revolution: A Report by the Council of Rome*. New York: Pantheon Books.

Kirk, D. 1996. 'Demographic Transition Theory'. *Population Studies* 50(3): 361–87.

Koeller, D. 2003. 'Immigration Act of 1995'. Available at: *http://www.then-again.info/webchron/usa/immigrationact.html* (accessed on 17 November 2013).

Koser, K. 2007. *International Migration: A Very Short Introduction*. Oxford University Press.

————. 2013. 'The Business Case for Migration: Engaging with the Private Sector to Encourage More Proactive Migration Policies in the Interest of Economic Growth and Prosperity'. International Organisation for Migration (IOM). Available at: *http://www.iom.int/cms/en/sites/iom/home/what-we-do/migration-policy-and-research/migration-policy-1/migration-policy-practice/issues/october-november-2013/the-business-case-for-migration.html*.

Kotz, D. M. 2002. 'Globalization and Neoliberalism'. *Rethinking Marxism* 14(2): 64–79.

Kouchner, B. 2013. Opinion. *Financial Times*, 22 October.

Kudaisya, M. 2011. *The Oxford India Anthology of Business History*. Oxford University Press.

Kumar, K. S. and I. S. Rajan. 2014. *Emigration in 21st-Century India: Governance, Legislation, Institutions*. Routledge India.

Kundu, A., P. C. Mohanan, and K. Varghese. 2013. *Spatial and Social Inequalities in Human Development: India in the Global Context*. UNDP India.

Kundu, A. and K. Varghese. 2010. 'Regional Inequality and "Inclusive" Growth in India under Globalization'. IHD and Oxfam India Working Paper Series, New Delhi.

Kutler, S. 2003. 'Immigration Act of 1965'. *Dictionary of American History*, third edition, vol. 4 (New York: Charles Scribner's Sons), p. 230.

Kuznetsov, Y. 2006a. 'International Migration of Talent, Diaspora Networks and Development'. *Innovation: Management, Policy and Practice* 8(12).

————. 2006b. 'Work Globally, Develop Locally: Diaspora Networks as Springboards of Knowledge-Based Development'. *Innovation: Management, Policy and Practice* 8(1–2).

LaGraffe, D. 2012. 'The Youth Bulge in Egypt: An Intersection of Demographics, Security, and the Arab Spring'. *Journal of Strategic Security* 5(2): 9.

Lal, B. V. 1980. 'Leaves of the Banyan Tree: Origins and Background of Fiji's North Indian Indentured Migrants 1879–1916'. Australian National University. Google Books.

———. 2007. *The Encyclopedia of the Indian Diaspora*. Oxford University Press.

Laski, H. (ed.). 1948. *The Communist Manifesto: The Centenary Edition*. London: Allen and Unwin.

Le Goff, M. and R. J. Singh. 2013. 'Can Trade Reduce Poverty in Africa?' Number 114. Poverty Reduction and Economic Management Network (PREM).The World Bank.

Leblang, D., J. Fitzgerald, and J. Teets. 2007. 'Defying the Law of Gravity: The Political Economy of International Migration'. MS, Department of Political Science, University of Colorado, Boulder.

Lee, E. S. 1966. 'A Theory of Migration'. *Demography* 3(1): 47–57.

Lee, S. and N. Piper. 2013. 'Understanding Multiple Discrimination against Labour Migrants in Asia: An Intersectional Analysis'. Friedrich Ebert Stiftung, International Policy Analysis.

Lefebvre, R., E. Simonova, and L. Wang. 2012. *Labour Shortages in Skilled Trades: The Best Guestimate?* No. 120702.

Li, P. S. 2008. 'World Migration in the Age of Globalization: Policy Implications and Challenges'. *New Zealand Population Review* 33(34): 1–22.

Li, Wei and Lucia Lo. 2010. 'High Skilled Indian Migrations in Canada and the US'. IMDS, Working Paper No 4—2009.

Light, I., P. Bhachu, and S. Karageorgis. 1989. 'Migration Networks and Immigrant Entrepreneurship'. UCLA: Institute for Social Science Research. Available at: *http://escholarship.org/uc/item/50g990sk*.

Lipton, M. 1977. *Why Poor People Stay Poor: A Study of Urban Bias in World Development*. London: Temple Smith.

Lord Cornwallis. 1789. 'The Asiatic Journal and Monthly Register for British and Foreign India'. *China and Australasia*, vol. 26. Google Books.

MacDonald, A. 2013. 'Canada Seeks Immigrants Who Fit Better'. *The Wall Street Journal*. Available at: *http://online.wsj.com/news/articles/SB100014 24127887323980604579030964060914466* (accessed on 1 November 2013).

Maddison, A. 2001. *The World Economy: A Millennial Perspective*. Development Centre Studies, OECD, Paris. Available at: *http://blogs. lesechos.fr/IMG/pdf/Statistiques_historiques_OCDE_par_pays_ depuis_1820.pdf*.

———. 2006. *The World Economy*. Organisation for Economic Cooperation and Development, Indian Edition, 2007.

Madhaven, M. 1987. 'Indian Emigration'. In Sidney Klein (ed.), *The Economics of Mass Migration in the Twentieth Century*. New York: Dragon House.

Magubane, B. 1975. 'Bantustans and Migrant Labour in the Political Economy of South Africa'. In Helen. I. Safa et al. (eds), *Migration and Development: Implications for Ethnic Identity and Political Conflict*. Mouton Publishers.

Mahomet, D. 1793. *The Travels of Dean Mohamet*. University of California Press, UC Press e-books collection, 1982–2004.

Marcolini, A. 2013. 'Flying South'. Available at: *http://www.brazilinfocus. com/samba/culture-a-society/84-culture-a-society/268-flying-south?start=1* (accessed on 14 March 2013).

Martin, J. P. 2008. 'Migration and the Global Economy: Some Stylised Facts'. Paper From the Directorate for Employment, Labour and Social Affairs, OECD Publishing, Paris. Available at: *www. oecd.org/datao-ecd/27/54/40196342.pdf*.

Martin, P., S. Martin, and S. Cross. 2007. 'High-level Dialogue on Migration and Development'. *International Migration* 45(1): 7–25.

Massey, D. S., J. Arango, G. Hugo, A. Kouaouci, A. Pellegrino, and J. E. Taylor. 1993. "Theories of International Migration: A Review and Appraisal'. *Population and Development Review*, 431–66.

Mayda, Anna Maria and Krishna Patel. 2004. 'OECD Countries Migration Policy Changes' (Appendix to *International Migration: A Panel Data Analysis of Economic and Non-Economic Determinants*, by Anna Maria Mayda). Available at: http://www9.georgetown.edu/faculty/amm223/policychangesAppendix.pdf

McGreal, C. 2012. 'Sikhs Say Attacks on Community Are "Collateral Damage" of 9/11'. *The Guardian*. Available at: *http://www.theguardian. com/world/2012/aug/06/sikj-abuse-america-911* (accessed on 31 July 2013).

McKinsey Global Institute. 2012. 'The World at Work: Jobs, Pay and Skills for 3.5 Billion People'. *MGI, 2012*.

Meadows, D. H., D. L. Meadows, J. Randers and W. W. Behrens III. 1972. *The Limits to Growth*. Washington, D.C.: Potomac Associates.

Menon, S. 2010. 'UID an Assault on Individual Liberty, say Activists'. *The Business Standard*. Available at: *http://www.business-standard.com/ article/economy-policy/uid-an-assault-on-individual-liberty-say-activ-ists-110090400043_1.html*.

Messerlin, P. 2010. *The Trade Regime and the Future of WTO in Peace and Prosperity through World Trade*. Cambridge University Press.

Migration News. 2002. 'World Migration Organisation?' 9(9). Available at: http://migration.ucdavis.edu/mn/more.php?id=2819_0_5_0 (accessed on 15 June 2013).

Ministry of Overseas Indian Affairs (MOIA). 2012. 'Population of Non-Resident Indians'. Available at: *http://moia.gov.in/writereaddata/pdf/NRISPIOS-Data%2815-06-12%29new.pdf.*

Moggridge, D. 1980. *The Collected Writings of John Maynard Keynes,* Vol. XXV: 'Activities 1940–1944, Shaping the Post-War World: The Clearing Union'.

———. 1983. 'Keynes as an Investor'. *The Collected Works of John Maynard Keynes,* 12, 1–113.

Mora, C. and N. Piper. 2011. 'Notions of Rights and Entitlements among Peruvian Female Workers in Chile' 13(1): 5–18.

Moses, J. W. and B. Letnes. 2004. 'The Economic Costs to International Labor Restrictions: Revisiting the Empirical Discussion'. *World Development* 32(10): 1609–26.

Motiram, S. and K. Naraparaju. 2013. *Growth and Deprivation in India: What Does Recent Data Say?* No. 2013-005, Indira Gandhi Institute of Development Research, Mumbai, India.

Murphy, K. 2006. *France's New Law: Control Immigration Flows, Court the Highly Skilled.* Migration Policy Institute, November.

Myers, K. and N. Conte. 2013. *Building New Skills: Immigration and Workforce.*

Nayyar, D. 2003. 'Globalization and Development'. In H. J. Chang (ed.), *Rethinking Development Economics.* Anthem Press.

Nayyar, D. 2008. 'International Migration and Economic Development'. In N. Serra and J. E. Stiglitz (eds), *The Washington Consensus Reconsidered: Towards a New Global Governance.* Oxford University Press.

Nekola, J. C., C. D. Allen, J. H. Brown, J. R. Burger, A. D. Davidson, T. S. Fristoe, and J. G. Okie. 2013. 'The Malthusian–Darwinian Dynamic and the Trajectory of Civilization'. *Trends in Ecology & Evolution* 28(3): 127–30.

Nett, R. 1971. 'The Civil Right We Are Not Ready For: The Right of Free Movement of People on the Face of the Earth'. *Ethics* 81(3): 212–27.

Newland, K. 2005. *The Governance of International Migration: Mechanisms, Processes and Institutions.* GCIM.

Nielson, J. 2003. *Labour Mobility in Regional Trade Agreements: Moving People to Deliver Services.* Washington, D.C.: World Bank.

Nilekani, N. 2013. *Imagining India: Ideas for the New Century.* Penguin UK.

NSSO. 2010a. 'Employment–Unemployment Survey Report (NSS) 66th Round (July 2009–June 2010): Employment, Unemployment and Household Consumer Expenditure'.

———. 2010b. 'Migration in India, 2007–08 (64th Round)'. New Delhi: Ministry of Statistics and Programme Implementation, Government of India.

————. 2013. Report No. 551 on Vocational Education in India. Ministry of Statistics and Programme Implementation.

OECD. 2006. *International Migration Outlook*. Annual Report, 2006. Paris.

————. 2009. *The Future of International Migration to OECD Countries*. OECD.

————. 2012. 'Looking to 2060: Long-Term Global Growth Prospects'. OECD Economic Policy Papers, Number 3.

————. 2013a. *International Migration Outlook 2013*. Available at: *http:// www.oecd.org/els/mig/imo2013.htm*.

————. 2013b. *Perspectives on Global Development: Industrial Policies in a Changing World*. OECD, Pocket Edition, 2013.

Ohmae, K. 1995. *The End of the Nation State: The Rise of Regional Economies. How New Engines of Prosperity are Reshaping Global Markets*. New York.

O'Rourke, K. H. 2004. *The Era of Migration: Lessons for Today*. No. 4498, CEPR Discussion Papers.

O'Rourke, K. and R. Sinnott. 2003. *Migration Flows: Political Economy of Migration and the Empirical Challenges*.

Ortega, F. and G. Peri. 2012. *The Effect of Trade and Migration on Income*. No. w18193, National Bureau of Economic Research.

Pâecoud, A. and P. F. Guchteneire (eds). 2007. *Migration without Borders: Essays on the Free Movement of People*. Berghahn Books.

Pearson, M. 2012. 'From War to Peace: European Union Accepts Nobel Prize'. CNN. Available at: *http://edition.cnn.com/2012/12/10/world/ nobel-peace-prize* (accessed on 7 June 2013).

Pebbles, P. 2001. *The Plantation Tamils of Ceylon*. New York: Leicester University Press.

Piketty, T. 2014. *Capital in the Twenty-First Century*.

Piper, N. 2005. 'Gender and Migration'. Policy Analysis and Research Programme, Global Commission on International Migration.

Polanyi, K. 2001. *The Great Transformation: The Political and Economic Origins of Our Time*. Beacon Press.

Pratto, F., D. G. Tatar, and S. Conway-Lanz (1999). 'Who Gets What and Why: Determinants of Social Allocations'. *Political Psychology* 20(1): 127–50.

Pritchett, L. 1997. 'Divergence, Big Time'. *The Journal of Economic Perspectives* 11(3): 3–17.

————. 2006. *Let Their People Come: Breaking the Gridlock on International Labor Mobility*. Centre for Global Development.

Putterman, L. and D. N. Weil. 2010. 'Post-1500 Population Flows and the Long-run Determinants of Economic Growth and Inequality'. *The Quarterly Journal of Economics* 125(4): 1627–82.

Queiroz, B., C. Turra, and E. Perez. 2006. *The Opportunities We Cannot Forgo: Economic Consequences of Population Changes in Brazil.* XV Encontro Nacional de Estudos Populacionais, ABEP.

Raghuram, P. 2008. 'Governing the Mobility of Skills'. In Christina Gabrielle and Helene Pellerin (eds), *Governing International Labour Migration: Current Issues, Challenges and Dilemmas.* New York: Routledge.

Rajan, I. S. *Kerala Migration Survey, 2011.* Centre for Development Studies.

Ravenstein, E. G. 1885. 'The Laws of Migration'. *Journal of the Royal Statistical Society* 48(2): 167–227.

———. 1889. 'The Laws of Migration'. *Journal of the Royal Statistical Society* 52: 214–301.

Reddy, Y. V. 2006. 'Dynamics of Balance of Payments in India, First Diamond Jubilee'. Diamond Jubilee Celebrations of the Department of Commerce, Osmania University.

Reimers, D. M. 1992. *Still the Golden Door: The Third World Comes to America.* Columbia University Press.

Rekacewicz, P. 2013. 'Mapping Europe's War on Immigration'. *Le monde diplomatique.* Available at: *http://mondediplo.com/blogs/ mapping-europe-s-war-on-immigration?utm_content=buffer512b2&utm_ source=buffer&utm_medium=twitter&utm_campaign=Buffer* (accessed on 1 November 2013).

Report of the Commissioners, 1848. Royal Commission appointed to inquire into the treatment of immigrants in Mauritius, 1848. Google Books.

Report of the Government Medical Inspector of Emigrants, 1870. In L. G. Sarup, *Colonial Emigration: 19th–20th Century,* vol I. Aldrich International, 2006.

Report of the High Level Panel on the post-2015 Development Agenda. Available at: *http://www.post2015hlp.org/the-report/.*

Ricupero, R. 2001. In United Nations Publication, *Asia-Pacific Population Journal* 20(3):158.

Roberts, A. 2002. 'Towards a World Community? The United Nations and International Law'. In M. E. Howard and W. R. Louis (eds-), *The Oxford History of the Twentieth Century.* Oxford University Press.

Robinson, J. (ed.). 1979. *Aspects of·Development and Underdevelopment.* CUP Archive.

Rodrik, D. 1997. 'Has Globalisation Gone Too Far?' (Institute for International Economics). Excerpted in F. J. Lechner and J. Boli (eds), *The Globalization Reader* (Oxford: Blackwell, 2004).

———. 2001. 'Comments at the Conference on Immigration Policy and the Welfare State'. Paper presented at the Conference on Immigration Policy and the Welfare State, Trieste, Italy.

————. 2007. 'The New York Times Gets It Wrong on Immigration'. Dani Rodrik's weblog. Available at: *http://rodrik.typepad.com/dani_rodriks_weblog/2007/05/the_new_york_ti.html* (accessed on 28 May 2013).

————. 2008. *One Economics, Many Recipes: Globalization, Institutions, and Economic Growth*. Princeton University Press.

Rosso, A., C. Rienzo, J. Portes. 2012. *The Economic Impact of Migration Liberalisation: Evidence and Issues*. NIESR.

Russeau, S. S. K. 2013. *How the Kafala System Is Failing Domestic Workers in the Middle East*. Inter Press Service.

Saha, K. C. 2012. *Irregular Migration from India to the EU: Punjab & Haryana Case Study*. CARIM-India Research Report—2012/28.

Said, E. W. 1985 [1978]). *Orientalism*. New York: Random House.

Saikia, D. 2012. *Indian Economy after Liberalisation: Performance and Challenges*. New Delhi: SSDN Publishers and Distributors.

Sarup, L.G. 2006. *Colonial Emigration 19th–20th Century*, vol. I. Aldrich International.

Sasikumar, S. K. and R. Thimothy 2012. *Migration of Women Workers from South Asia to the Gulf* . V. V. Giri Labour National Labour Institute, Noida, and UN Women South Asia Sub Regional Office, New Delhi.

Sassen, S. 1996. *Losing Control? Sovereignty in an Age of Globalization*. Columbia University Press.

Saxenian, A. 1999. *Silicon Valley's New Immigrant Entrepreneurs*. Public Policy Institute of California.

Schumpeter, J. 1942. 1975. *Capitalism, Socialism and Democracy*. New York: Harper, 1975.

Shachar, A. 2006. 'Race for Talent: Highly Skilled Migrants and Competitive Immigration Regimes'. *The NYUL Rev*. 81, 148.

Shah, N. M. 2008. 'Irregular Migration and Some Negative Consequences for Development: Asia-GCC Context'. Discussion paper prepared for the Civil Society Days of the Global Forum on Migration and Development, Manila, October 2008.

Shearmur, R. 2006. 'The New Knowledge Aristocracy: The Creative Class, Mobility and Urban Growth'. *Work Organisation, Labour and Globalisation* 1(1): 31–47.

Shih, Susan. 'Immigration Act of 1965'. Purdue University. Available at: *http://web.ics.purdue.edu/~willough/immgact.htm*.

Singer, A. and J. Wilson. 2013. *The 10 Traits of Globally Fluent Metropolitan Areas: Immigration, Opportunity and Appeal*. Brookings Institution Blog. Available at: *http://www.brookings.edu/blogs/the-avenue/posts/2013/08/01-global-metro-traits-singer-wilson*.

Skeldon, R. 1990. *Population Mobility in Developing Countries*. Belhaven Press.

———. 1997. *Migration and Development: A Global Perspective*.

Skerry, P. 2013. 'Splitting the Difference on Illegal Immigration'. *National Affairs* (Winter).

Slaughter, A. M. 2009. *A New World Order*. Princeton University Press.

Smith, A. 1937 (1776). *The Wealth of Nations*. New York: Modern Library.

Solimano, A. and N. Watts. 2005. *International Migration Capital Flows and the Global Economy: A Long-Run View*, vol. 35. United Nations Publications.

Somerville, W. and A. Dudhwar. 2010. 'Indian Emigration to the United Kingdom'. IMDS Working Paper No 21.

Sripad, S. M. A. X. and K. Naraparaju. 2013. *Growth and Deprivation in India: What Does Recent Data Say?* No. 287, ECINEQ, Society for the Study of Economic Inequality.

Stark, O. 1991. *The Migration of Labor*. Cambridge and Oxford: Blackwell.

Stark, O., and D. E. Bloom. 1985. 'The New Economics of Labor Migration'. *The American Economic Review* 173–8.

Statistical update on employment in the informal economy ILO–Department of Statistics, 2012, India's Economic Survey.

Stiglitz, J. 2002. 'Globalism's Discontents'. *The American Prospect* 13(1): A16–A21. Reprinted in F. J. Lechnerand J. Boli (eds), *The Globalization Reader* (Oxford: Blackwell, 2008).

Sutherland, P. and W. L. Swing. 2014. 'Migration on the Move'. *Project Syndicate*. Available at: *http://www.project-syndicate.org/commentary/peter-sutherland-and-william-l--swing-explain-why-migration-is-likely-to-gain-a-prominent-place-in-the-post-2015-development-agenda*.

Sutherland, P. 2014. 'Migration Is Development'. *Project Syndicate*. Available at: *http://www.project-syndicate.org/commentary/migrants-and-the-post-2015-global-development-agenda-by-peter-sutherland*.

Taylor, A. M. and J. G. Williamson. 1997. 'Convergence in the Age of Mass Migration'. *European Review of Economic History* 1(1): 27–63.

The Economist. 2013. 'The World's Next Leap Forward: Towards the End of World Poverty'. Available at: *http://www.economist.com/news/leaders/21578665-nearly-1-billion-people-have-been-taken-out-extreme-poverty-20-years-world-should-aim?spc=scode&spv=xm&ah=9d7f7ab9455 10a56fa6d37c30b6f1709* (accessed on 11 June 2013).

The Leitch Review of Skills 2006. *Prosperity for all in the Global Economy-World Class Skills*.

The National Archives of the Government of the UK. 'Abolition of Slavery'. Available at: *nationalarchives.gov.uk*.

The New York Times. 2007. 'The Immigration Deal'. 20 May. Available at: *http://www.nytimes.com/2007/05/20/opinion/20sun1.html?_r=2&oref= slogin&* (accessed on 28 May 2013).

———. 2013. 'France Says Deportation of Roma Girl was Legal'. 19 October. Available at: *http://www.nytimes.com/2013/10/20/world/ europe/france-says-deportation-of-roma-girl-was-legal.html* (accessed on 4 November 2013).

———. 2014. 'Does Immigration Mean France Is 'Over?' Available at: *http://opinionator.blogs.nytimes.com/2014/01/05/does-immigration-mean- france-is-over/?_php=true&_type=blogs&_r=0.*

The Secretary-General Address to the High-Level Dialogue of the General Assembly on International Migration and Development, 14 September, New York, available at *http://www.un.org/migration/sg-speech.html.*

Todaro, M. P. 1969. 'A Model of Labor Migration and Urban Unemployment in Less-developed Countries'. *American Economic Review* 59:138–48.

Todaro, M. P. and S. C. Smith 2011. *Economic Development.* Pearson Higher Ed.

Trachtman, J. P. 2009. 'Introduction: Toward the Fourth Freedom'. In *International Law of Economic Migration*, 1–29. Upjohn Institute of Employment Research.

Turner, G. 2007. *A Comparison of the Limits to Growth with Thirty Years of Reality.* CSIRO Sustainable Ecosystems.

Turra, C. and B. Lanza. 2012. *Window of Opportunity: Socioeconomic Consequences of Demographic Changes in Brazil and Mexico.* CEDEPLAR: Universidade Federal de Minas Gerais.

Ugur, M. 2007. 'Migration without Borders: The Ethics, Economics and Governance of Free Movement. In *Economics and Governance of Free Movement*, 65–94.

UN. 2013. *Report of the Special Rapporteur on the Human Rights of Migrants: Promotion and Protection of Human Rights—Human Rights Questions, including Alternative Approaches for Improving the Effective Enjoyment of Human Rights and Fundamental Freedom.* Advance Unedited Version.

UN ECOSOC. 2013. 'Millennium Development Goals and the Post-2015 Development Agenda'. Available at: *http://www.un.org/en/ecosoc/about/ mdg.shtml.*

UN HLD. 2006. 'Sixty-first Session, Agenda Item 55 (b): Globalization and Interdependence—International Migration and Development Summary of the High-level Dialogue on International Migration and Development. Note by the President of the General Assembly'.

———. 2006. 'Compendium of Recommendations on International Migration and Development: The United Nations Development Agenda and the Global Commission on International Migration Compared'. New York.

UN-DESA. 2013b. 'International Migration 2013: Migrants by Origin and Destination'. UN Population Facts No. 2013/3, September 2013. Available at: *http://www.un.org/en/development/desa/population/publications/ pdf/popfacts/popfacts_2013-3.pdf* (accessed on 15 September 2013).

————. 2013b. MPI Tabulation. Available at: http://www.migrationpolicy. org/programs/data-hub.

————. (2013a). 'Number of International Migrants Rises above 232 Million'. Available at: *http://www.un.org/en/development/desa/news/popu- lation/number-of-international-migrants-rises.html*.

UNESCO. 2013. 'Social Inclusion of Internal Migrants in India'. Internal Migration in India Initiative. Available at: *http://unesdoc.unesco.org/ images/0022/002237/223702e.pdf*

UNFPA. 2004a. 'Investing in People: National Progress in Implementing the ICPD Programme of Action (1994–2004).' Available at: *http:// www.unfpa.org/upload/lib_pub_file/278_filename_icpd04_summary.pdf* (accessed on: 14 June 2013).

————. 2004b. 'Meeting the Challenges of Migration: Progress since the ICPD.' Available at: *http://www.unfpa.org/webdav/site/global/shared/ documents/publications/2004/migration_icpd.pdf* (accessed on 17 July 2013).

UNGA. 1948. *Universal Declaration of Human Rights.*

UNGA HLD. 2006.

UNGA HLD. 2013. Available at *http://www.un.org/esa/population/meetings/ HLD2013/mainhld2013.html.*

UNGA HLD. 2014.

United Nations. 'Open Working Group on Sustainable Development Goals'. Available at: *http://sustainabledevelopment.un.org/index.php?menu=1549.*

United Nations. 'The Universal Declaration of Human Rights'. Available at: *http://www.un.org/en/documents/udhr/.*

United Nations Development Programme. 1999. *UNDP Human Development Report 1999.*

————. 2009. *Human Development Report: Overcoming Barriers: Human Mobility and Development. 2009.* United Nations Development Programme.

United Nations General Assembly. 1948. *Universal Declaration of Human Rights.* Resolution adopted by the General Assembly, 10(12).

United Nations General Assembly. 'United Nations Millennium Declaration, 55/2'. Adopted by the United Nations General Assembly, September 2000.

United Nations Population Division DESA. 'World Population Ageing 1950–2050'. Available at http://www.un.org/esa/population/publications/worldageing19502050/.

United Nations. 2014. *World Economic and Social Survey 2014: International Migration*. Department of Economic and Social Affairs.

US State Department. 'Annual Reports of Non-immigrant Visas Issued by Classification and Nationality 2003 to 2012'. Available at: *Travel. state.gov*.

Varma, R. 2007. 'Changing Borders and Realities: Emigration of Indian Scientists and Engineers to the United States'. *Perspectives on Global Development and Technology* 6(4): 539–56.

Verhofstadt. 2007. Address at the inaugural session at the first GFMD meeting at Brussels, 2007.

Wade, R. 1990. *Governing the Market: Economic Theory and the Role of Government in East Asian Industrialization*. Princeton University Press.

Wadhwa, V. 2012. *The Immigrant Exodus: Why America Is Losing the Global Race to Capture Entrepreneurial Talent*. Wharton Digital Press.

Wadhwa, V., S. Jain, A. Saxenian, G. Gereffi, and H. Wang. 2011. 'The Grass Is Indeed Greener in India and China for Returnee Entrepreneurs: America's New Immigrant Entrepreneurs', Part VI. Available at SSRN 1824670.

Watt, N. 2012. 'Ed Miliband: Every Briton Should Speak English'. *The Guardian*. Available at *http://www.guardian.co.uk/politics/2012/dec/14/miliband-english-language-integration* (accessed on 23 July 2013).

Weiner, M. 1996. 'Ethics, National Sovereignty and the Control of Immigration'. *International Migration Review* 30(1): 171–97.

Wickramasekara, P. 2011. 'International Labour Migration: The Missing Link in Globalization', SSRN. *Transnationalism and Migration*.

Wolpert, S. A. 1991. *India*. University of California Press (updated edition, 1999).

World Bank. 1989. *Sub-Saharan Africa: From Crisis to Sustainable Development—A Long-term Perspective Study*. Washington, DC.

World Bank. 2006. *Global Economic Prospects 2006: Economic Implications of Remittances and Migration*, Chapter 2, pp. 25–51.

World Economic Forum. 2012. *The Global Competitiveness Report 2012–13*. WEF Geneva.

WTO Agreement, 1995.

Yuval-Davis, N. 2006. 'Belonging and the Politics of Belonging'. *Patterns of Prejudice* 40(3): 197–214.

Zelinsky, Z. 1971. 'The Hypothesis of the Mobility Transition'. *Geographical Review* 61: 219–49.

Index

About the Authors

Gurucharan Gollerkeri is a senior civil servant of the Indian Administrative Service. He is currently serving as Secretary to the Government of India in New Delhi.

Natasha Chhabra is a migration researcher. She was a research assistant at the India Centre for Migration, Government of India, New Delhi, and now leads the work of the International Migration vertical at the Federation of Indian Chambers of Commerce and Industry (FICCI) in New Delhi.